STAR WARS®
EPISODE I
ADVENTURES

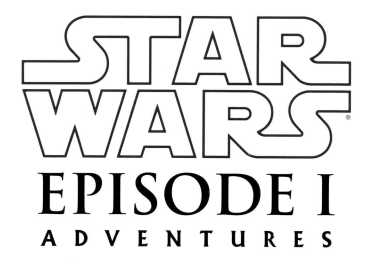

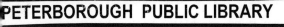

STAR WARS

EPISODE I

ADVENTURES

Scripts	Inks
HENRY GILROY	CHRIS CHUCKRY
MARK SCHULTZ	GEORGE FREEMAN
TIMOTHY TRUMAN	P. CRAIG RUSSELL
RYDER WINDHAM	HOWARD M. SHUM

Pencils	Colors
STEVE CRESPO	CHRIS CHUCKRY
MARTIN EGELAND	HAROLD MACKINNON
GALEN SHOWMAN	DAVE NESTELLE
ROBERT TERANISHI	LISA STAMP

Lettering
VICKIE WILLIAMS

Cover Art
HUGH FLEMING

STAR WARS
EPISODE I
THE PHANTOM MENACE
3D

DARK HORSE BOOKS®

Collection designer
KAT LARSON

Original series editor
PEET JANES

Collection assistant editor
FREDDYE LINS

Collection editor
RANDY STRADLEY

President and publisher
MIKE RICHARDSON

Special thanks to Joanne Chan Taylor, Leland Chee, Troy Alders, Carol Roeder,
Jann Moorhead, and David Anderman at Lucas Licensing.

This volume collects *Star Wars: Episode I—Anakin Skywalker*; *Star Wars: Episode I—Queen Amidala*; *Star Wars: Episode I—Qui-Gon Jinn*; *Star Wars: Episode I—Obi-Wan Kenobi*; and *Star Wars: Episode I #1/2*, all originally published by Dark Horse Comics.

STAR WARS: EPISODE I ADVENTURES

MIKE RICHARDSON president and publisher **NEIL HANKERSON** executive vice president **TOM WEDDLE** chief financial officer **RANDY STRADLEY** vice president of publishing **MICHAEL MARTENS** vice president of book trade sales **ANITA NELSON** vice president of business affairs **MICHA HERSHMAN** vice president of marketing **DAVID SCROGGY** vice president of product development **DALE LAFOUNTAIN** vice president of information technology **DARLENE VOGEL** senior director of print, design, and production **KEN LIZZI** general counsel **DAVEY ESTRADA** editorial director **SCOTT ALLIE** senior managing editor **CHRIS WARNER** senior books editor **DIANA SCHUTZ** executive editor **CARY GRAZZINI** director of print and development **LIA RIBACCHI** art director **CARA NIECE** director of scheduling

Published by Dark Horse Books
A division of Dark Horse Comics, Inc.
10956 SE Main Street
Milwaukie, OR 97222

DarkHorse.com
StarWars.com

To find a comics shop in your area, call the Comic Shop
Locator Service toll-free at 1-888-266-4226.

First paperback edition: March 2000
Second paperback edition: January 2012
ISBN 978-1-59582-842-2

1 3 5 7 9 10 8 6 4 2
Printed at 1010 Printing International, Ltd., Guangdong Province, China

CONTENTS

THE RISE OF THE EMPIRE
1000–0 YEARS BEFORE *STAR WARS: A NEW HOPE*

The events in this story take place approximately
thirty-two years before the Battle of Yavin.

After the seeming final defeat of the Sith, the Republic
enters a state of complacency. In the waning years of
the Republic, the Senate is rife with corruption, and
the ambitious Senator Palpatine has himself elected
Supreme Chancellor.

EPISODE I—ANAKIN SKYWALKER

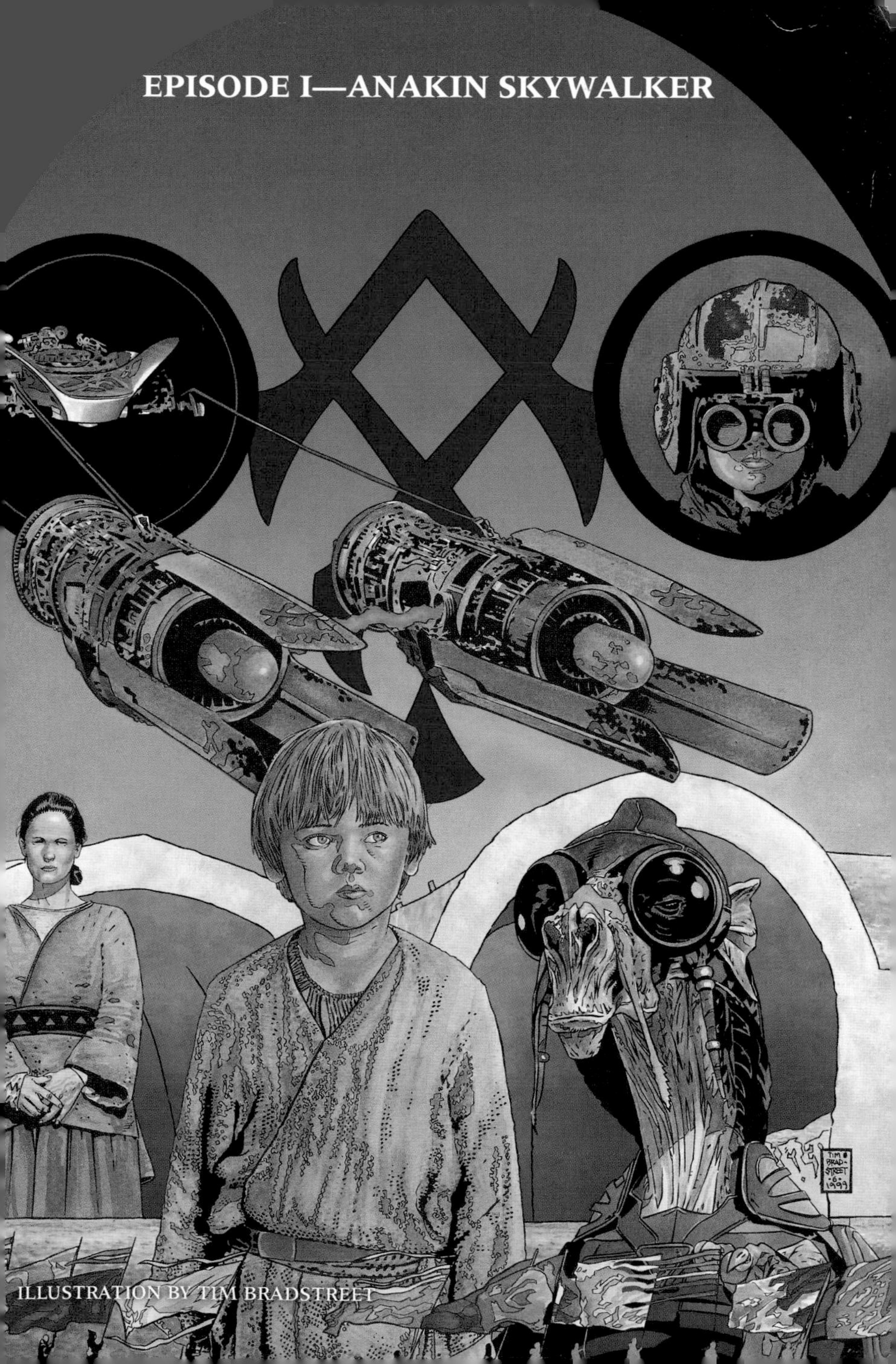

ILLUSTRATION BY TIM BRADSTREET

Script
TIMOTHY TRUMAN

Pencils
STEVE CRESPO

Inks
GEORGE FREEMAN

Colors
DAVE NESTELLE

Lettering
VICKIE WILLIAMS

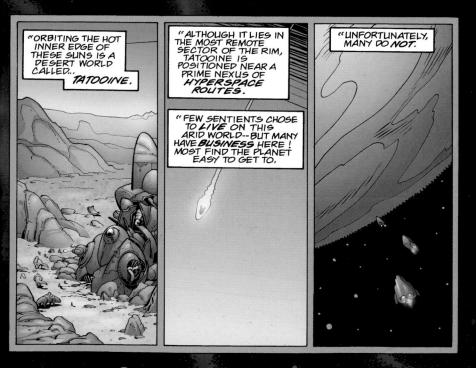

"*THE OUTER RIM* IS A FORBIDDEN, FOREBODING, LARGELY UNEXPLORED SECTOR--A GALACTIC *FRONTIER*, LYING FAR FROM THE LIGHT AND ENLIGHTENMENT OF THE *REPUBLIC*.

"ON THE FURTHEST CUSP OF THE RIM, THE TWIN SUNS *TATOO 1* AND *TATOO 2* LEND THEIR MALIGNANT BLAZE TO THE PLANETS BENEATH THEIR SWAY.

"ORBITING THE HOT INNER EDGE OF THESE SUNS IS A DESERT WORLD CALLED...

TATOOINE.

"ALTHOUGH IT LIES IN THE MOST REMOTE SECTOR OF THE RIM, TATOOINE IS POSITIONED NEAR A PRIME NEXUS OF *HYPERSPACE ROUTES*.

"FEW SENTIENTS CHOSE TO *LIVE* ON THIS ARID WORLD--BUT MANY HAVE *BUSINESS* HERE! MOST FIND THE PLANET EASY TO GET TO,

"UNFORTUNATELY, MANY DO *NOT*.

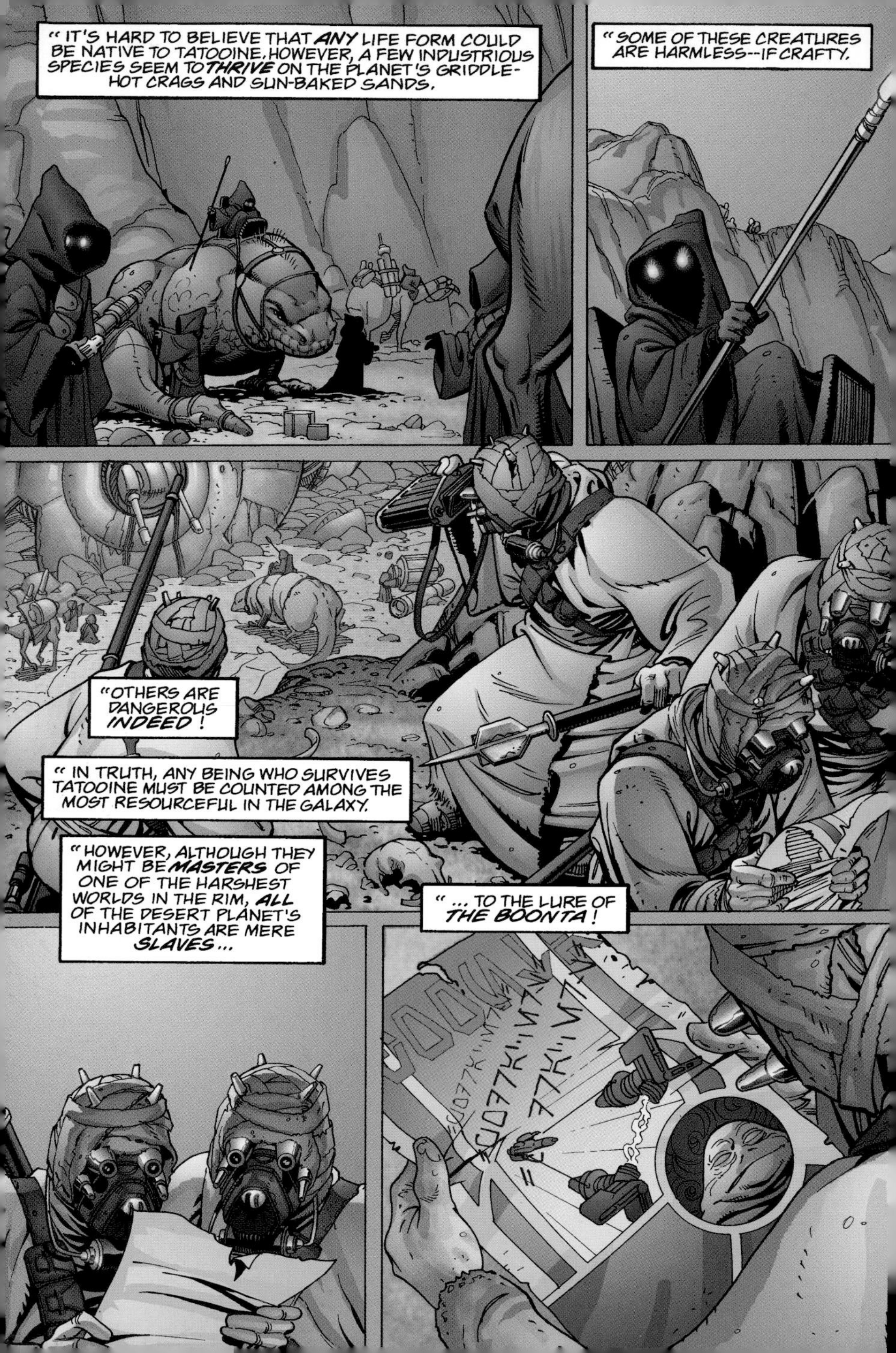
"IT'S HARD TO BELIEVE THAT ANY LIFE FORM COULD BE NATIVE TO TATOOINE. HOWEVER, A FEW INDUSTRIOUS SPECIES SEEM TO THRIVE ON THE PLANET'S GRIDDLE-HOT CRAGS AND SUN-BAKED SANDS.
"SOME OF THESE CREATURES ARE HARMLESS--IF CRAFTY.
"OTHERS ARE DANGEROUS INDEED!
"IN TRUTH, ANY BEING WHO SURVIVES TATOOINE MUST BE COUNTED AMONG THE MOST RESOURCEFUL IN THE GALAXY.
"HOWEVER, ALTHOUGH THEY MIGHT BE MASTERS OF ONE OF THE HARSHEST WORLDS IN THE RIM, ALL OF THE DESERT PLANET'S INHABITANTS ARE MERE SLAVES...
"...TO THE LURE OF THE BOONTA!

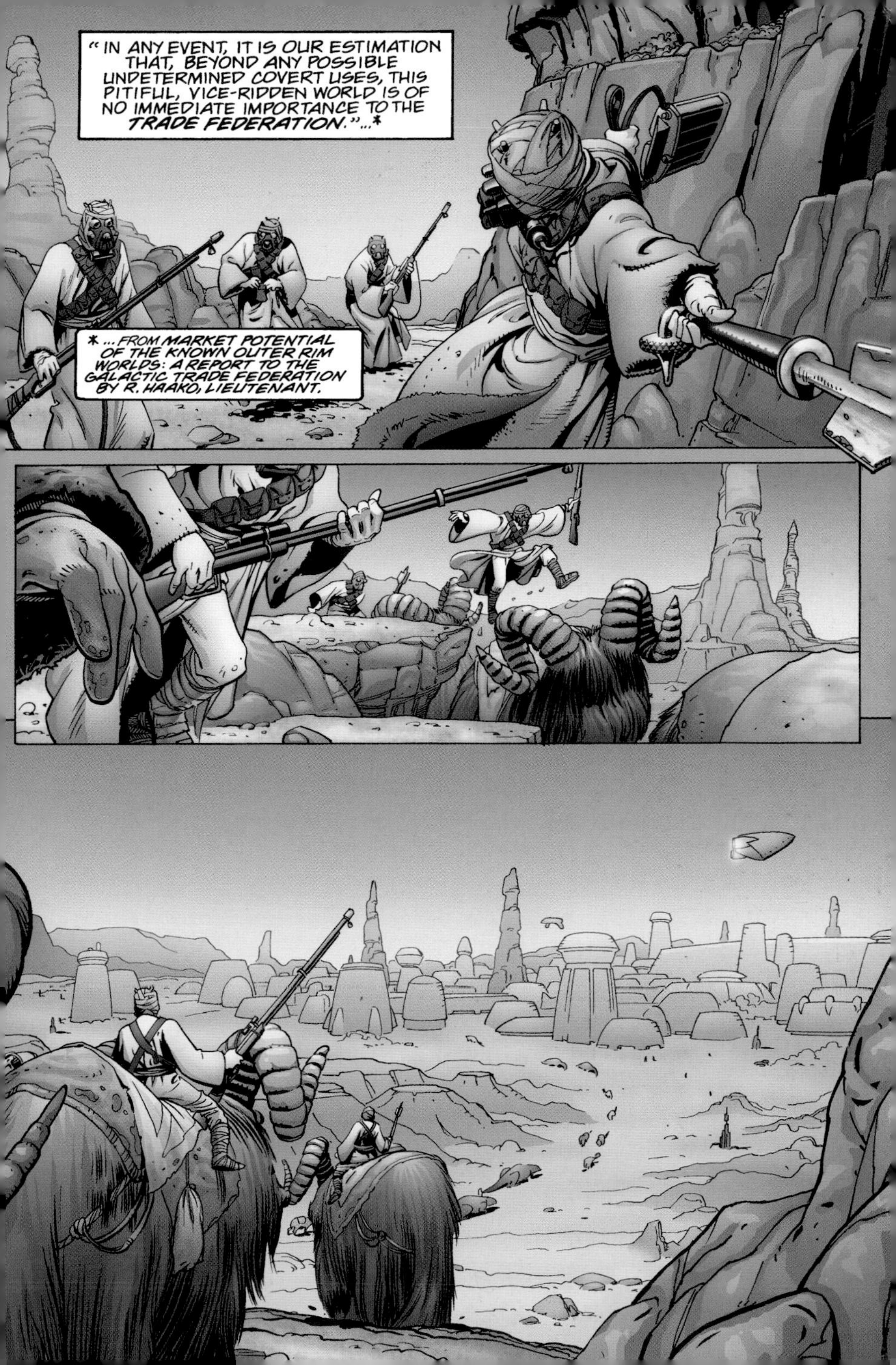
"IN ANY EVENT, IT IS OUR ESTIMATION THAT, BEYOND ANY POSSIBLE UNDETERMINED COVERT USES, THIS PITIFUL, VICE-RIDDEN WORLD IS OF NO IMMEDIATE IMPORTANCE TO THE TRADE FEDERATION."...*
*...FROM MARKET POTENTIAL OF THE KNOWN OUTER RIM WORLDS: A REPORT TO THE GALACTIC TRADE FEDERATION BY R. HAAKO, LIEUTENANT.

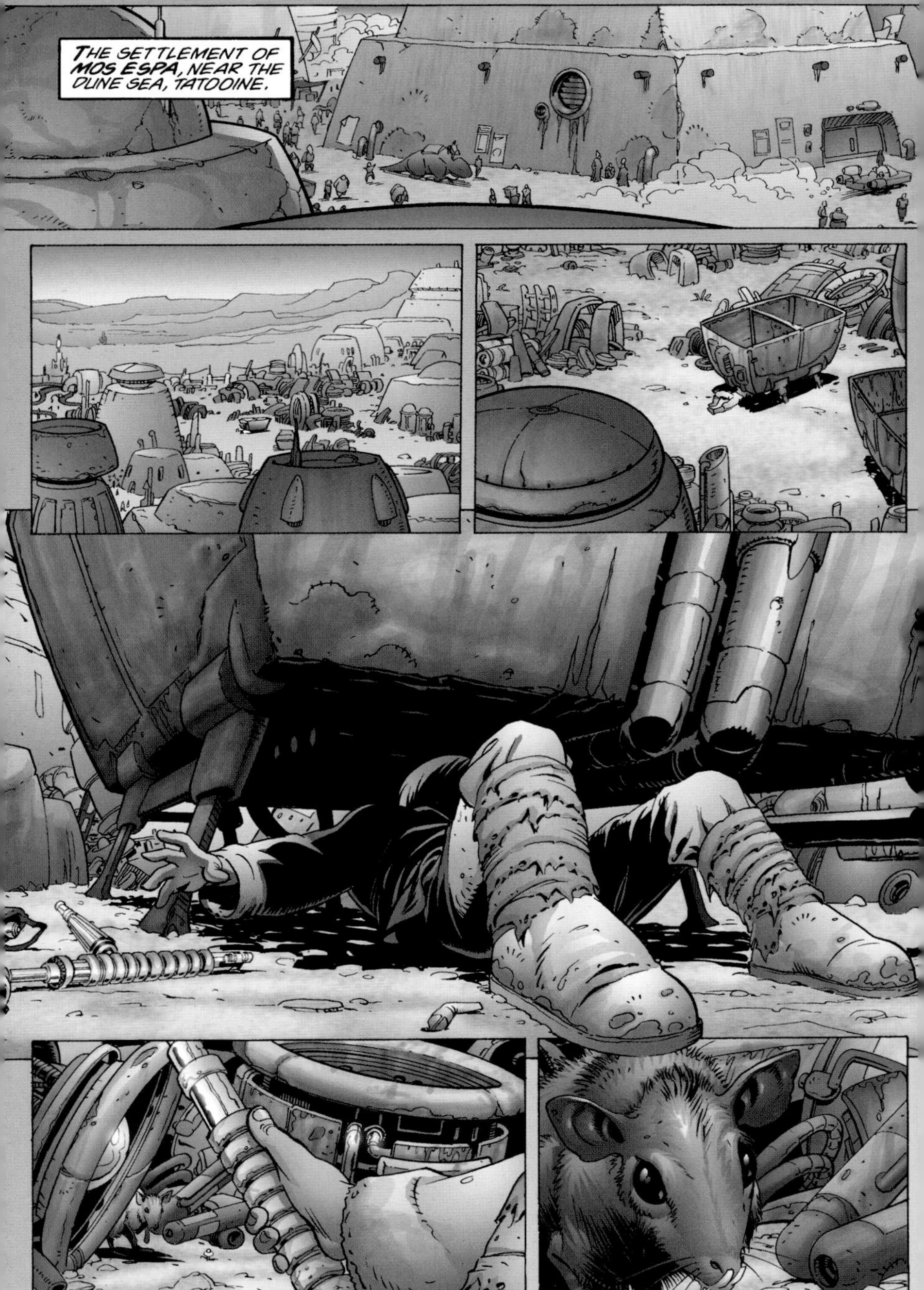
THE SETTLEMENT OF MOS ESPA, NEAR THE DUNE SEA, TATOOINE.

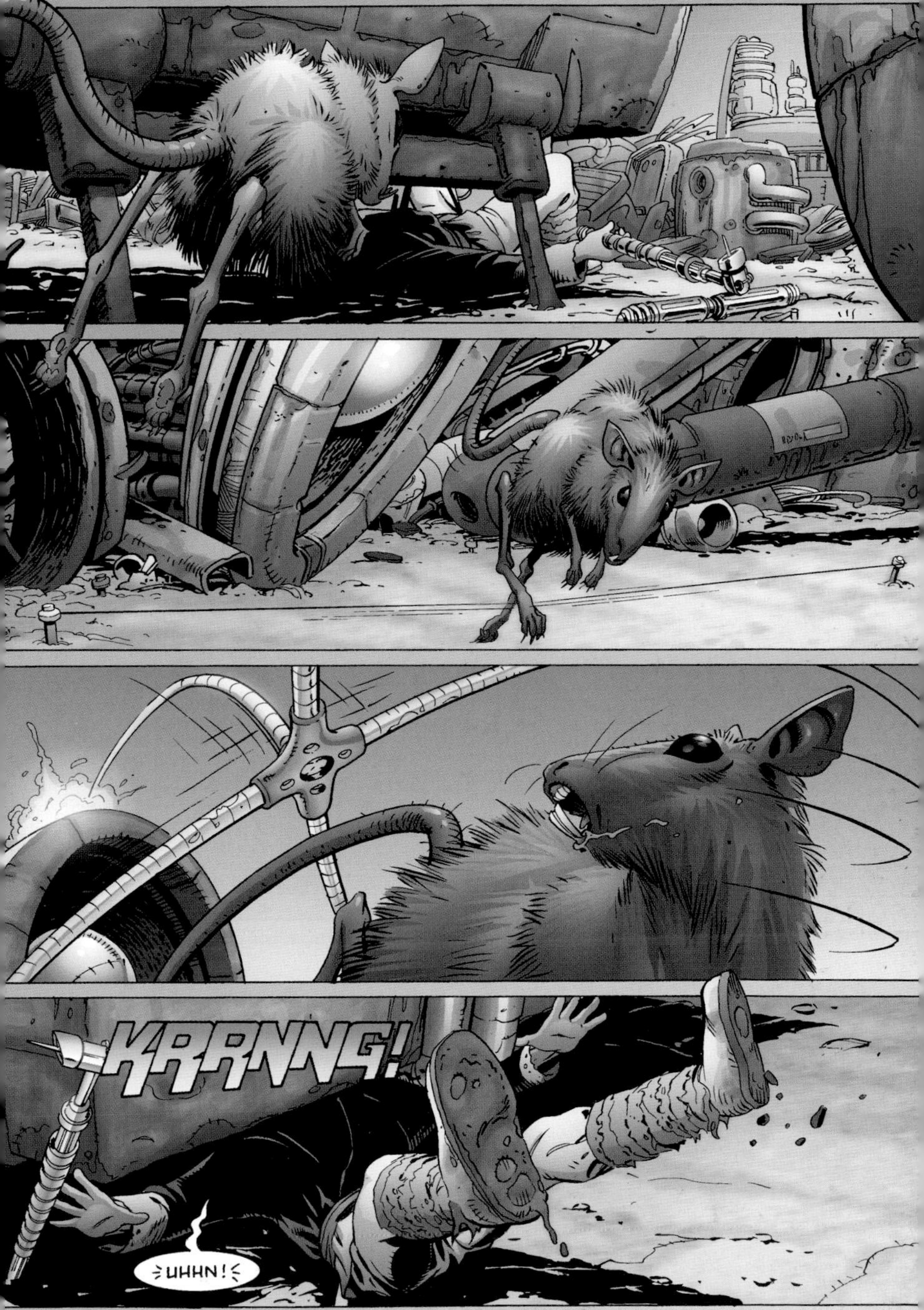
KRRNNG!
UHHN!

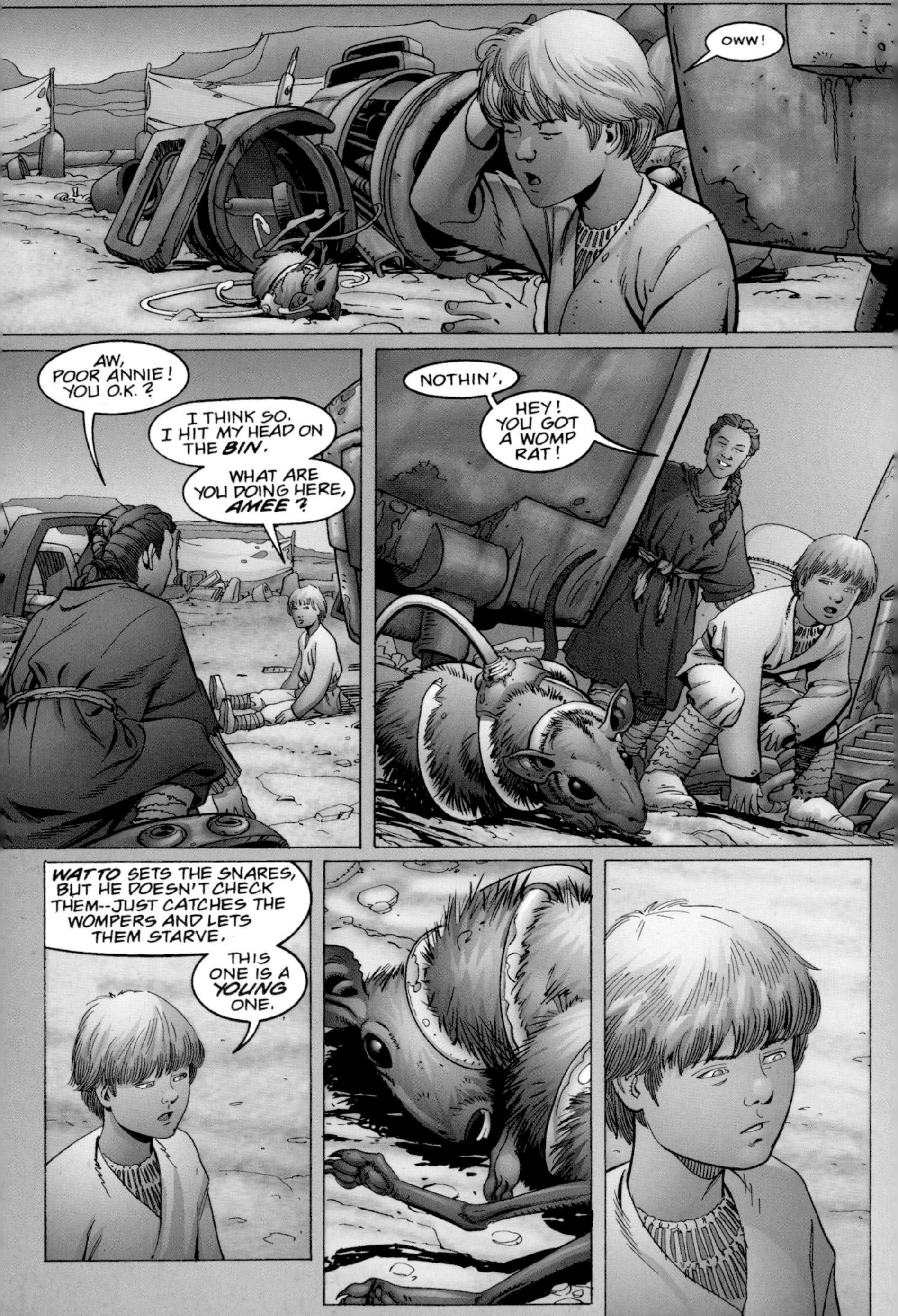
OWW!
AW, POOR ANNIE! YOU O.K.?
I THINK SO. I HIT MY HEAD ON THE BIN.
WHAT ARE YOU DOING HERE, AMEE?
NOTHIN'.
HEY! YOU GOT A WOMP RAT!
WATTO SETS THE SNARES, BUT HE DOESN'T CHECK THEM--JUST CATCHES THE WOMPERS AND LETS THEM STARVE.
THIS ONE IS A YOUNG ONE.

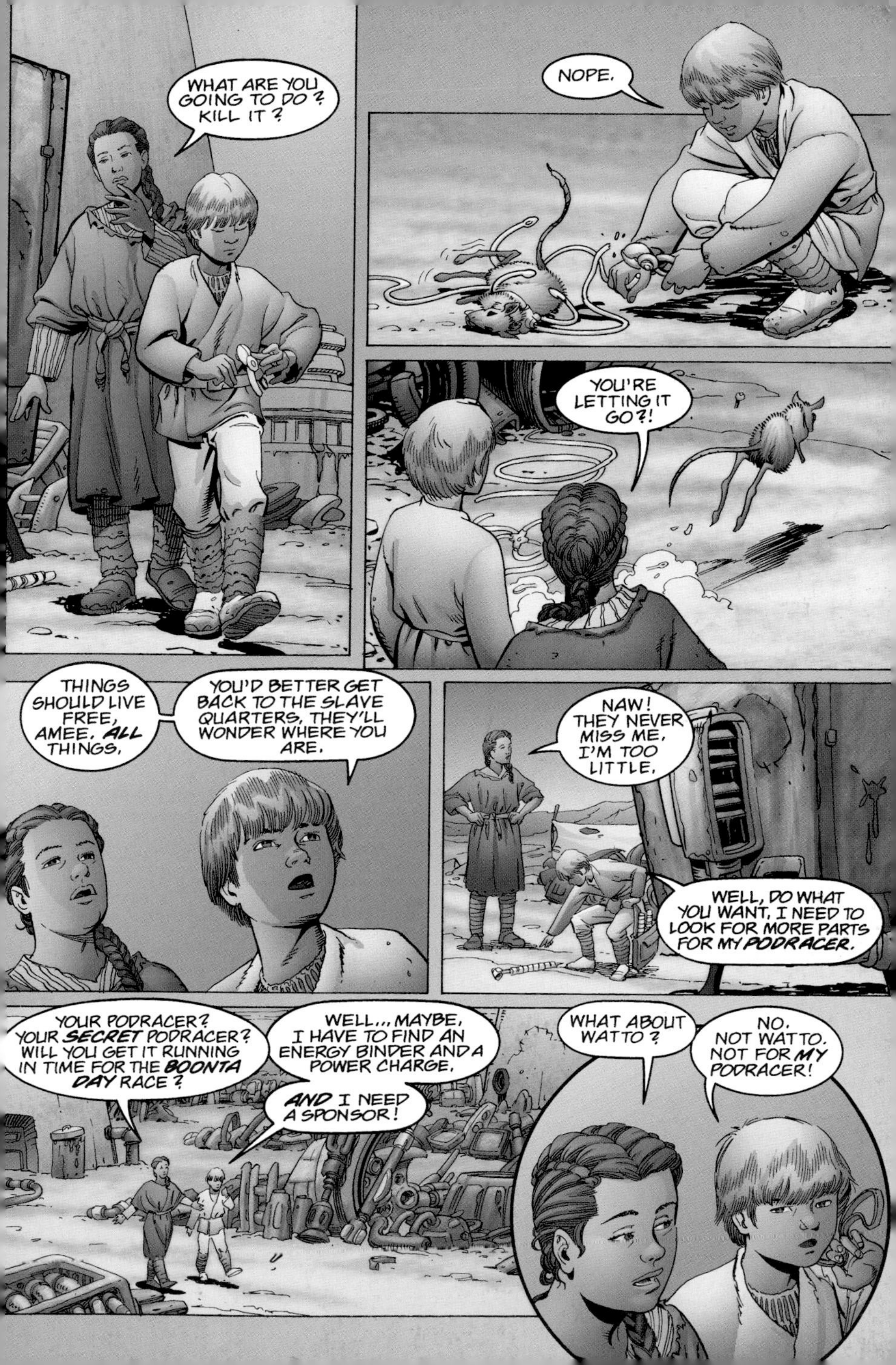
WHAT ARE YOU GOING TO DO? KILL IT?
NOPE.
YOU'RE LETTING IT GO?!
THINGS SHOULD LIVE FREE, AMEE. ALL THINGS.
YOU'D BETTER GET BACK TO THE SLAVE QUARTERS. THEY'LL WONDER WHERE YOU ARE.
NAW! THEY NEVER MISS ME. I'M TOO LITTLE.
WELL, DO WHAT YOU WANT. I NEED TO LOOK FOR MORE PARTS FOR MY PODRACER.
YOUR PODRACER? YOUR SECRET PODRACER? WILL YOU GET IT RUNNING IN TIME FOR THE BOONTA DAY RACE?
WELL... MAYBE. I HAVE TO FIND AN ENERGY BINDER AND A POWER CHARGE.
AND I NEED A SPONSOR!
WHAT ABOUT WATTO?
NO. NOT WATTO. NOT FOR MY PODRACER!

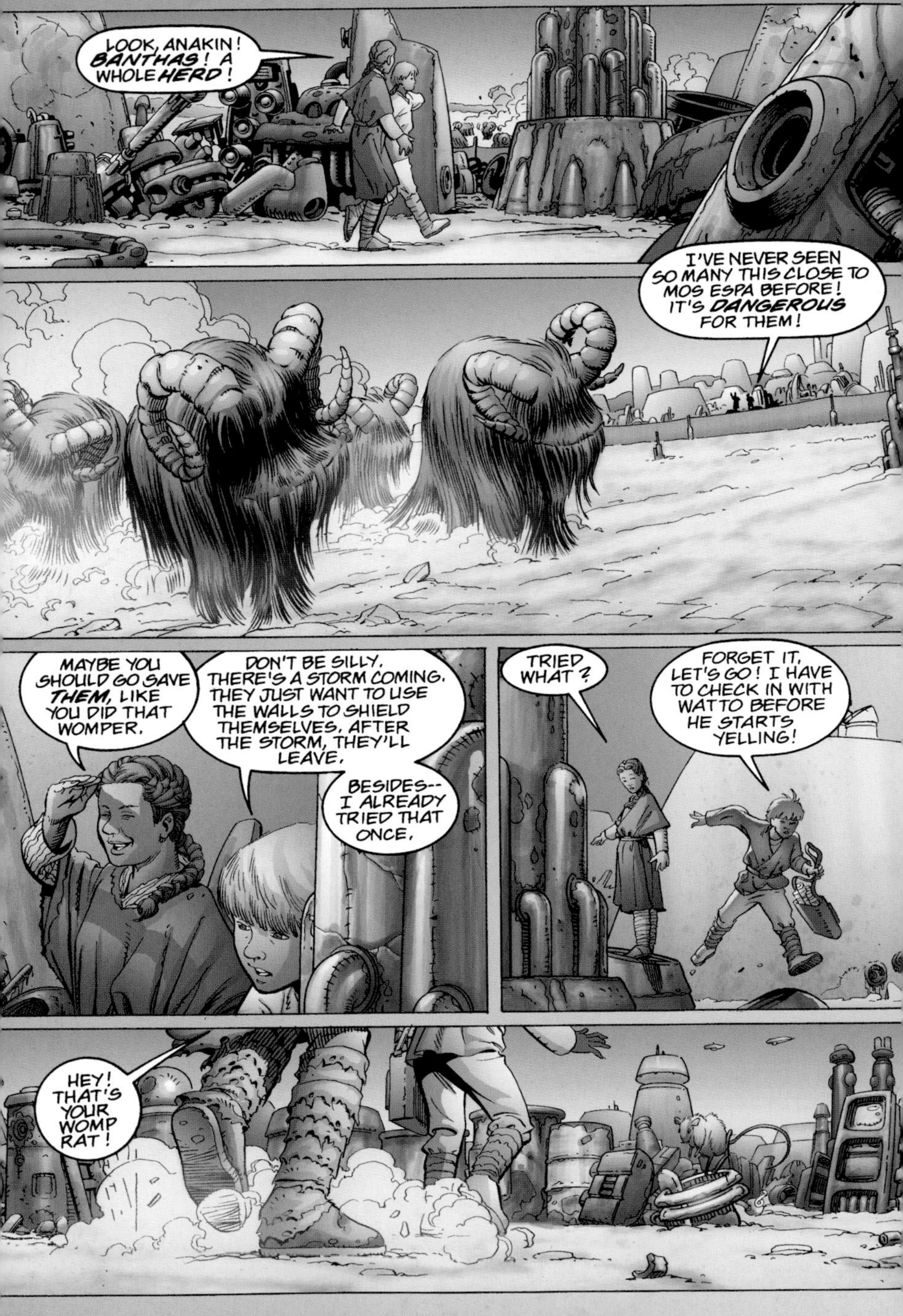
LOOK, ANAKIN! BANTHAS! A WHOLE HERD!
I'VE NEVER SEEN SO MANY THIS CLOSE TO MOS ESPA BEFORE! IT'S DANGEROUS FOR THEM!
MAYBE YOU SHOULD GO SAVE THEM, LIKE YOU DID THAT WOMPER.
DON'T BE SILLY. THERE'S A STORM COMING. THEY JUST WANT TO USE THE WALLS TO SHIELD THEMSELVES. AFTER THE STORM, THEY'LL LEAVE.
BESIDES-- I ALREADY TRIED THAT ONCE.
TRIED WHAT?
FORGET IT, LET'S GO! I HAVE TO CHECK IN WITH WATTO BEFORE HE STARTS YELLING!
HEY! THAT'S YOUR WOMP RAT!

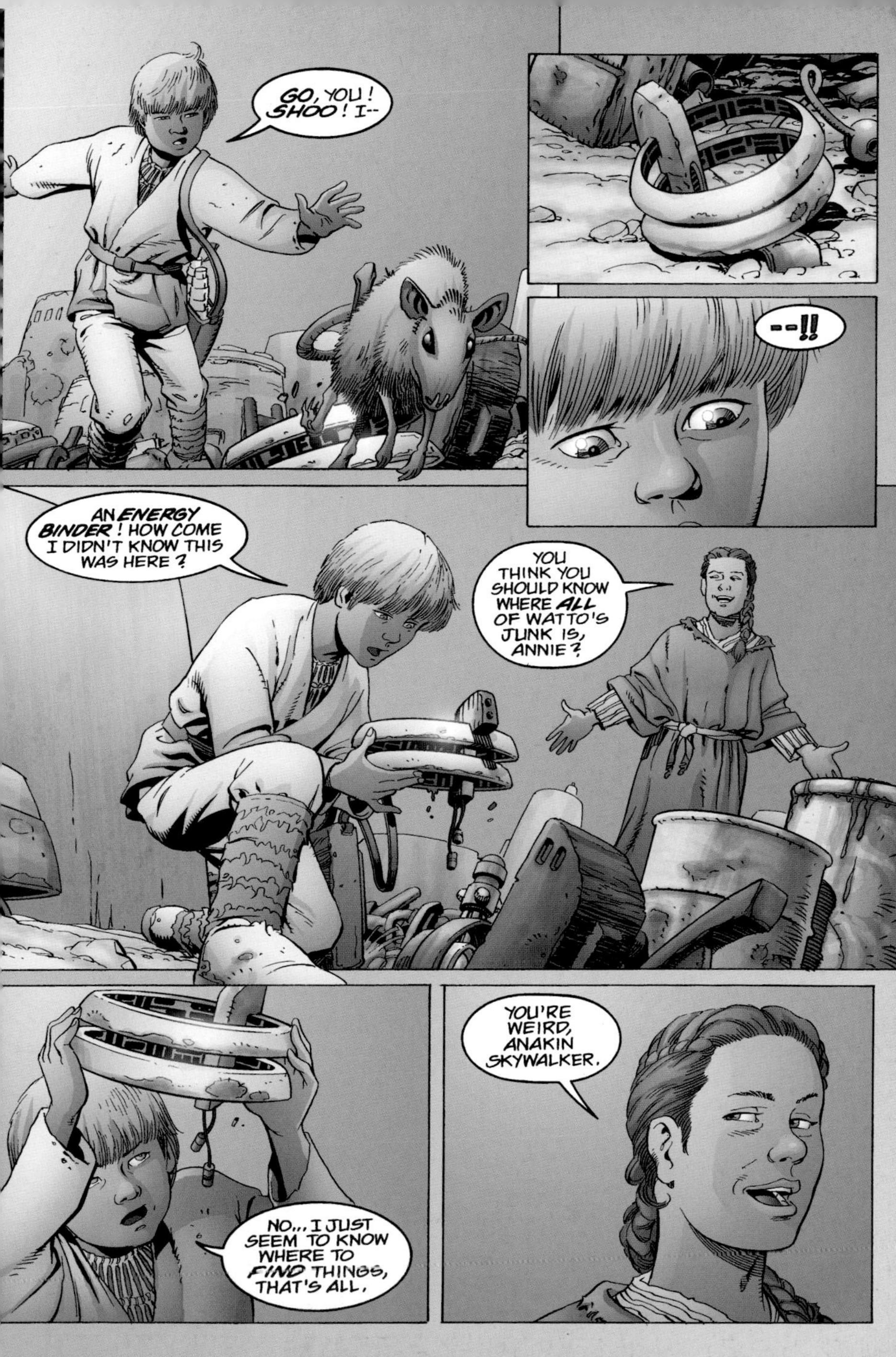
GO, YOU! SHOO! I--
--!!
AN ENERGY BINDER! HOW COME I DIDN'T KNOW THIS WAS HERE?
YOU THINK YOU SHOULD KNOW WHERE ALL OF WATTO'S JUNK IS, ANNIE?
NO... I JUST SEEM TO KNOW WHERE TO FIND THINGS, THAT'S ALL.
YOU'RE WEIRD, ANAKIN SKYWALKER.

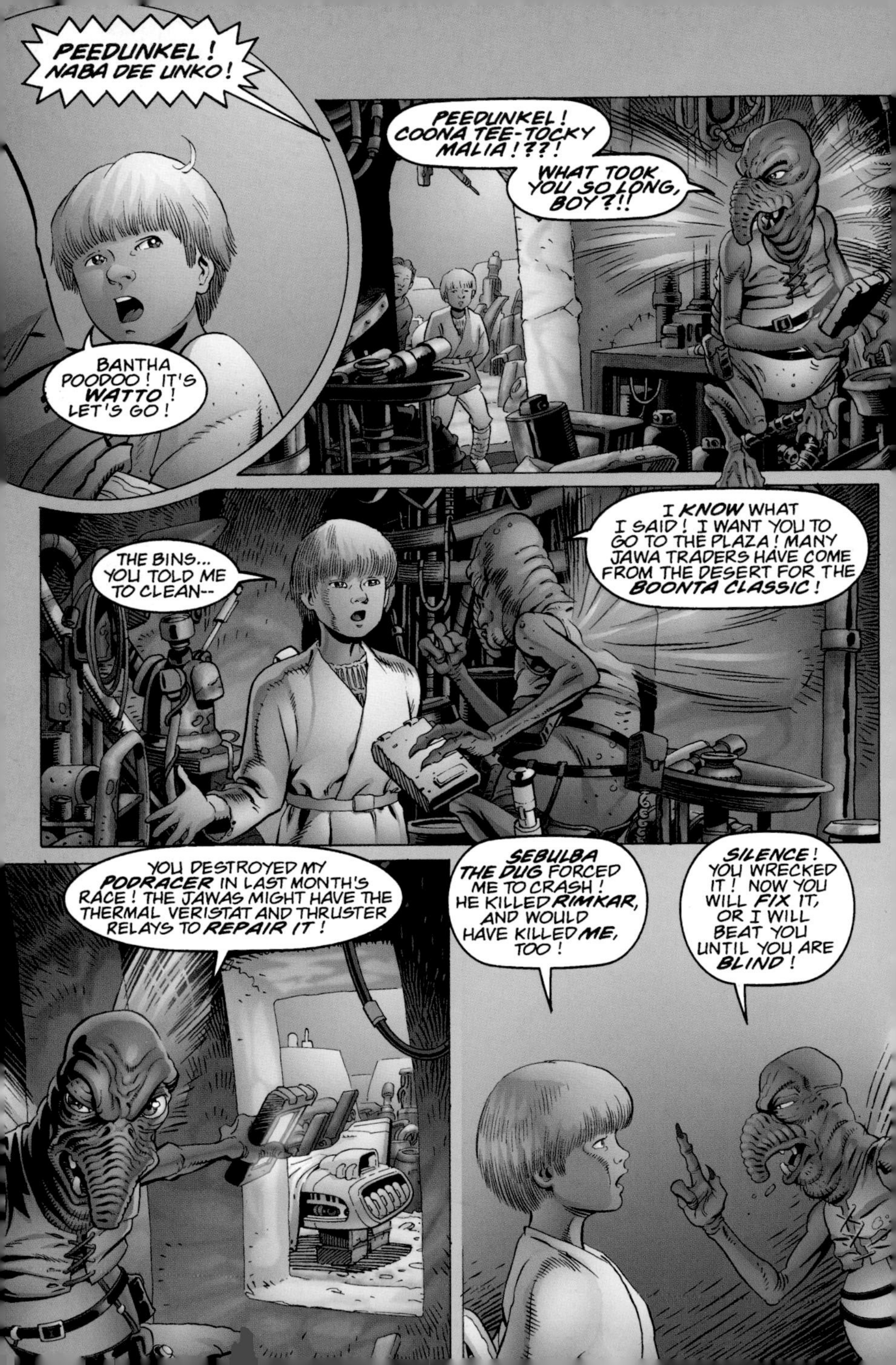
PEEDUNKEL! NABA DEE UNKO!
BANTHA POODOO! IT'S WATTO! LET'S GO!
PEEDUNKEL! COONA TEE-TOCKY MALIA!??!
WHAT TOOK YOU SO LONG, BOY?!!
THE BINS... YOU TOLD ME TO CLEAN--
I KNOW WHAT I SAID! I WANT YOU TO GO TO THE PLAZA! MANY JAWA TRADERS HAVE COME FROM THE DESERT FOR THE BOONTA CLASSIC!
YOU DESTROYED MY PODRACER IN LAST MONTH'S RACE! THE JAWAS MIGHT HAVE THE THERMAL VERISTAT AND THRUSTER RELAYS TO REPAIR IT!
SEBULBA THE DUG FORCED ME TO CRASH! HE KILLED RIMKAR, AND WOULD HAVE KILLED ME, TOO!
SILENCE! YOU WRECKED IT! NOW YOU WILL FIX IT, OR I WILL BEAT YOU UNTIL YOU ARE BLIND!

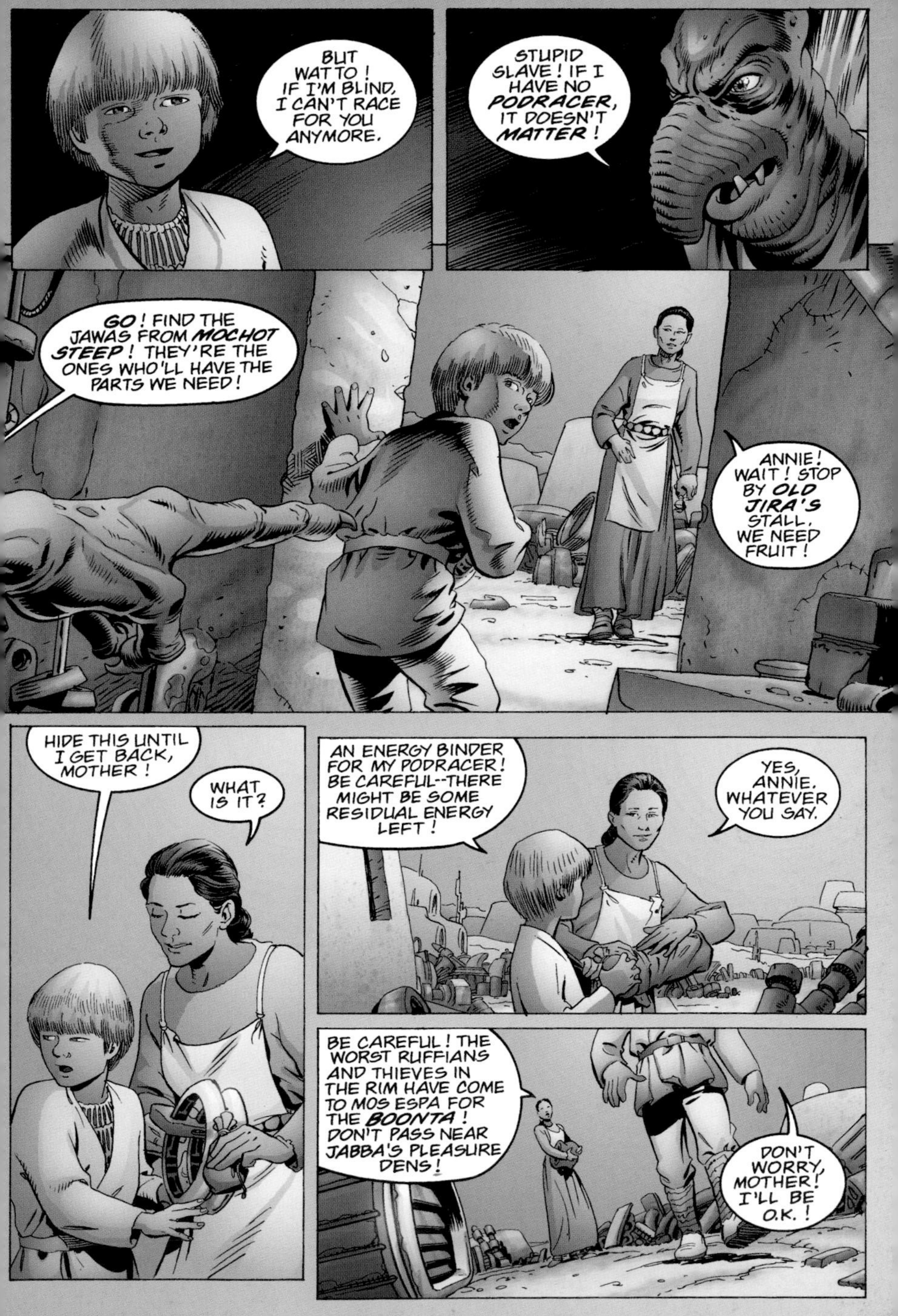
BUT WATTO! IF I'M BLIND, I CAN'T RACE FOR YOU ANYMORE.
STUPID SLAVE! IF I HAVE NO PODRACER, IT DOESN'T MATTER!
GO! FIND THE JAWAS FROM MOCHOT STEEP! THEY'RE THE ONES WHO'LL HAVE THE PARTS WE NEED!
ANNIE! WAIT! STOP BY OLD JIRA'S STALL. WE NEED FRUIT!
HIDE THIS UNTIL I GET BACK, MOTHER!
WHAT IS IT?
AN ENERGY BINDER FOR MY PODRACER! BE CAREFUL--THERE MIGHT BE SOME RESIDUAL ENERGY LEFT!
YES, ANNIE. WHATEVER YOU SAY.
BE CAREFUL! THE WORST RUFFIANS AND THIEVES IN THE RIM HAVE COME TO MOS ESPA FOR THE BOONTA! DON'T PASS NEAR JABBA'S PLEASURE DENS!
DON'T WORRY, MOTHER! I'LL BE O.K.!

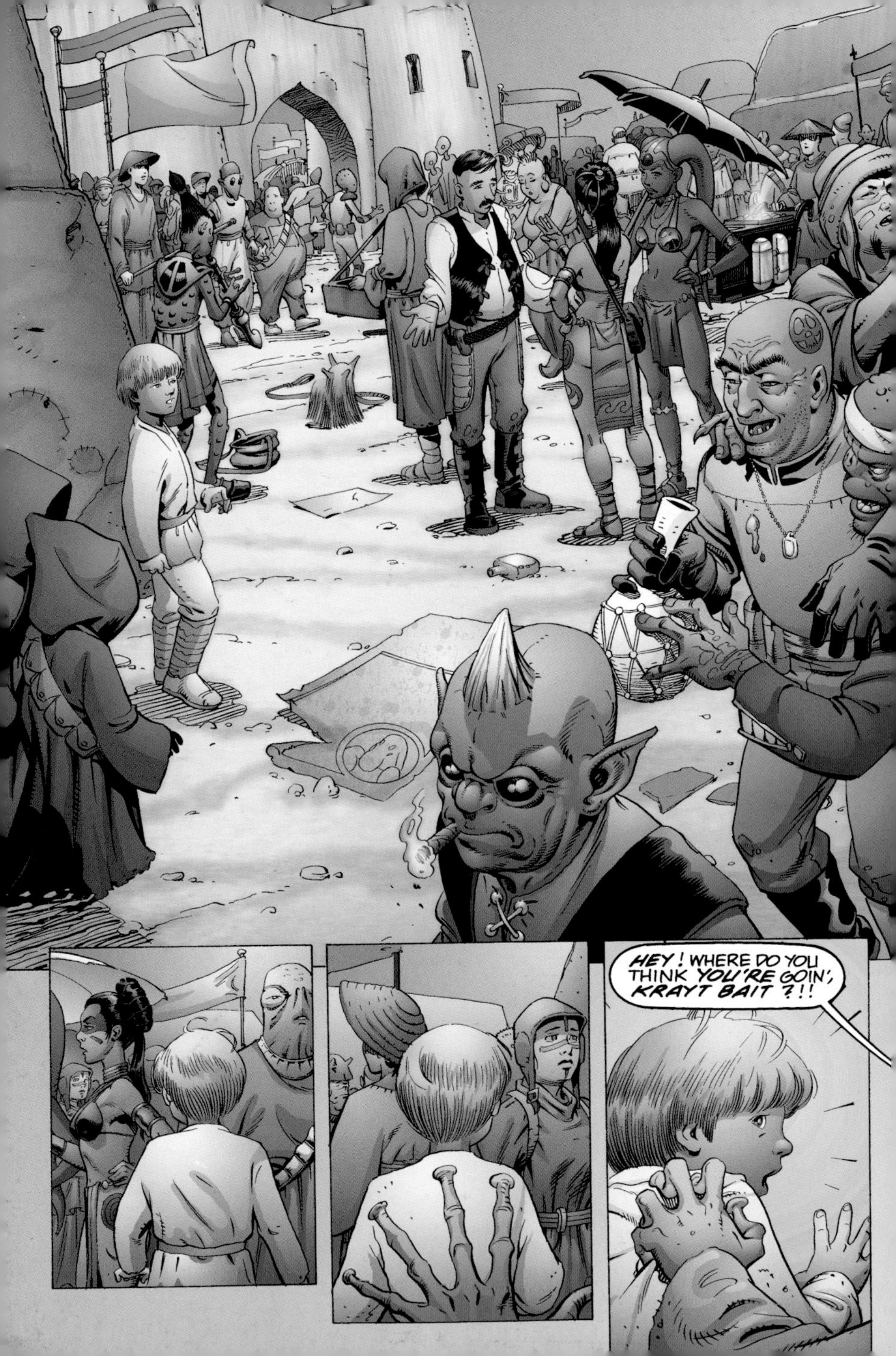
HEY! WHERE DO YOU THINK YOU'RE GOIN', KRAYT BAIT?!!

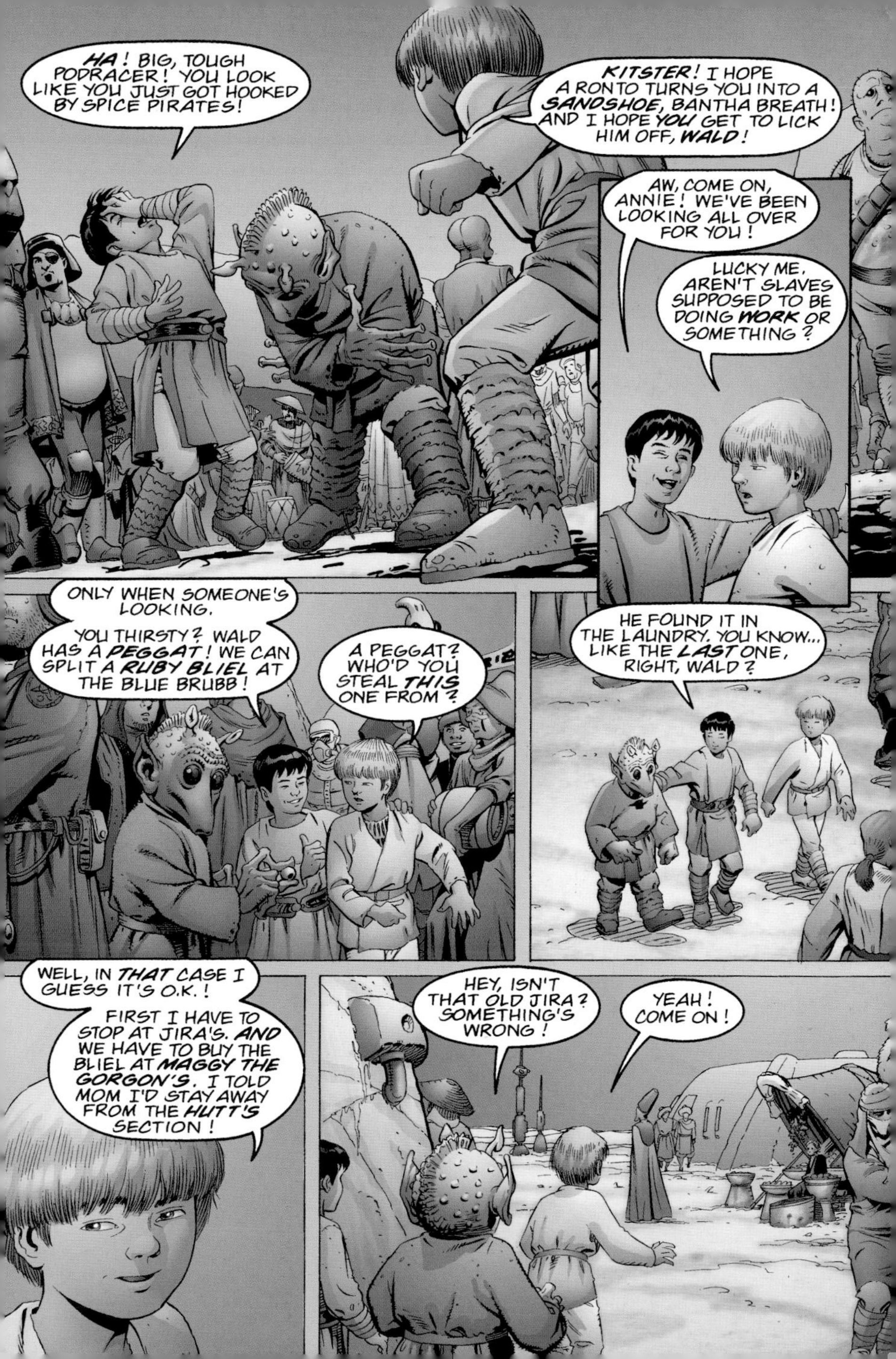
HA! BIG, TOUGH PODRACER! YOU LOOK LIKE YOU JUST GOT HOOKED BY SPICE PIRATES!
KITSTER! I HOPE A RONTO TURNS YOU INTO A SANDSHOE, BANTHA BREATH! AND I HOPE YOU GET TO LICK HIM OFF, WALD!
AW, COME ON, ANNIE! WE'VE BEEN LOOKING ALL OVER FOR YOU!
LUCKY ME. AREN'T SLAVES SUPPOSED TO BE DOING WORK OR SOMETHING?
ONLY WHEN SOMEONE'S LOOKING.
YOU THIRSTY? WALD HAS A PEGGAT! WE CAN SPLIT A RUBY BLIEL AT THE BLUE BRUBB!
A PEGGAT? WHO'D YOU STEAL THIS ONE FROM?
HE FOUND IT IN THE LAUNDRY. YOU KNOW... LIKE THE LAST ONE, RIGHT, WALD?
WELL, IN THAT CASE I GUESS IT'S O.K.!
FIRST I HAVE TO STOP AT JIRA'S. AND WE HAVE TO BUY THE BLIEL AT MAGGY THE GORGON'S. I TOLD MOM I'D STAY AWAY FROM THE HUTT'S SECTION!
HEY, ISN'T THAT OLD JIRA? SOMETHING'S WRONG!
YEAH! COME ON!

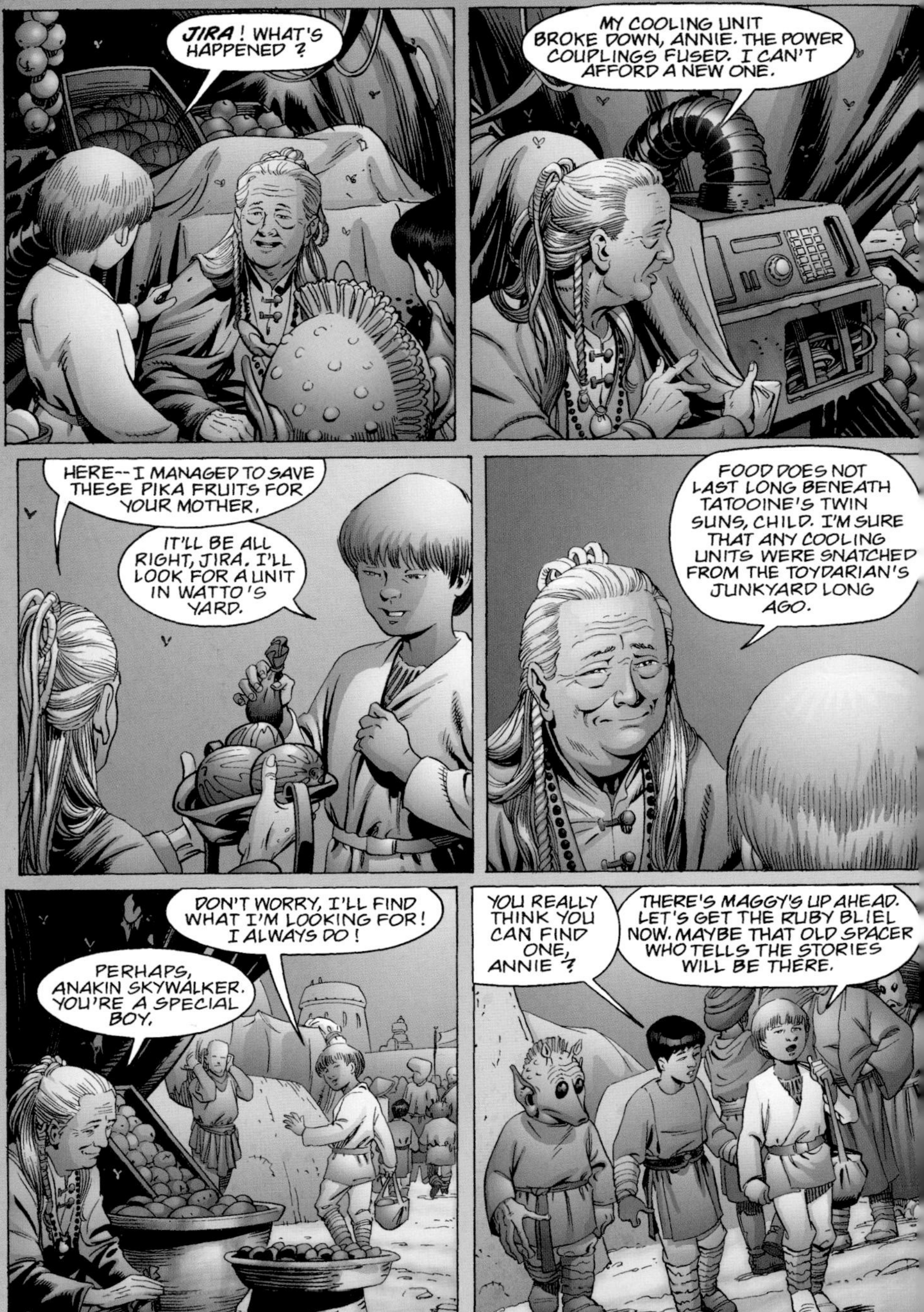
JIRA! WHAT'S HAPPENED?
MY COOLING UNIT BROKE DOWN, ANNIE. THE POWER COUPLINGS FUSED. I CAN'T AFFORD A NEW ONE.
HERE-- I MANAGED TO SAVE THESE PIKA FRUITS FOR YOUR MOTHER.
IT'LL BE ALL RIGHT, JIRA. I'LL LOOK FOR A UNIT IN WATTO'S YARD.
FOOD DOES NOT LAST LONG BENEATH TATOOINE'S TWIN SUNS, CHILD. I'M SURE THAT ANY COOLING UNITS WERE SNATCHED FROM THE TOYDARIAN'S JUNKYARD LONG AGO.
DON'T WORRY, I'LL FIND WHAT I'M LOOKING FOR! I ALWAYS DO!
PERHAPS, ANAKIN SKYWALKER. YOU'RE A SPECIAL BOY.
YOU REALLY THINK YOU CAN FIND ONE, ANNIE?
THERE'S MAGGY'S UP AHEAD. LET'S GET THE RUBY BLIEL NOW. MAYBE THAT OLD SPACER WHO TELLS THE STORIES WILL BE THERE.

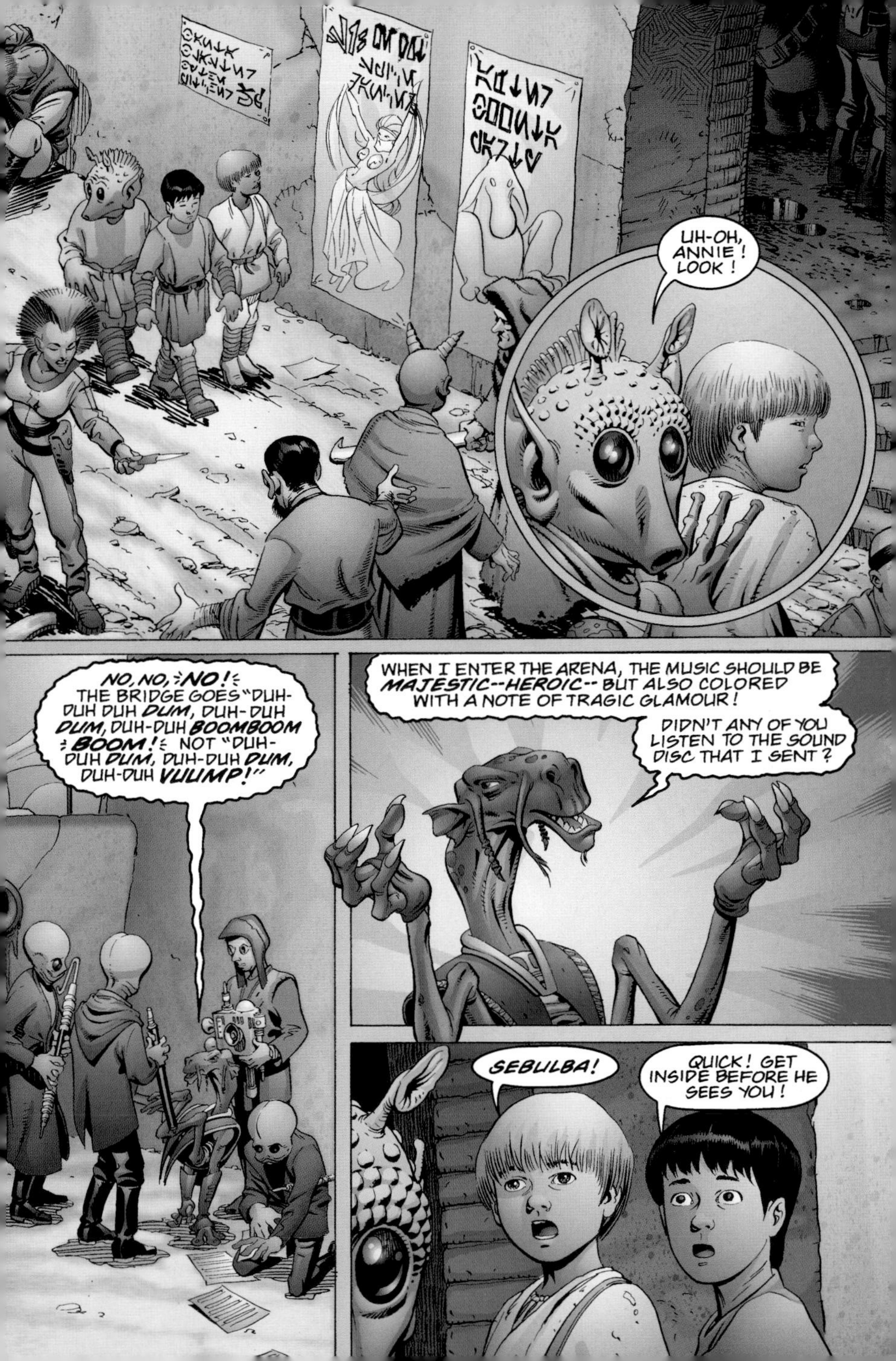
UH-OH, ANNIE! LOOK!
NO, NO, NO! THE BRIDGE GOES "DUH-DUH DUH DUM, DUH-DUH DUM, DUH-DUH BOOMBOOM BOOM!" NOT "DUH-DUH DUM, DUH-DUH DUM, DUH-DUH VUUMP!"
WHEN I ENTER THE ARENA, THE MUSIC SHOULD BE MAJESTIC--HEROIC-- BUT ALSO COLORED WITH A NOTE OF TRAGIC GLAMOUR!
DIDN'T ANY OF YOU LISTEN TO THE SOUND DISC THAT I SENT?
SEBULBA!
QUICK! GET INSIDE BEFORE HE SEES YOU!

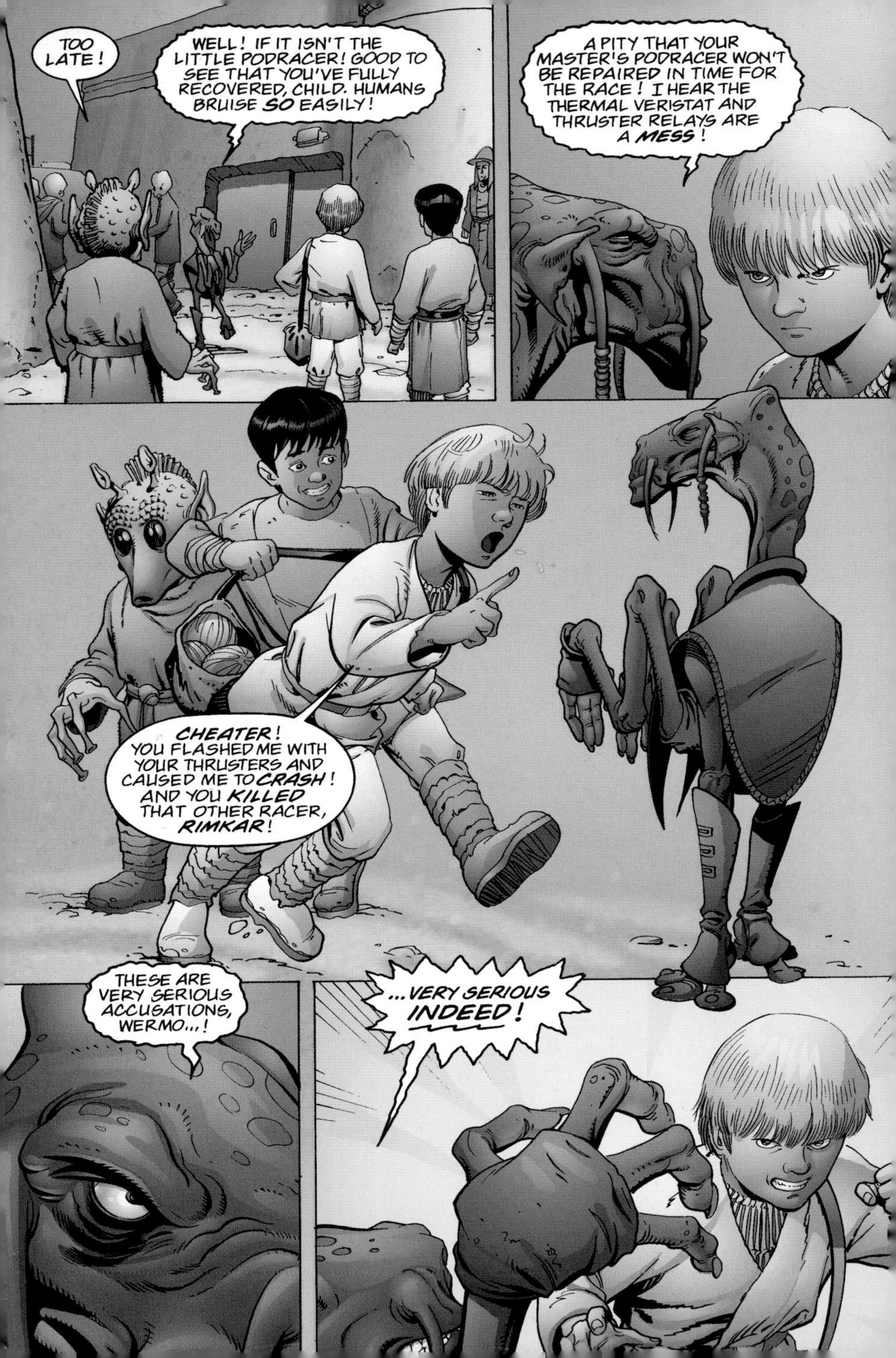
TOO LATE!
WELL! IF IT ISN'T THE LITTLE PODRACER! GOOD TO SEE THAT YOU'VE FULLY RECOVERED, CHILD. HUMANS BRUISE SO EASILY!
A PITY THAT YOUR MASTER'S PODRACER WON'T BE REPAIRED IN TIME FOR THE RACE! I HEAR THE THERMAL VERISTAT AND THRUSTER RELAYS ARE A MESS!
CHEATER! YOU FLASHED ME WITH YOUR THRUSTERS AND CAUSED ME TO CRASH! AND YOU KILLED THAT OTHER RACER, RIMKAR!
THESE ARE VERY SERIOUS ACCUSATIONS, WERMO...!
...VERY SERIOUS INDEED!

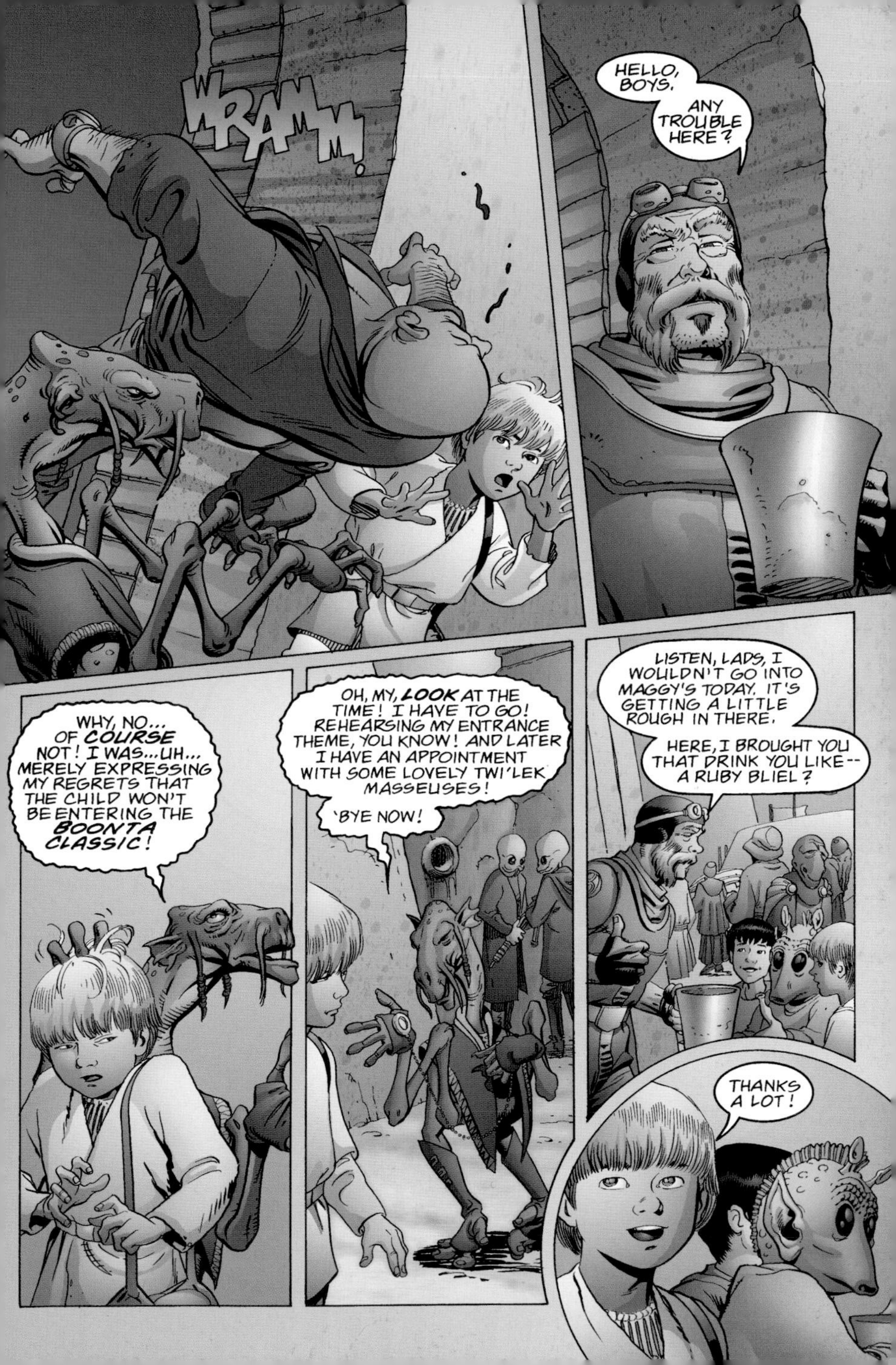
WRAMM!
HELLO, BOYS.
ANY TROUBLE HERE?
WHY, NO... OF COURSE NOT! I WAS...UH... MERELY EXPRESSING MY REGRETS THAT THE CHILD WON'T BE ENTERING THE BOONTA CLASSIC!
OH, MY, LOOK AT THE TIME! I HAVE TO GO! REHEARSING MY ENTRANCE THEME, YOU KNOW! AND LATER I HAVE AN APPOINTMENT WITH SOME LOVELY TWI'LEK MASSEUSES!
'BYE NOW!
LISTEN, LADS, I WOULDN'T GO INTO MAGGY'S TODAY. IT'S GETTING A LITTLE ROUGH IN THERE.
HERE, I BROUGHT YOU THAT DRINK YOU LIKE-- A RUBY BLIEL?
THANKS A LOT!

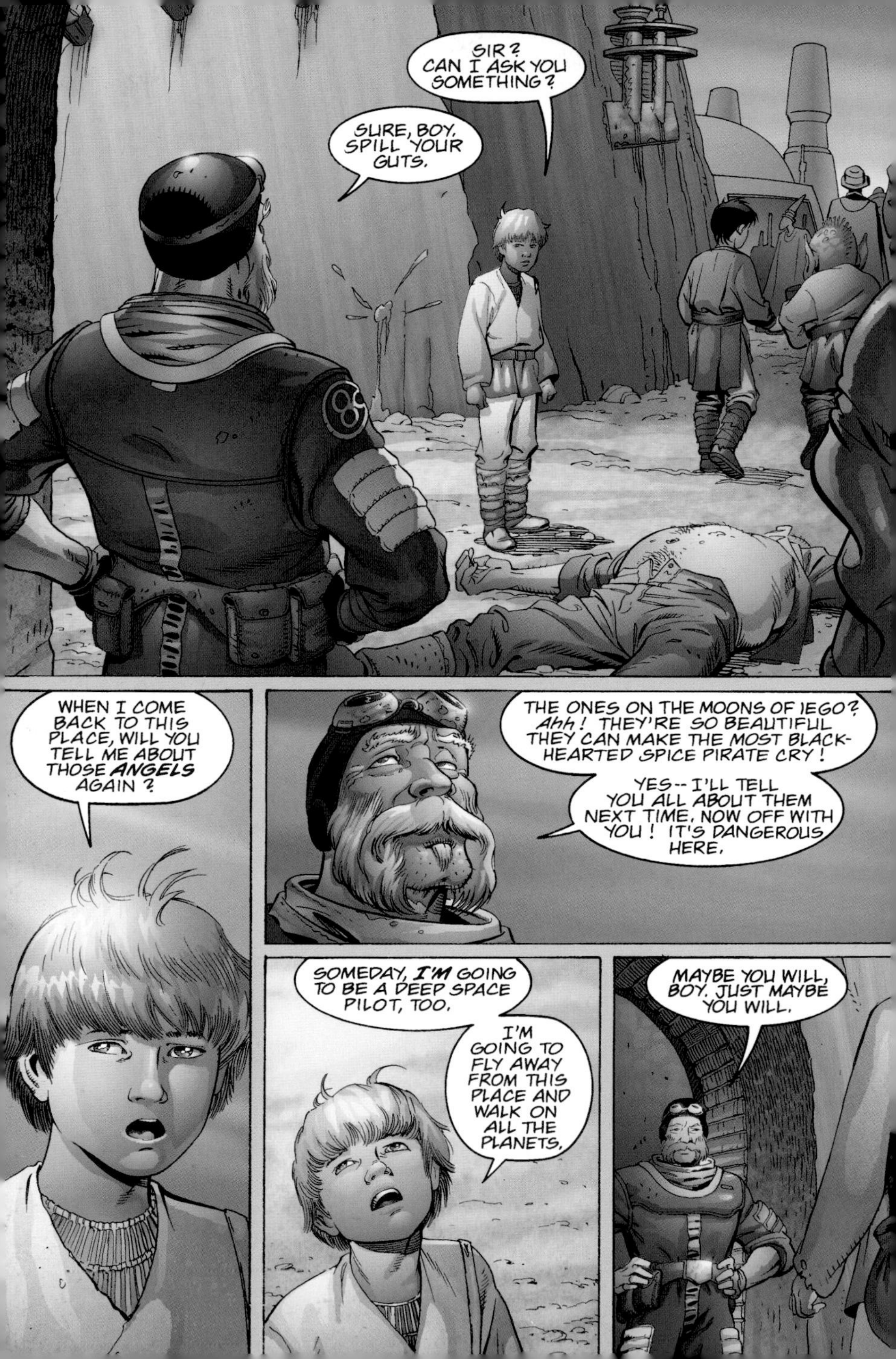
SIR? CAN I ASK YOU SOMETHING?
SURE, BOY. SPILL YOUR GUTS.
WHEN I COME BACK TO THIS PLACE, WILL YOU TELL ME ABOUT THOSE ANGELS AGAIN?
THE ONES ON THE MOONS OF IEGO? Ahh! THEY'RE SO BEAUTIFUL THEY CAN MAKE THE MOST BLACK-HEARTED SPICE PIRATE CRY!
YES-- I'LL TELL YOU ALL ABOUT THEM NEXT TIME. NOW OFF WITH YOU! IT'S DANGEROUS HERE.
SOMEDAY, I'M GOING TO BE A DEEP SPACE PILOT, TOO.
I'M GOING TO FLY AWAY FROM THIS PLACE AND WALK ON ALL THE PLANETS.
MAYBE YOU WILL, BOY. JUST MAYBE YOU WILL.

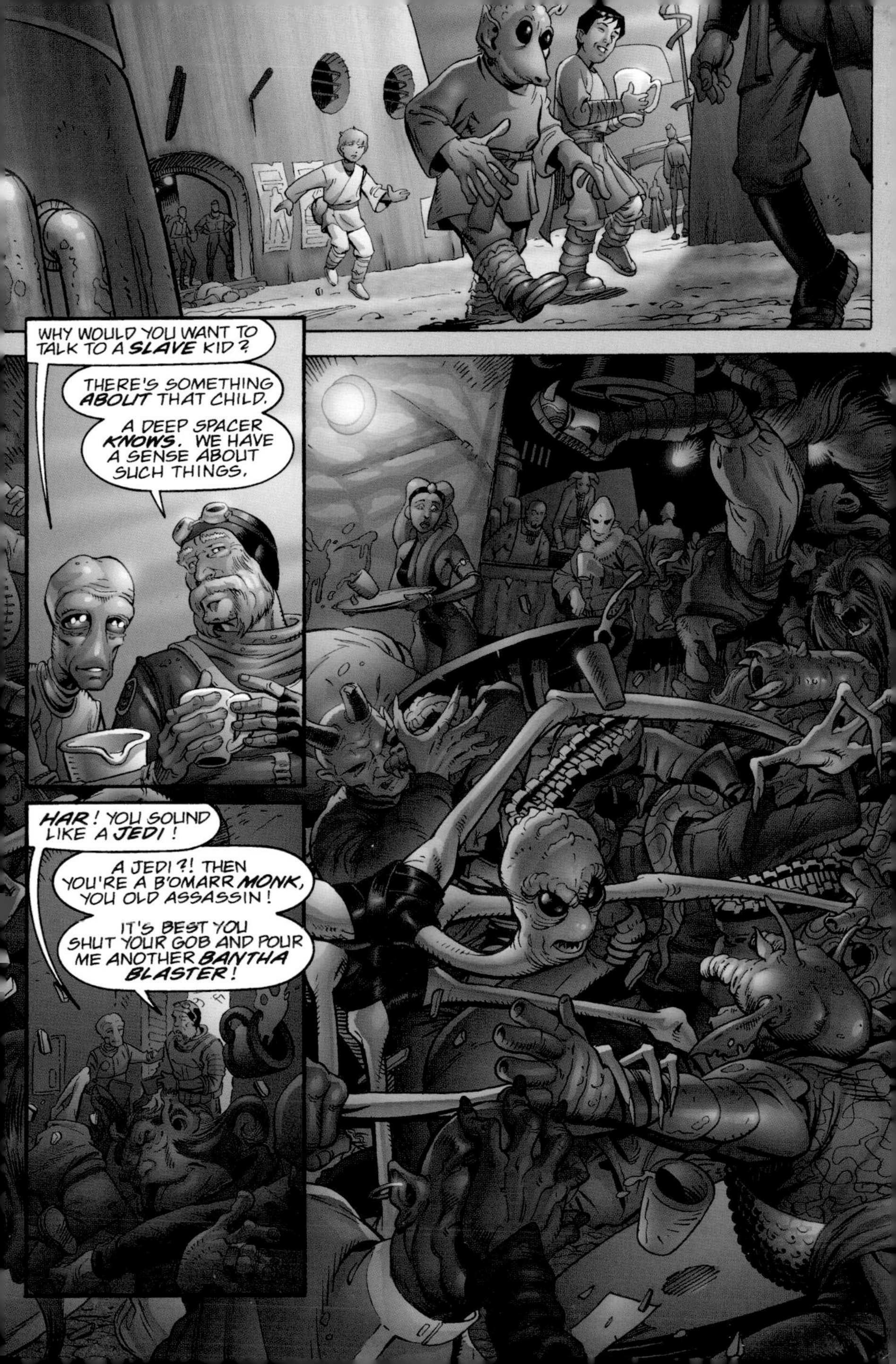
WHY WOULD YOU WANT TO TALK TO A SLAVE KID?
THERE'S SOMETHING ABOUT THAT CHILD.
A DEEP SPACER KNOWS. WE HAVE A SENSE ABOUT SUCH THINGS.
HAR! YOU SOUND LIKE A JEDI!
A JEDI?! THEN YOU'RE A B'OMARR MONK, YOU OLD ASSASSIN!
IT'S BEST YOU SHUT YOUR GOB AND POUR ME ANOTHER BANTHA BLASTER!

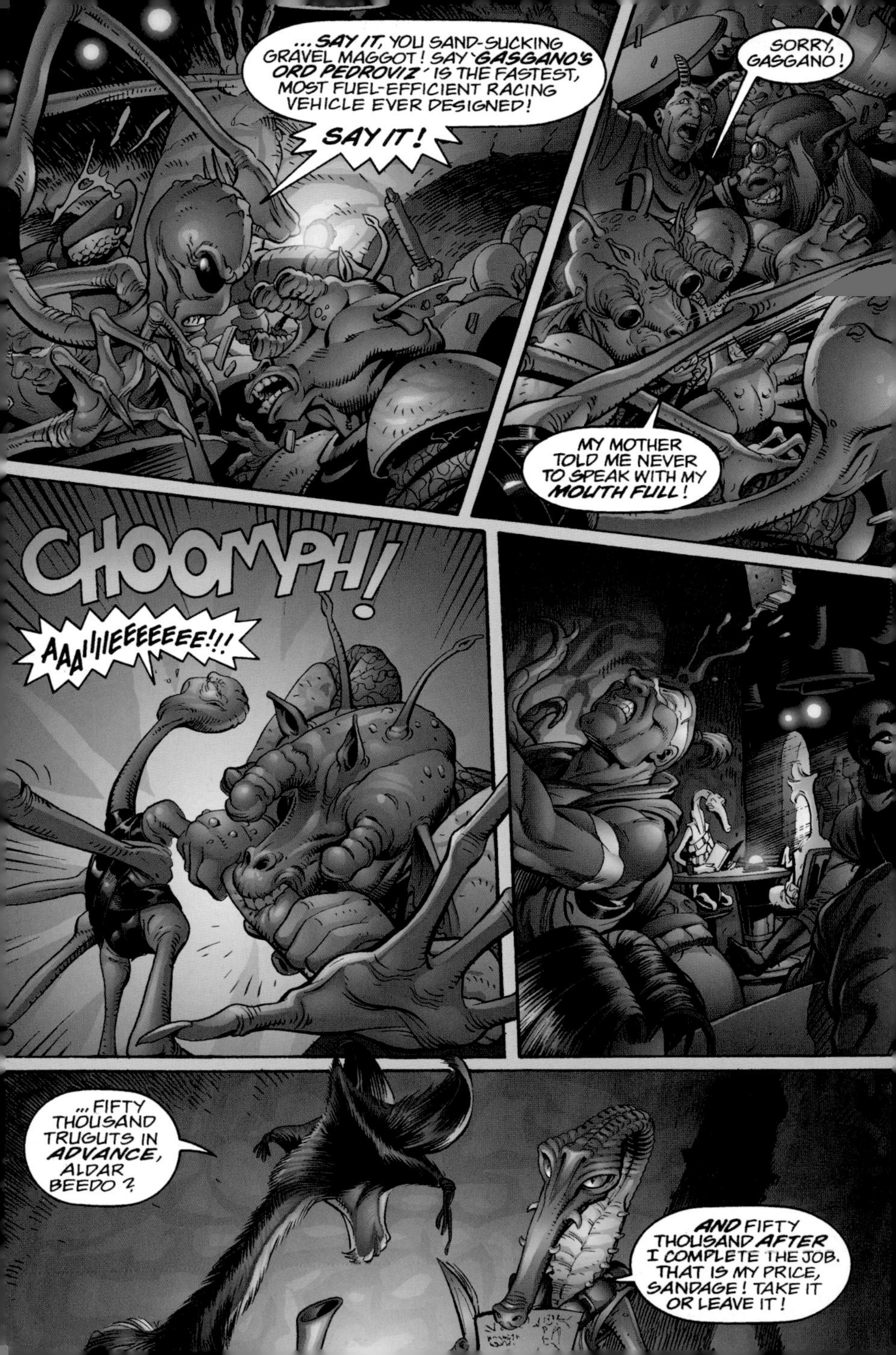

... SAY IT, YOU SAND-SUCKING GRAVEL MAGGOT! SAY 'GASGANO'S ORD PEDROVIZ' IS THE FASTEST, MOST FUEL-EFFICIENT RACING VEHICLE EVER DESIGNED!
SAY IT!
SORRY, GASGANO!
MY MOTHER TOLD ME NEVER TO SPEAK WITH MY MOUTH FULL!
CHOOMPH!
AAAIIIIEEEEEEE!!!
... FIFTY THOUSAND TRUGUTS IN ADVANCE, ALDAR BEEDO?
AND FIFTY THOUSAND AFTER I COMPLETE THE JOB. THAT IS MY PRICE, SANDAGE! TAKE IT OR LEAVE IT!

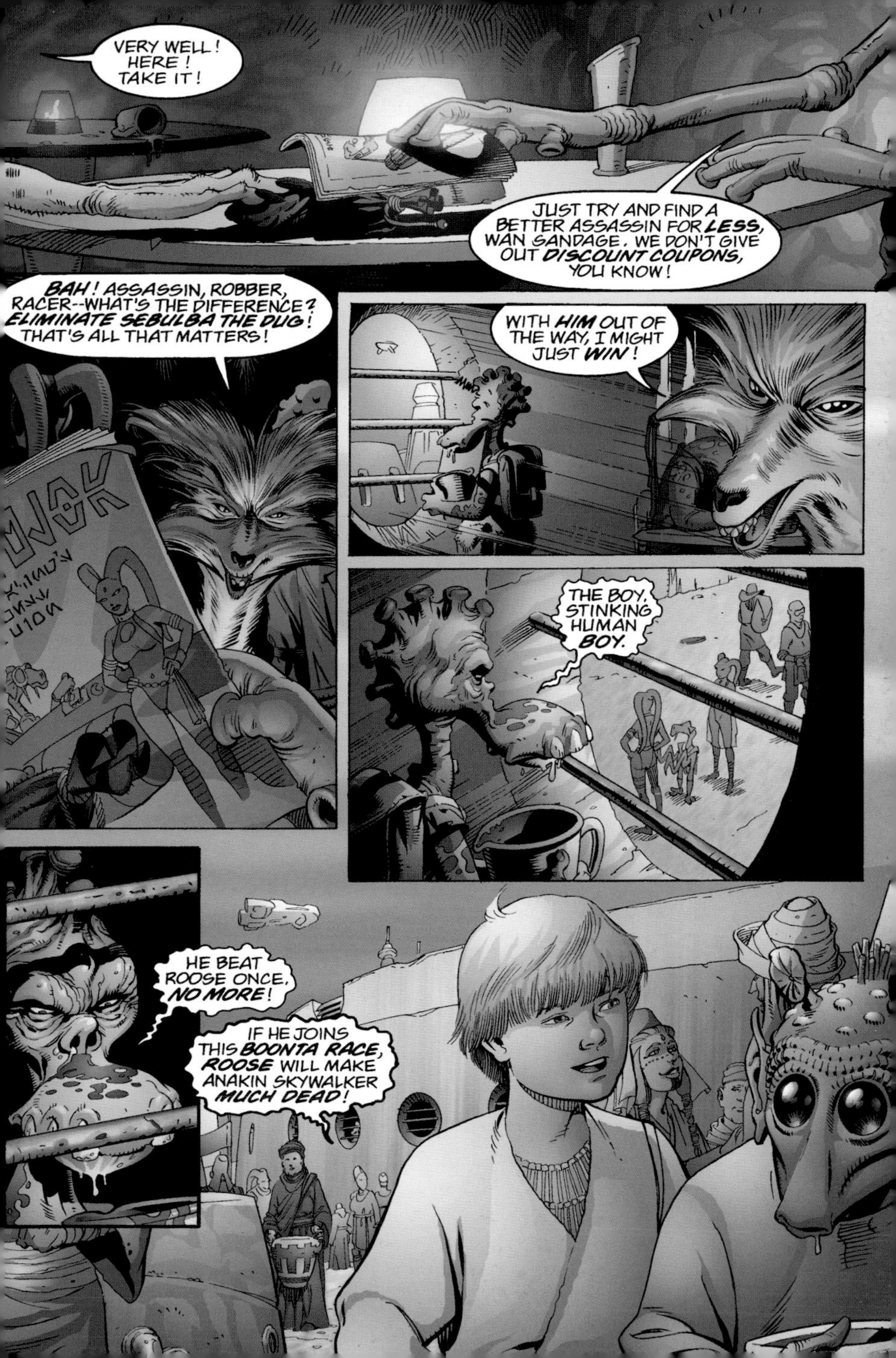
VERY WELL! HERE! TAKE IT!
JUST TRY AND FIND A BETTER ASSASSIN FOR LESS, WAN SANDAGE. WE DON'T GIVE OUT DISCOUNT COUPONS, YOU KNOW!
BAH! ASSASSIN, ROBBER, RACER--WHAT'S THE DIFFERENCE? ELIMINATE SEBULBA THE DUG! THAT'S ALL THAT MATTERS!
WITH HIM OUT OF THE WAY, I MIGHT JUST WIN!
THE BOY. STINKING HUMAN BOY.
HE BEAT ROOSE ONCE, NO MORE!
IF HE JOINS THIS BOONTA RACE, ROOSE WILL MAKE ANAKIN SKYWALKER MUCH DEAD!

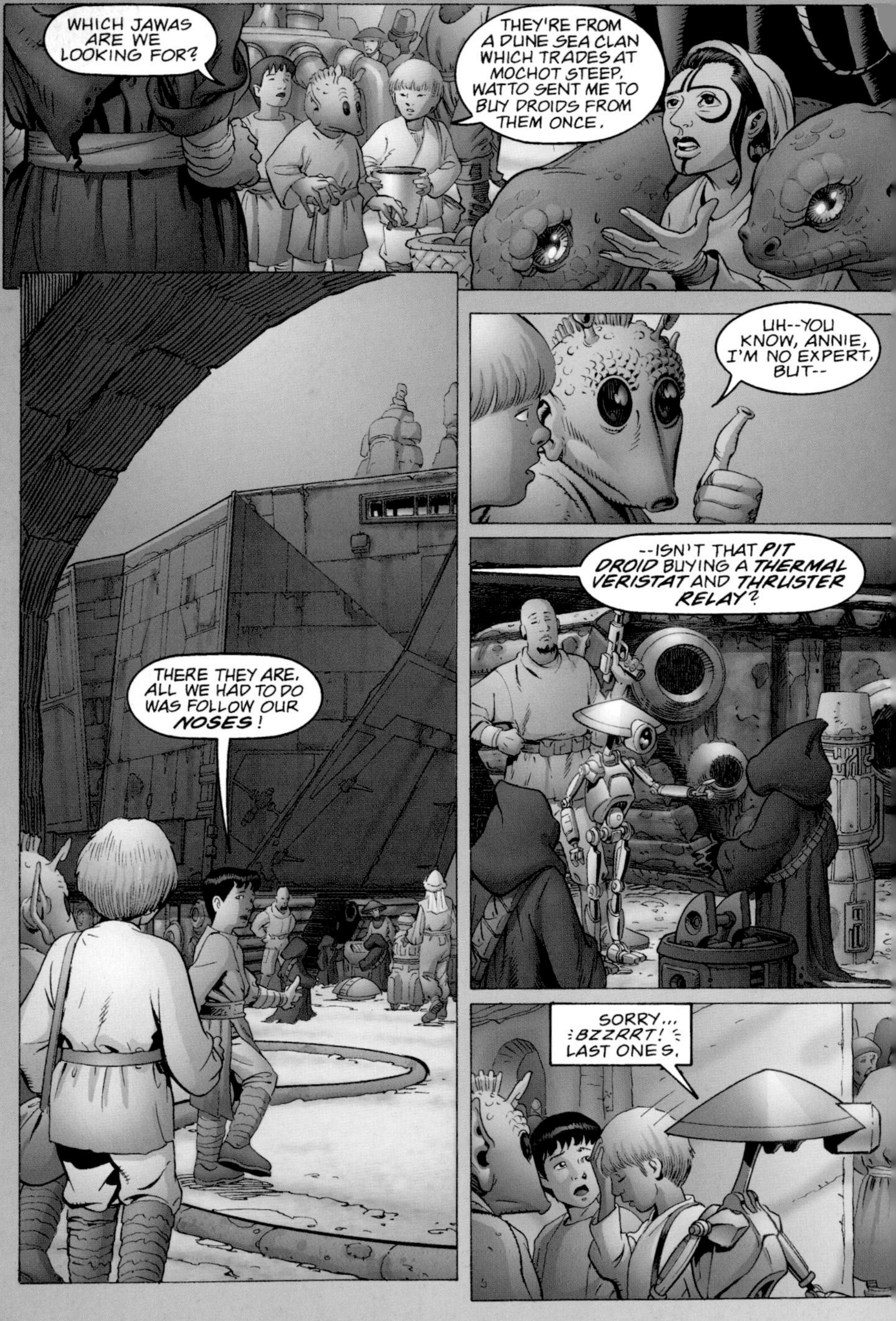
WHICH JAWAS ARE WE LOOKING FOR?
THEY'RE FROM A DUNE SEA CLAN WHICH TRADES AT MOCHOT STEEP. WATTO SENT ME TO BUY DROIDS FROM THEM ONCE.
THERE THEY ARE. ALL WE HAD TO DO WAS FOLLOW OUR NOSES!
UH--YOU KNOW, ANNIE, I'M NO EXPERT, BUT--
--ISN'T THAT PIT DROID BUYING A THERMAL VERISTAT AND THRUSTER RELAY?
SORRY... BZZRRT! LAST ONES.

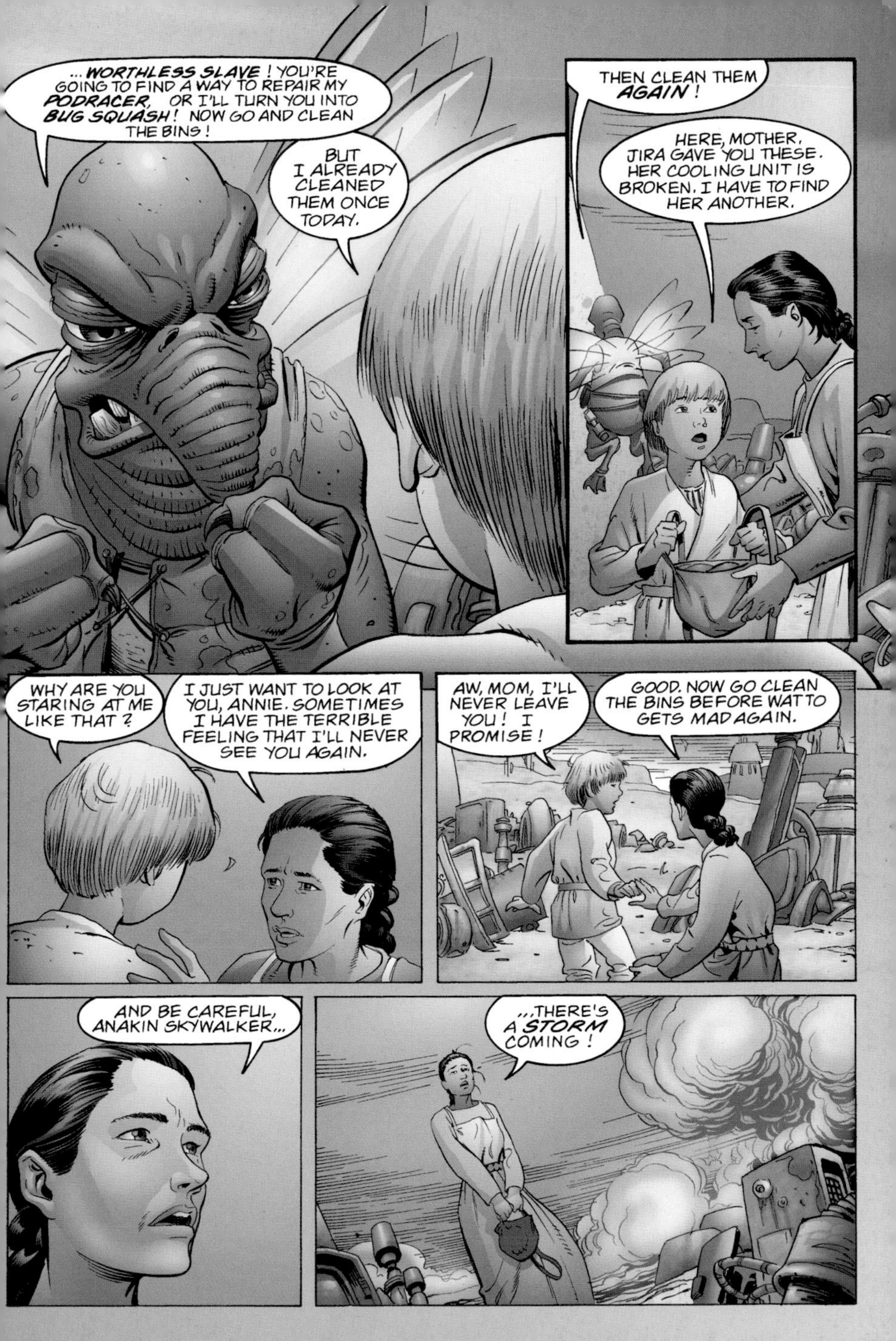
...WORTHLESS SLAVE! YOU'RE GOING TO FIND A WAY TO REPAIR MY PODRACER, OR I'LL TURN YOU INTO BUG SQUASH! NOW GO AND CLEAN THE BINS!
BUT I ALREADY CLEANED THEM ONCE TODAY.
THEN CLEAN THEM AGAIN!
HERE, MOTHER. JIRA GAVE YOU THESE. HER COOLING UNIT IS BROKEN. I HAVE TO FIND HER ANOTHER.
WHY ARE YOU STARING AT ME LIKE THAT?
I JUST WANT TO LOOK AT YOU, ANNIE. SOMETIMES I HAVE THE TERRIBLE FEELING THAT I'LL NEVER SEE YOU AGAIN.
AW, MOM, I'LL NEVER LEAVE YOU! I PROMISE!
GOOD. NOW GO CLEAN THE BINS BEFORE WATTO GETS MAD AGAIN.
AND BE CAREFUL, ANAKIN SKYWALKER...
...THERE'S A STORM COMING!

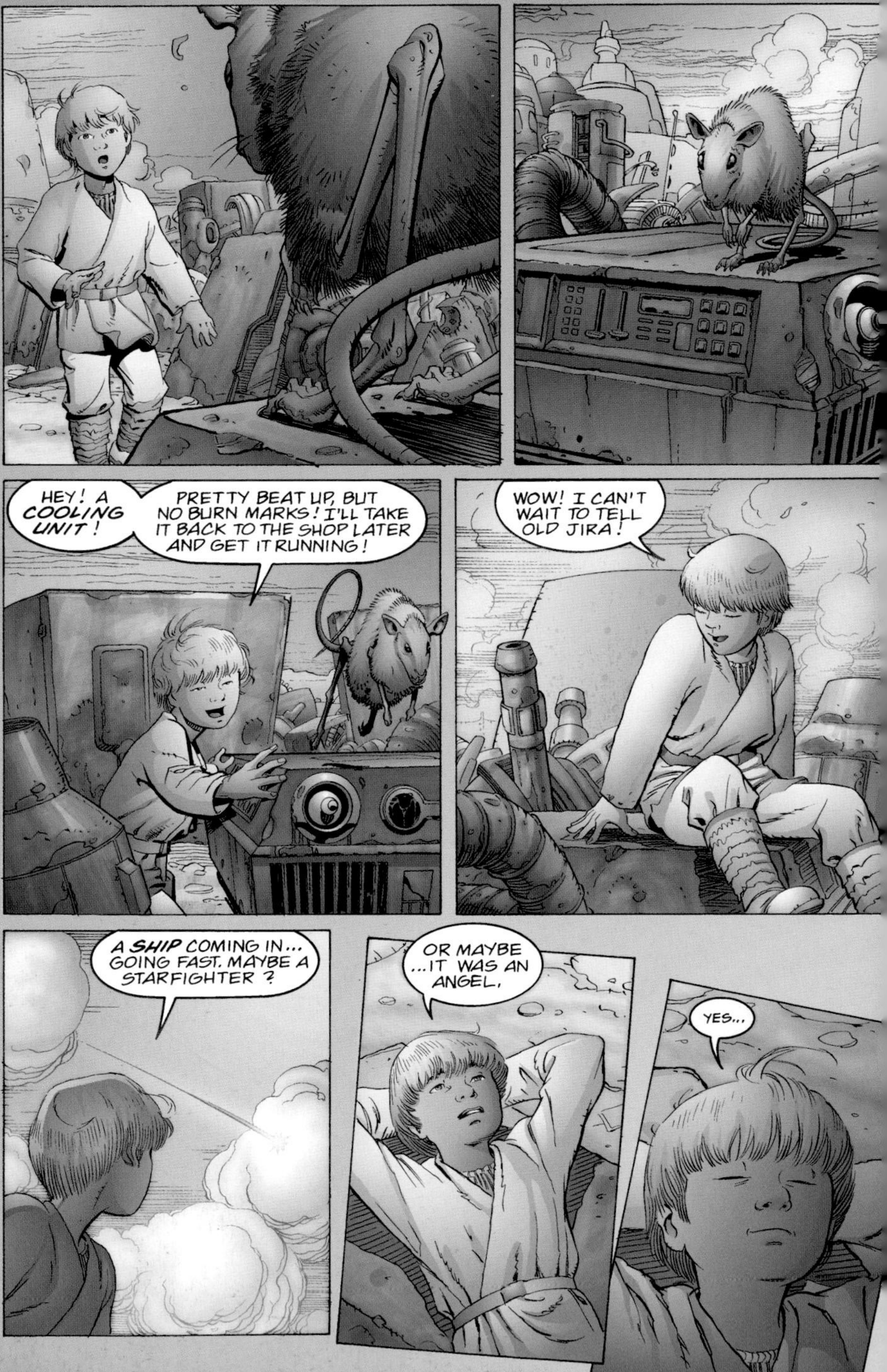
HEY! A COOLING UNIT!
PRETTY BEAT UP, BUT NO BURN MARKS! I'LL TAKE IT BACK TO THE SHOP LATER AND GET IT RUNNING!
WOW! I CAN'T WAIT TO TELL OLD JIRA!
A SHIP COMING IN... GOING FAST. MAYBE A STARFIGHTER?
OR MAYBE ...IT WAS AN ANGEL.
YES...

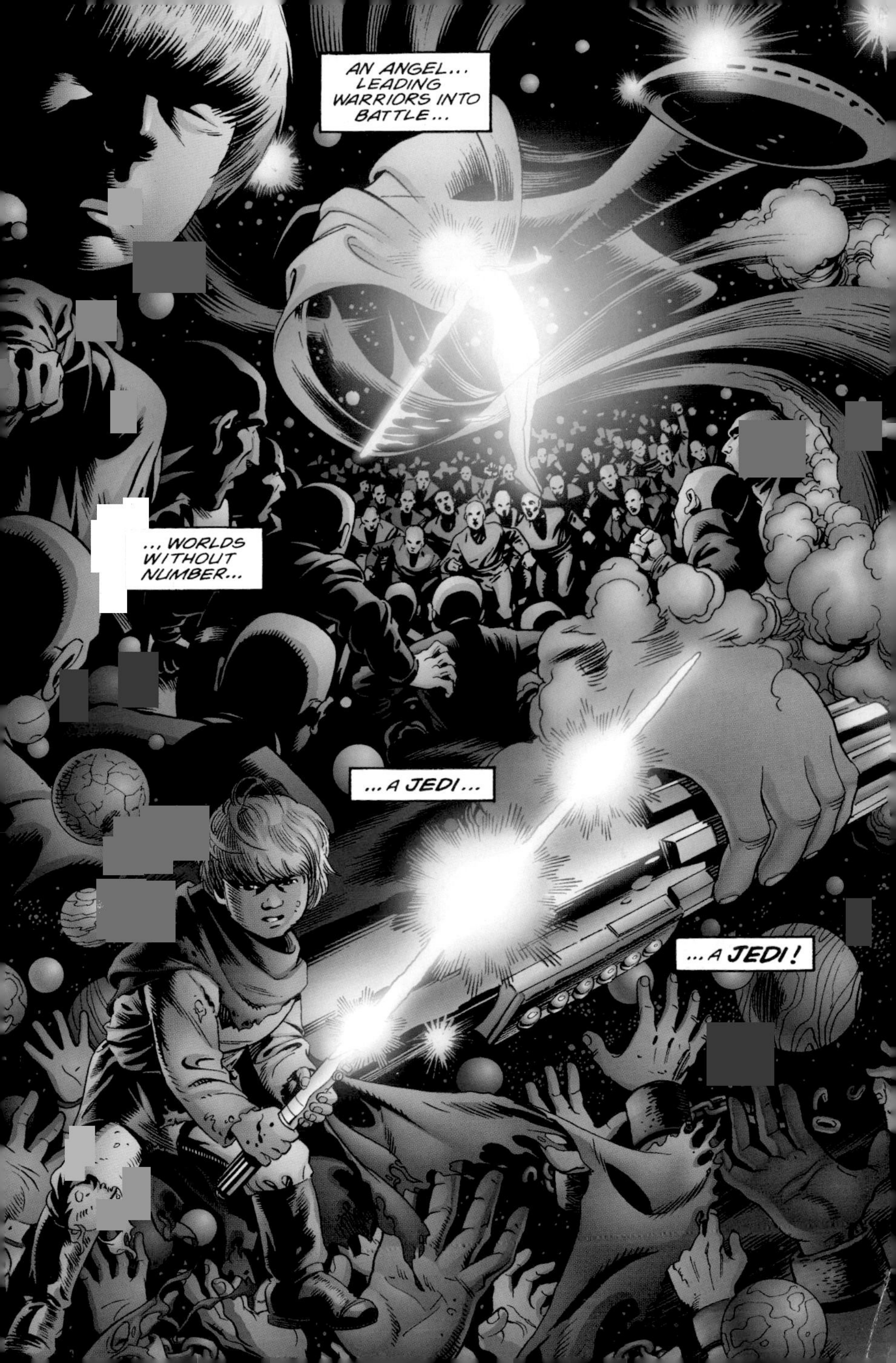
AN ANGEL... LEADING WARRIORS INTO BATTLE...
..., WORLDS WITHOUT NUMBER...
...A JEDI...
...A JEDI!

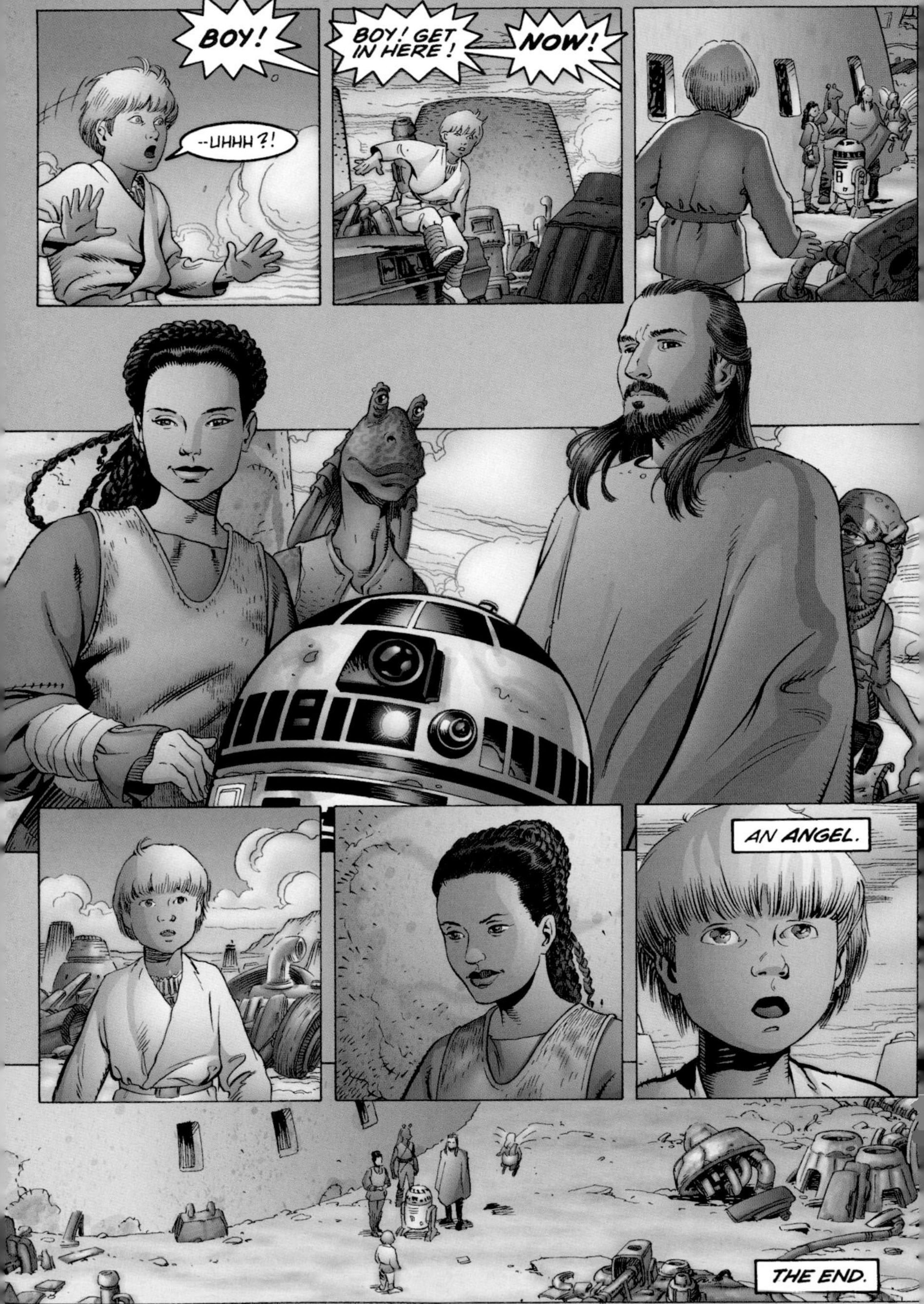
BOY!
--UHHH?!
BOY! GET IN HERE!
NOW!
AN ANGEL.
THE END.

EPISODE I—QUEEN AMIDALA

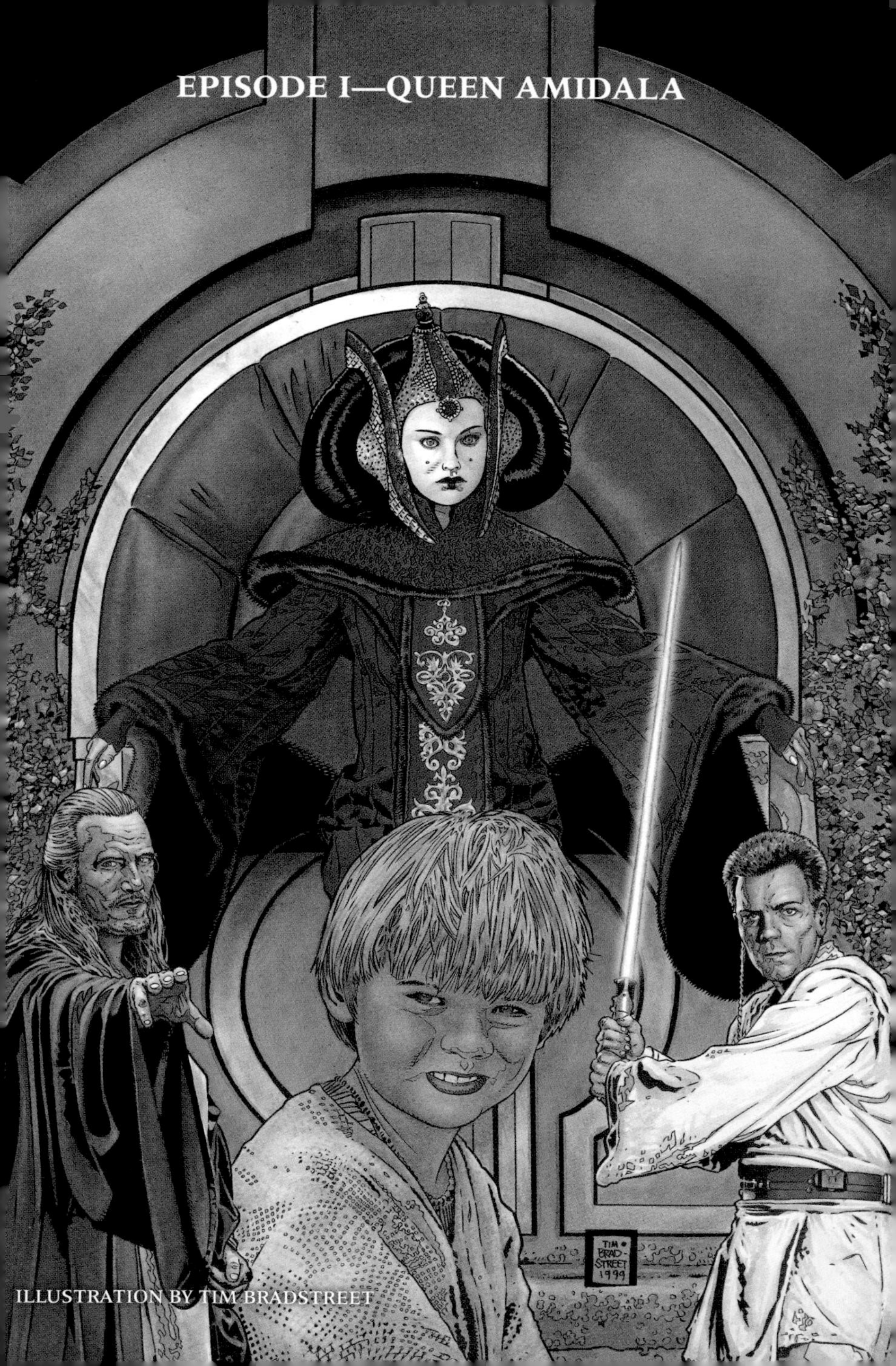
TIM BRADSTREET 1999

ILLUSTRATION BY TIM BRADSTREET

Script
MARK SCHULTZ

Pencils
GALEN SHOWMAN

Inks
P. CRAIG RUSSELL

Color rendering
LISA STAMP

Lettering
VICKIE WILLIAMS

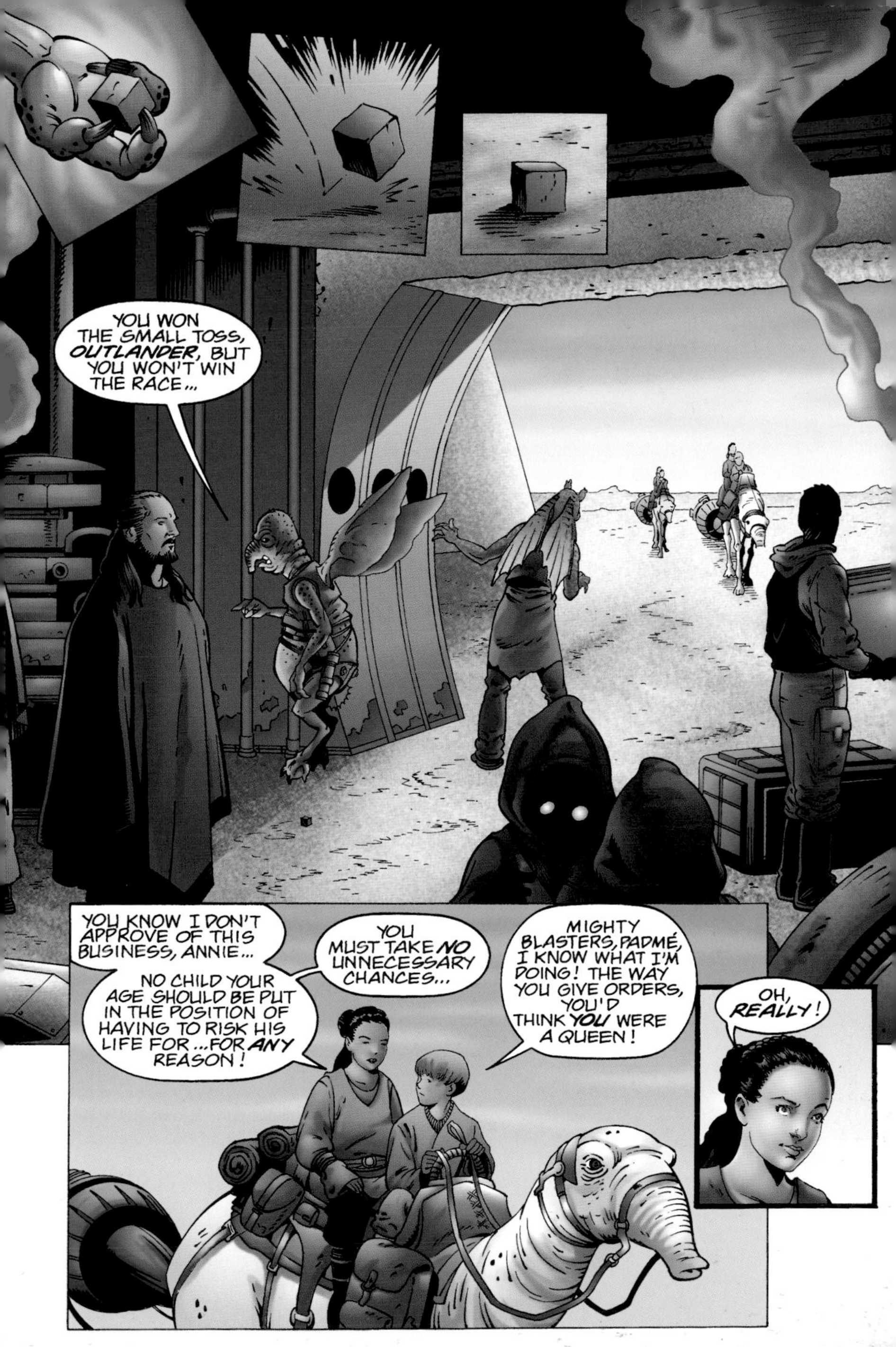
YOU WON THE SMALL TOSS, OUTLANDER, BUT YOU WON'T WIN THE RACE...
YOU KNOW I DON'T APPROVE OF THIS BUSINESS, ANNIE...
NO CHILD YOUR AGE SHOULD BE PUT IN THE POSITION OF HAVING TO RISK HIS LIFE FOR ...FOR ANY REASON!
YOU MUST TAKE NO UNNECESSARY CHANCES...
MIGHTY BLASTERS, PADMÉ, I KNOW WHAT I'M DOING! THE WAY YOU GIVE ORDERS, YOU'D THINK YOU WERE A QUEEN!
OH, REALLY!

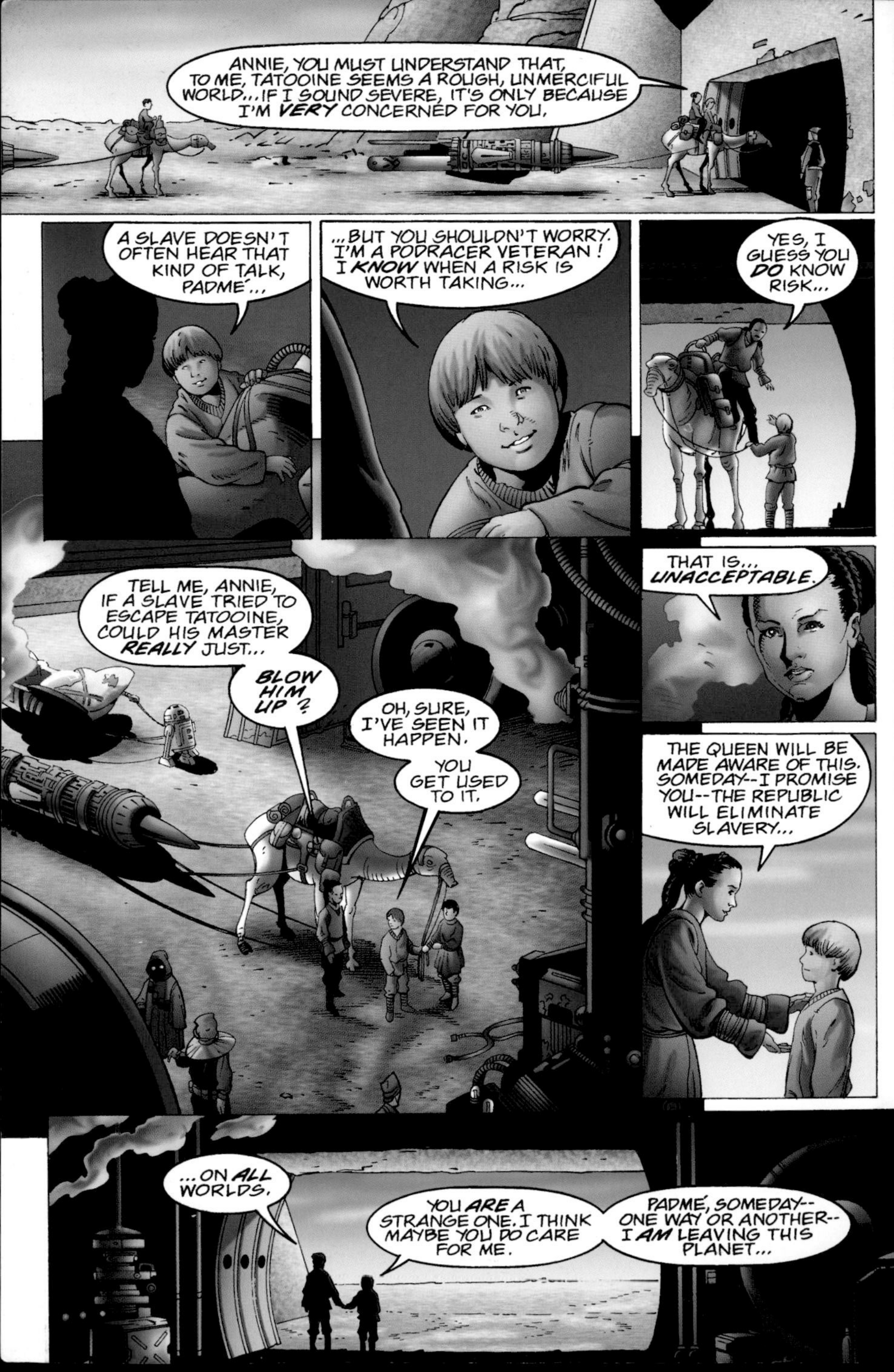
ANNIE, YOU MUST UNDERSTAND THAT, TO ME, TATOOINE SEEMS A ROUGH, UNMERCIFUL WORLD... IF I SOUND SEVERE, IT'S ONLY BECAUSE I'M **VERY** CONCERNED FOR YOU.
A SLAVE DOESN'T OFTEN HEAR THAT KIND OF TALK, PADMÉ...
...BUT YOU SHOULDN'T WORRY. I'M A PODRACER VETERAN! I **KNOW** WHEN A RISK IS WORTH TAKING...
YES, I GUESS YOU **DO** KNOW RISK...
TELL ME, ANNIE, IF A SLAVE TRIED TO ESCAPE TATOOINE, COULD HIS MASTER **REALLY** JUST...
BLOW HIM UP?
OH, SURE, I'VE SEEN IT HAPPEN.
YOU GET USED TO IT.
THAT IS... **UNACCEPTABLE**.
THE QUEEN WILL BE MADE AWARE OF THIS. SOMEDAY--I PROMISE YOU--THE REPUBLIC WILL ELIMINATE SLAVERY...
...ON **ALL** WORLDS.
YOU **ARE** A STRANGE ONE. I THINK MAYBE YOU DO CARE FOR ME.
PADMÉ, SOMEDAY-- ONE WAY OR ANOTHER-- I **AM** LEAVING THIS PLANET...

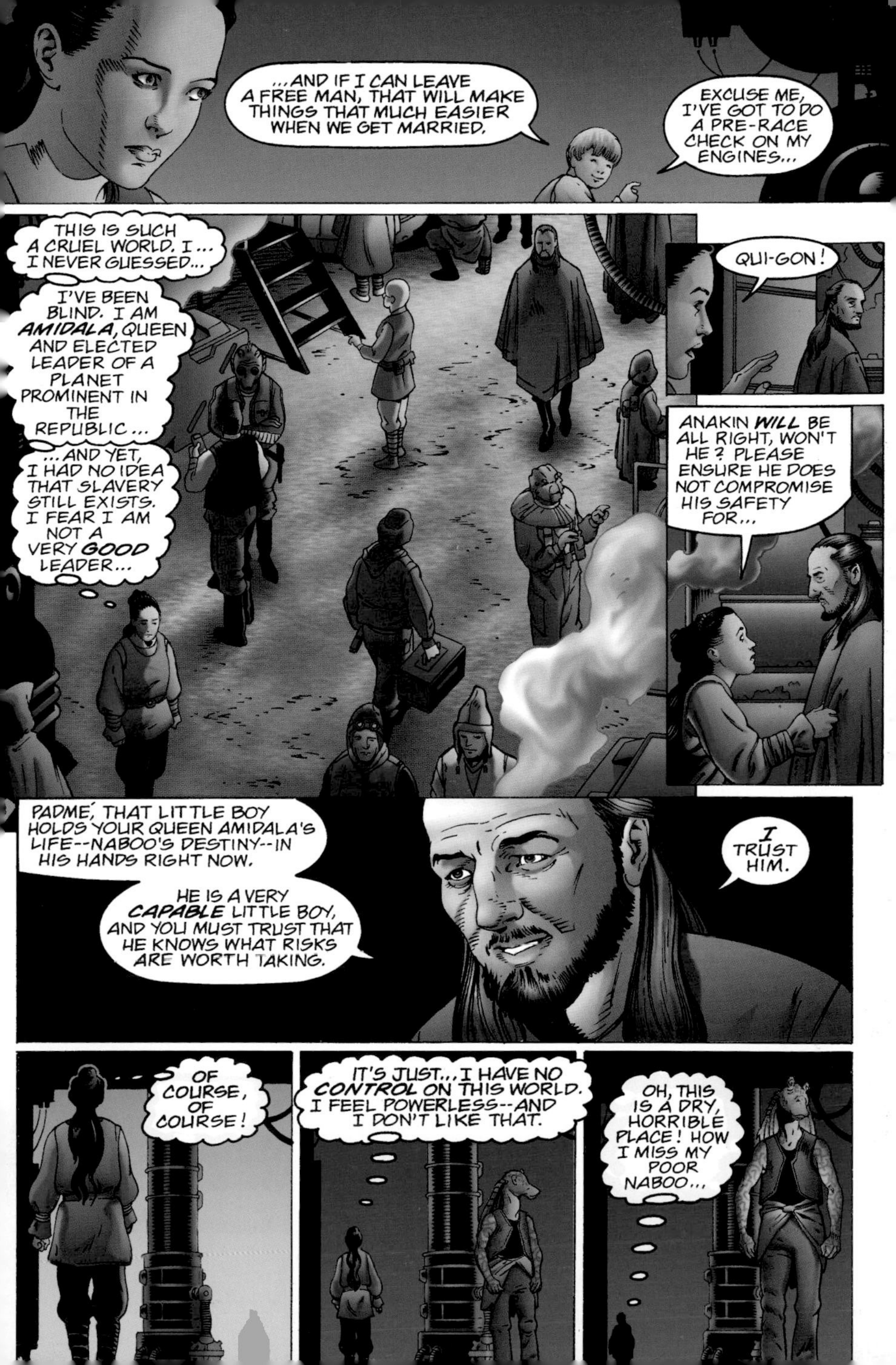
...AND IF I CAN LEAVE A FREE MAN, THAT WILL MAKE THINGS THAT MUCH EASIER WHEN WE GET MARRIED.
EXCUSE ME, I'VE GOT TO DO A PRE-RACE CHECK ON MY ENGINES...
THIS IS SUCH A CRUEL WORLD. I... I NEVER GUESSED...
I'VE BEEN BLIND. I AM AMIDALA, QUEEN AND ELECTED LEADER OF A PLANET PROMINENT IN THE REPUBLIC...
...AND YET, I HAD NO IDEA THAT SLAVERY STILL EXISTS. I FEAR I AM NOT A VERY GOOD LEADER...
QUI-GON!
ANAKIN WILL BE ALL RIGHT, WON'T HE? PLEASE ENSURE HE DOES NOT COMPROMISE HIS SAFETY FOR...
PADMÉ, THAT LITTLE BOY HOLDS YOUR QUEEN AMIDALA'S LIFE--NABOO'S DESTINY--IN HIS HANDS RIGHT NOW.
HE IS A VERY CAPABLE LITTLE BOY, AND YOU MUST TRUST THAT HE KNOWS WHAT RISKS ARE WORTH TAKING.
I TRUST HIM.
OF COURSE, OF COURSE!
IT'S JUST... I HAVE NO CONTROL ON THIS WORLD. I FEEL POWERLESS--AND I DON'T LIKE THAT.
OH, THIS IS A DRY, HORRIBLE PLACE! HOW I MISS MY POOR NABOO...

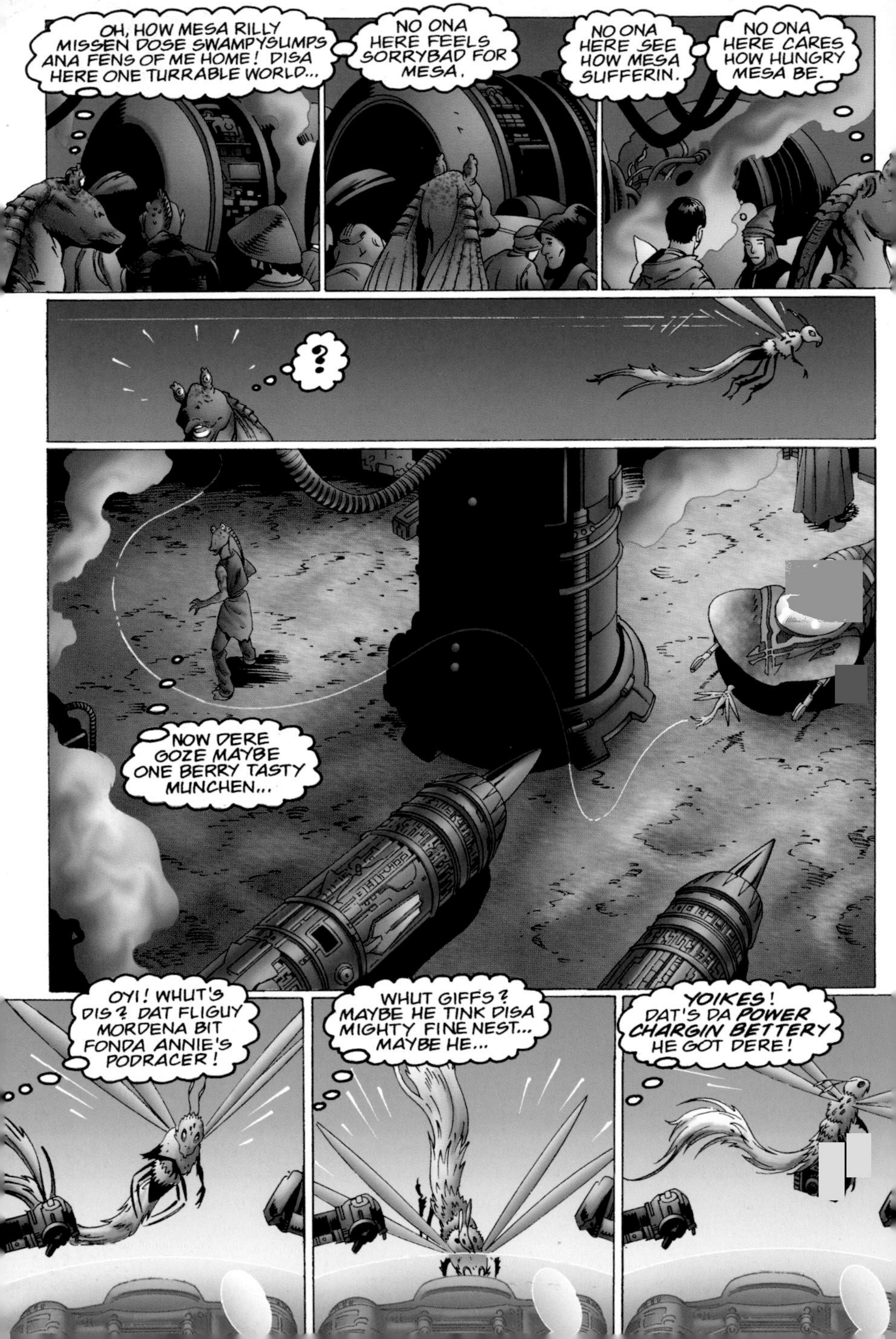

OH, HOW MESA RILLY MISSEN DOSE SWAMPYSUMPS ANA FENS OF ME HOME! DISA HERE ONE TURRABLE WORLD...
NO ONA HERE FEELS SORRYBAD FOR MESA.
NO ONA HERE SEE HOW MESA SUFFERIN.
NO ONA HERE CARES HOW HUNGRY MESA BE.
?
NOW DERE GOZE MAYBE ONE BERRY TASTY MUNCHEN...
OYI! WHUT'S DIS? DAT FLIGUY MORDENA BIT FONDA ANNIE'S PODRACER!
WHUT GIFFS? MAYBE HE TINK DISA MIGHTY FINE NEST... MAYBE HE...
YOIKES! DAT'S DA POWER CHARGIN BETTERY HE GOT DERE!

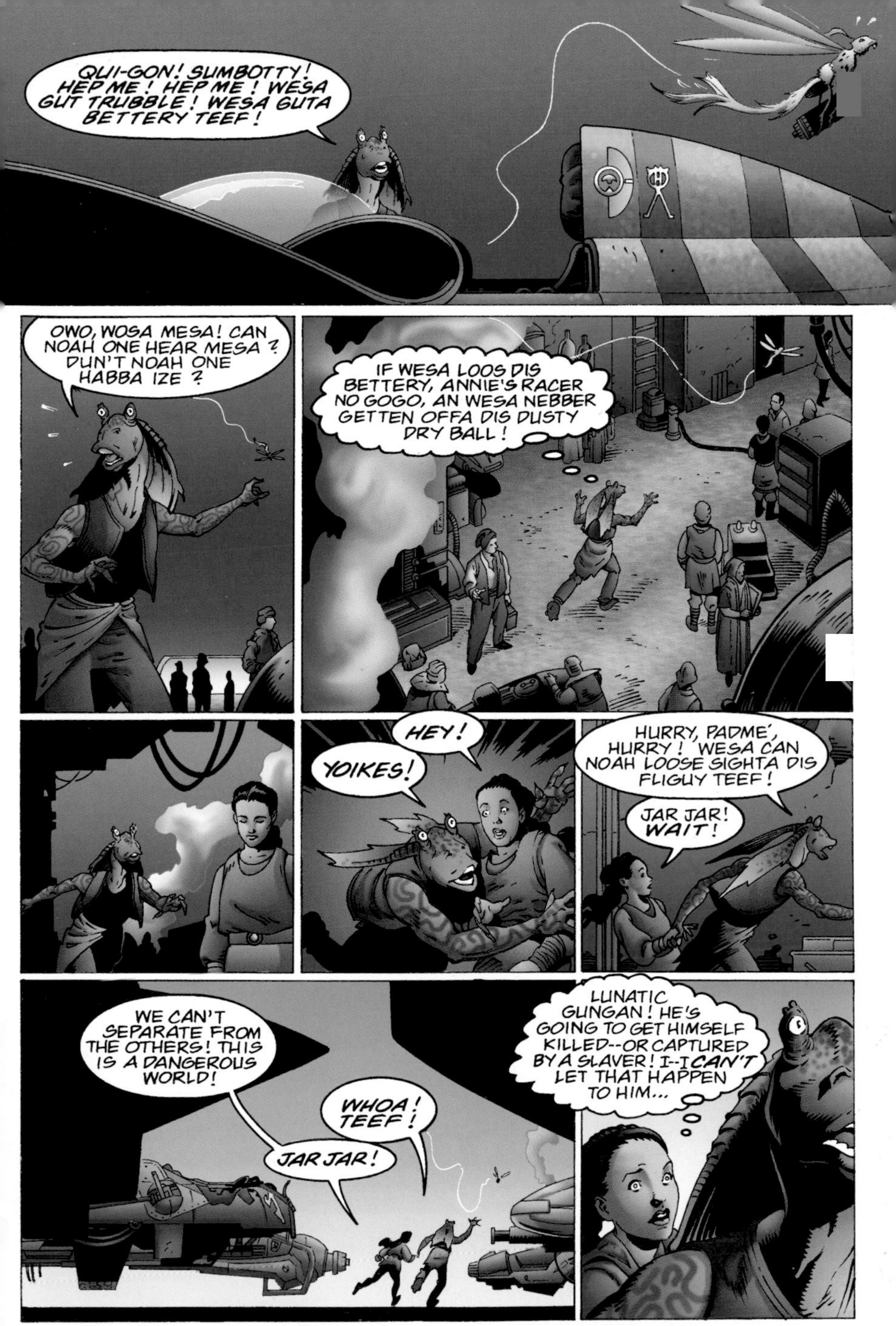
QUI-GON! SUMBOTTY! HEP ME! HEP ME! WESA GUT TRUBBLE! WESA GUTA BETTERY TEEF!
OWO, WOSA MESA! CAN NOAH ONE HEAR MESA? DUN'T NOAH ONE HABBA IZE?
IF WESA LOOS DIS BETTERY, ANNIE'S RACER NO GOGO, AN WESA NEBBER GETTEN OFFA DIS DUSTY DRY BALL!
HEY!
YOIKES!
HURRY, PADME', HURRY! WESA CAN NOAH LOOSE SIGHTA DIS FLIGUY TEEF!
JAR JAR! WAIT!
WE CAN'T SEPARATE FROM THE OTHERS! THIS IS A DANGEROUS WORLD!
WHOA! TEEF!
JAR JAR!
LUNATIC GUNGAN! HE'S GOING TO GET HIMSELF KILLED--OR CAPTURED BY A SLAVER! I--I CAN'T LET THAT HAPPEN TO HIM...

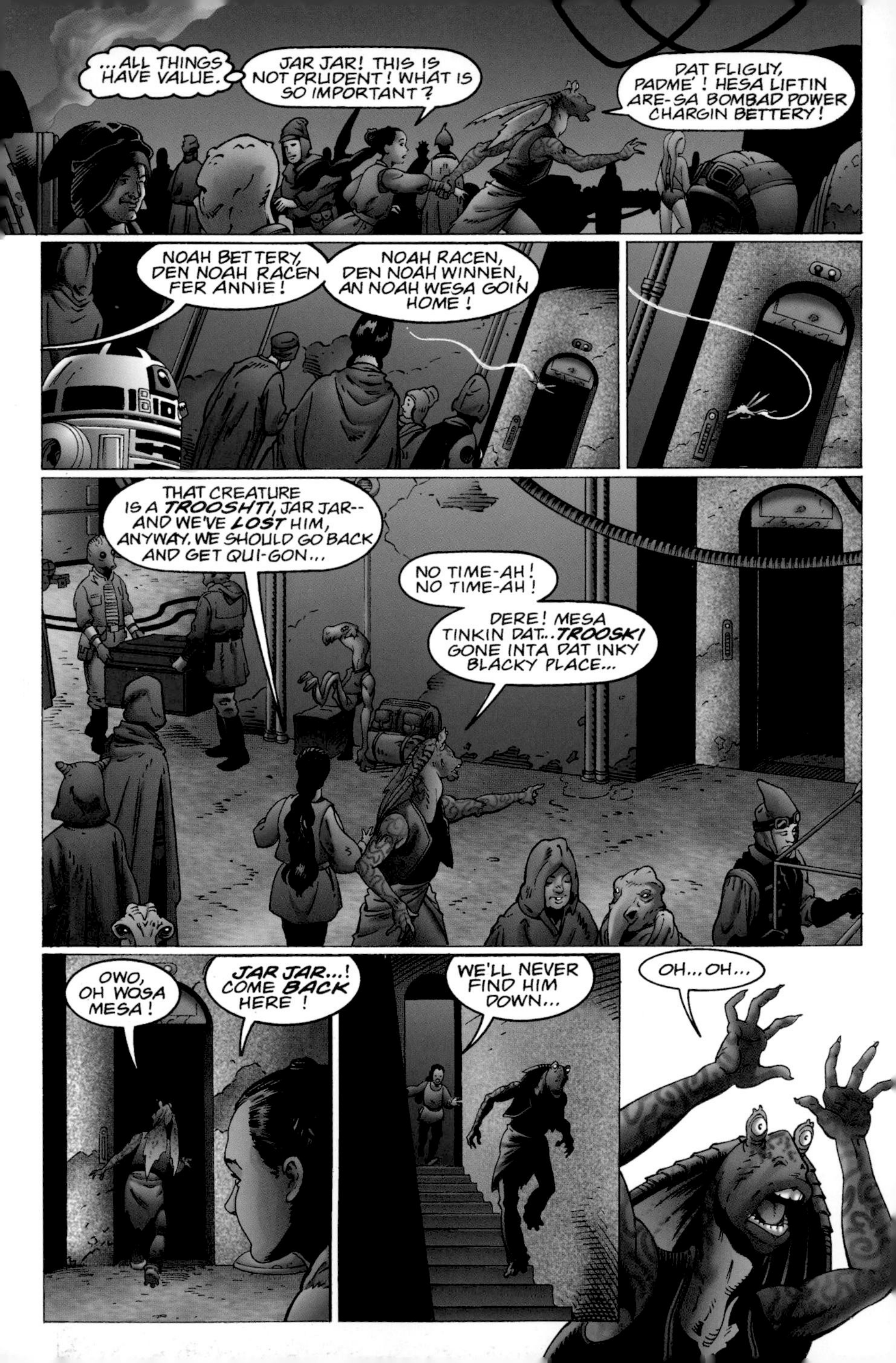
...ALL THINGS HAVE VALUE.
JAR JAR! THIS IS NOT PRUDENT! WHAT IS SO IMPORTANT?
DAT FLIGUY, PADME'! HESA LIFTIN ARE-SA BOMBAD POWER CHARGIN BETTERY!
NOAH BETTERY, DEN NOAH RACEN FER ANNIE!
NOAH RACEN, DEN NOAH WINNEN, AN NOAH WESA GOIN HOME!
THAT CREATURE IS A TROOSHTI, JAR JAR-- AND WE'VE LOST HIM, ANYWAY. WE SHOULD GO BACK AND GET QUI-GON...
NO TIME-AH! NO TIME-AH!
DERE! MESA TINKIN DAT...TROOSK! GONE INTA DAT INKY BLACKY PLACE...
OWO, OH WOSA MESA!
JAR JAR...! COME BACK HERE!
WE'LL NEVER FIND HIM DOWN...
OH...OH...

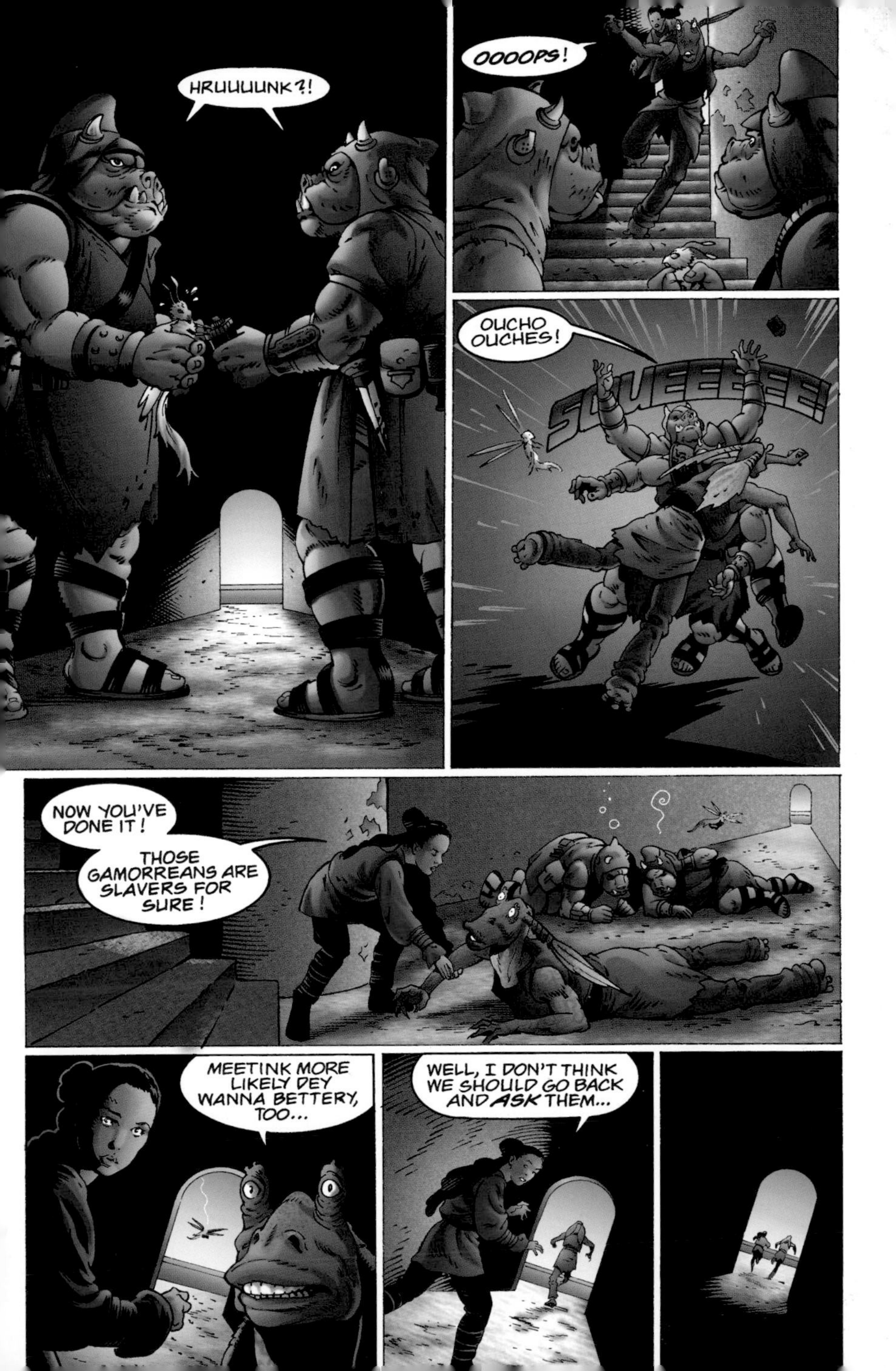
HRUUUUNK?!
OOOOPS!
OUCHO OUCHES!
NOW YOU'VE DONE IT!
THOSE GAMORREANS ARE SLAVERS FOR SURE!
MEETINK MORE LIKELY DEY WANNA BETTERY, TOO...
WELL, I DON'T THINK WE SHOULD GO BACK AND ASK THEM...

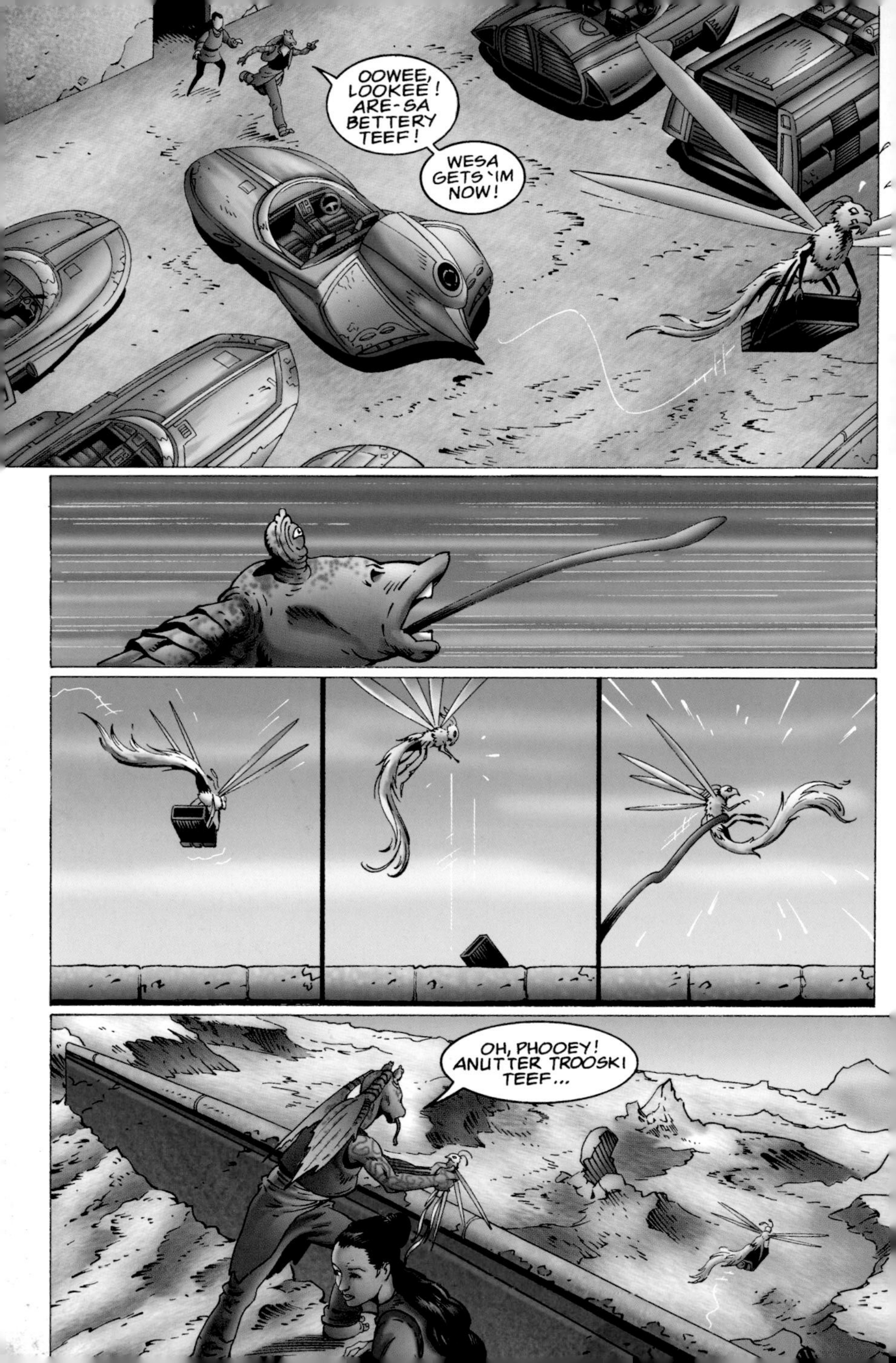
OOWEE, LOOKEE! ARE-SA BETTERY TEEF!
WESA GETS 'IM NOW!
OH, PHOOEY! ANUTTER TROOSKI TEEF...

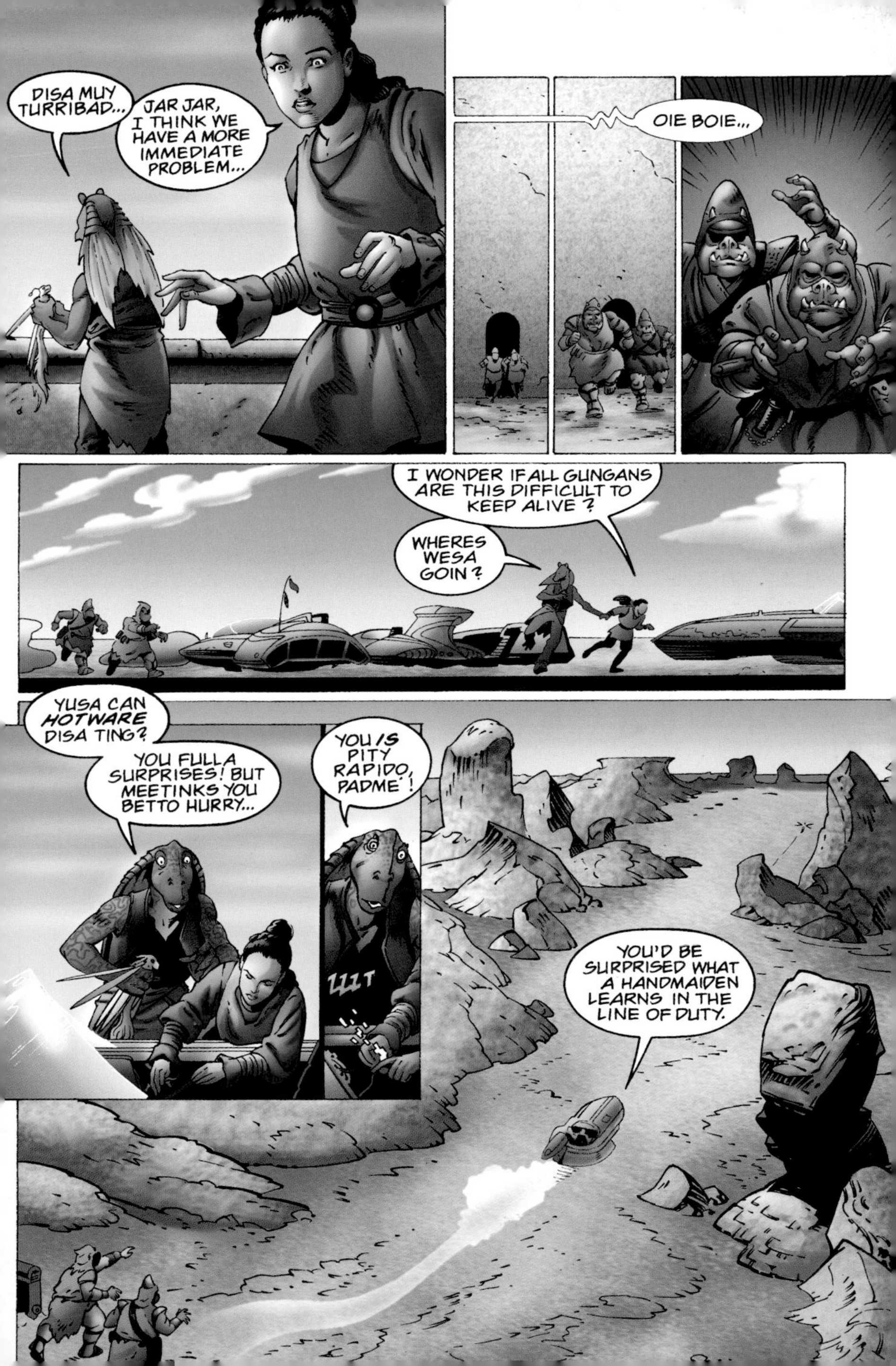
DISA MUY TURRIBAD...
JAR JAR, I THINK WE HAVE A MORE IMMEDIATE PROBLEM...
OIE BOIE...
I WONDER IF ALL GUNGANS ARE THIS DIFFICULT TO KEEP ALIVE ?
WHERES WESA GOIN ?
YUSA CAN HOTWARE DISA TING?
YOU FULLA SURPRISES! BUT MEETINKS YOU BETTO HURRY...
YOU IS PITY RAPIDO, PADME' !
ZZZT
YOU'D BE SURPRISED WHAT A HANDMAIDEN LEARNS IN THE LINE OF DUTY.

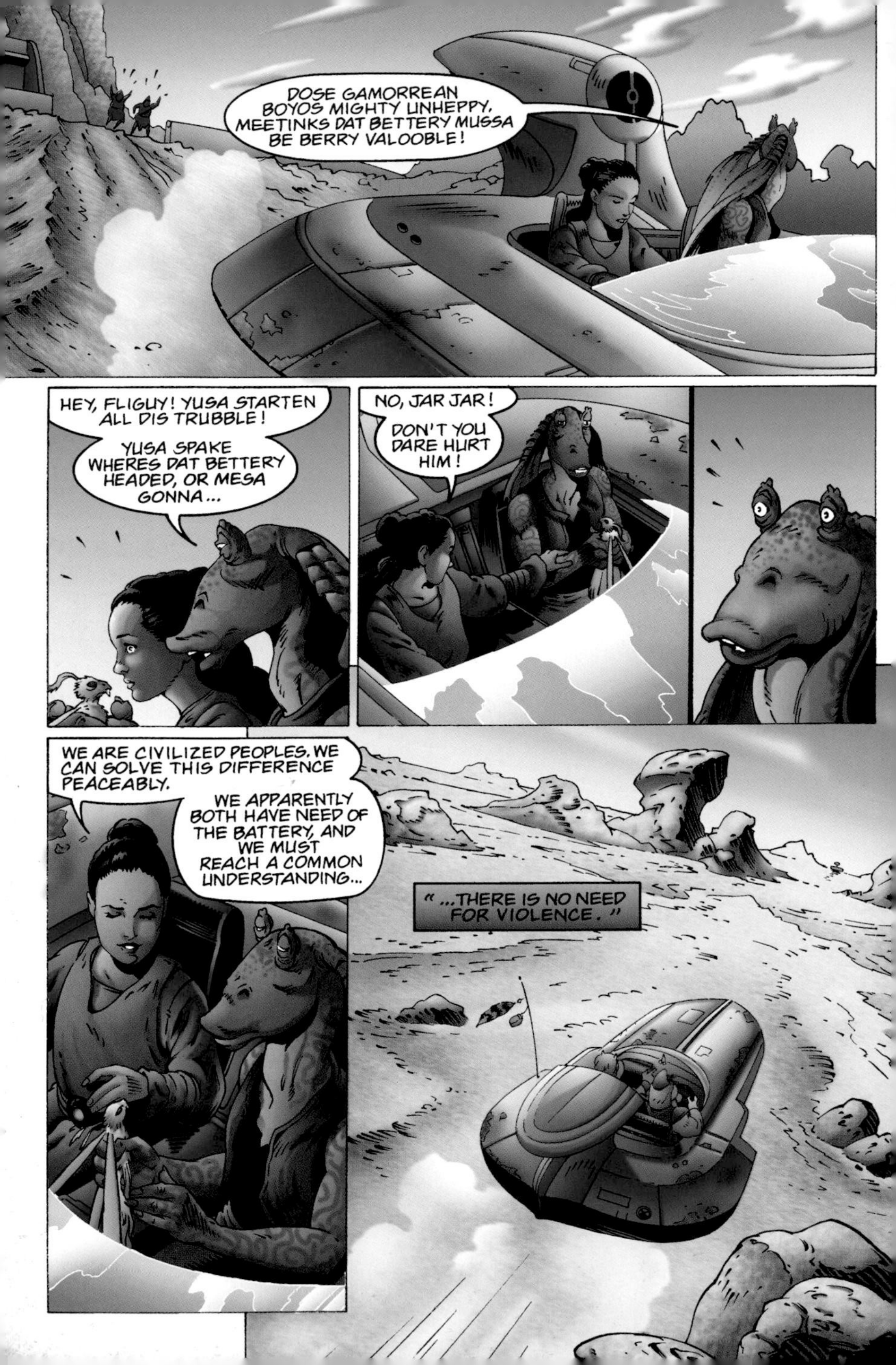
DOSE GAMORREAN BOYOS MIGHTY UNHEPPY. MEETINKS DAT BETTERY MUSSA BE BERRY VALOOBLE!
HEY, FLIGUY! YUSA STARTEN ALL DIS TRUBBLE!
YUSA SPAKE WHERES DAT BETTERY HEADED, OR MESA GONNA...
NO, JAR JAR!
DON'T YOU DARE HURT HIM!
WE ARE CIVILIZED PEOPLES. WE CAN SOLVE THIS DIFFERENCE PEACEABLY.
WE APPARENTLY BOTH HAVE NEED OF THE BATTERY, AND WE MUST REACH A COMMON UNDERSTANDING...
"...THERE IS NO NEED FOR VIOLENCE."

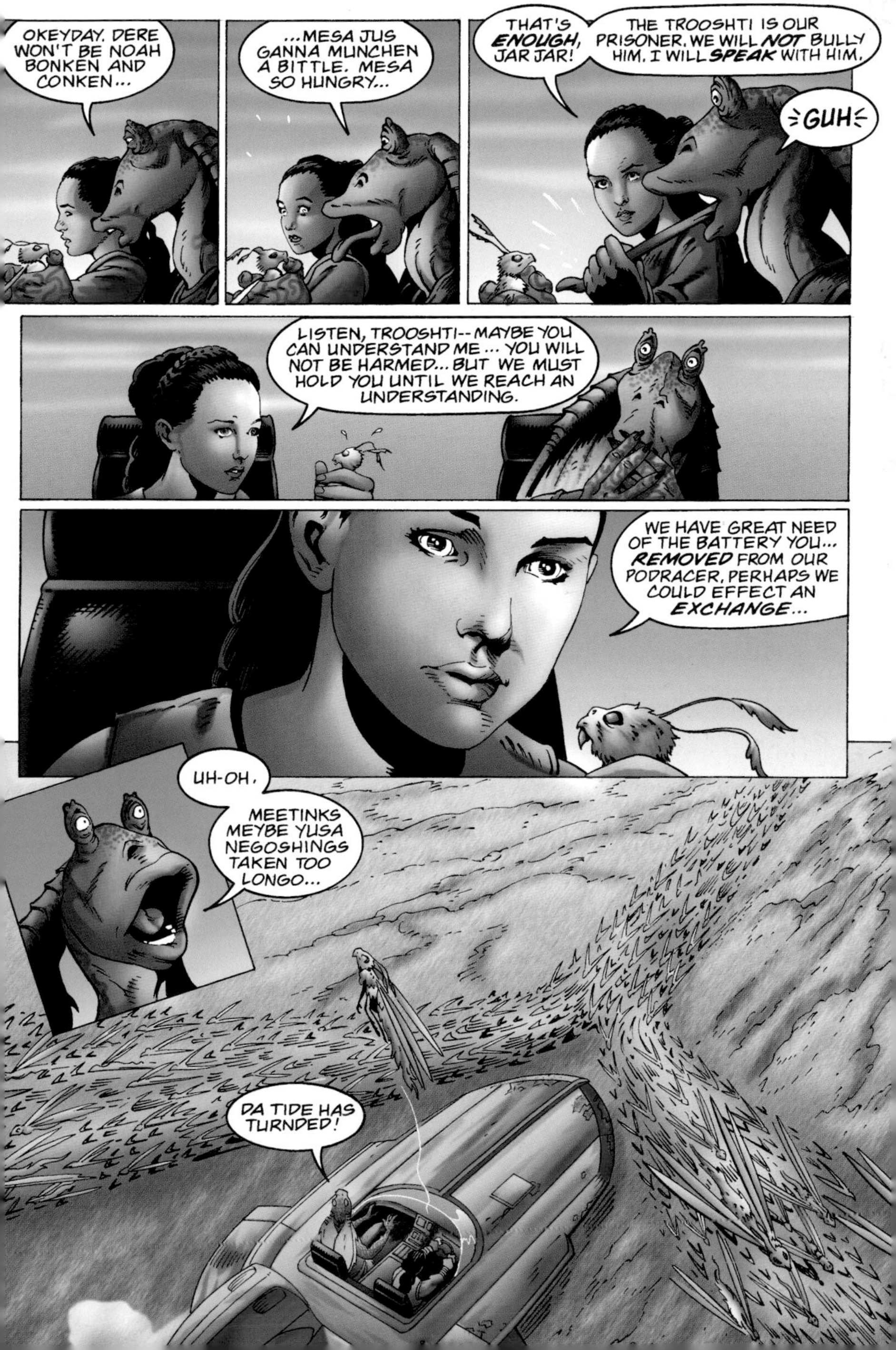
OKEYDAY. DERE WON'T BE NOAH BONKEN AND CONKEN...
...MESA JUS GANNA MUNCHEN A BITTLE. MESA SO HUNGRY...
THAT'S ENOUGH, JAR JAR!
THE TROOSHTI IS OUR PRISONER. WE WILL NOT BULLY HIM. I WILL SPEAK WITH HIM.
GUH
LISTEN, TROOSHTI-- MAYBE YOU CAN UNDERSTAND ME ... YOU WILL NOT BE HARMED... BUT WE MUST HOLD YOU UNTIL WE REACH AN UNDERSTANDING.
WE HAVE GREAT NEED OF THE BATTERY YOU... REMOVED FROM OUR PODRACER. PERHAPS WE COULD EFFECT AN EXCHANGE...
UH-OH.
MEETINKS MEYBE YUSA NEGOSHINGS TAKEN TOO LONGO...
DA TIDE HAS TURNDED!

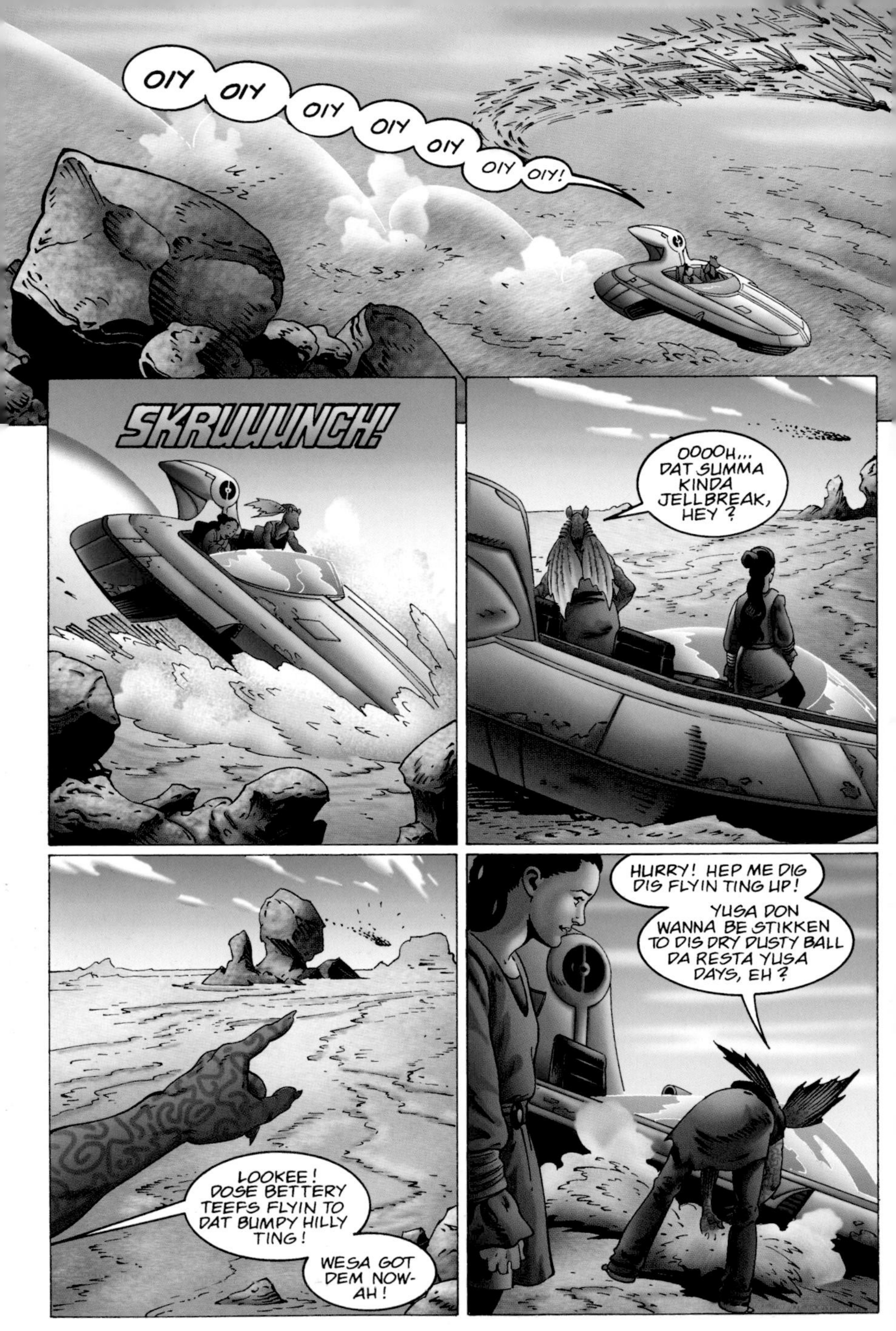
OIY OIY OIY OIY OIY OIY OIY!
SKRUUUNCH!
OOOOH... DAT SUMMA KINDA JELLBREAK, HEY?
LOOKEE! DOSE BETTERY TEEFS FLYIN TO DAT BUMPY HILLY TING!
WESA GOT DEM NOW-AH!
HURRY! HEP ME DIG DIS FLYIN TING UP!
YUSA DON WANNA BE STIKKEN TO DIS DRY DUSTY BALL DA RESTA YUSA DAYS, EH?

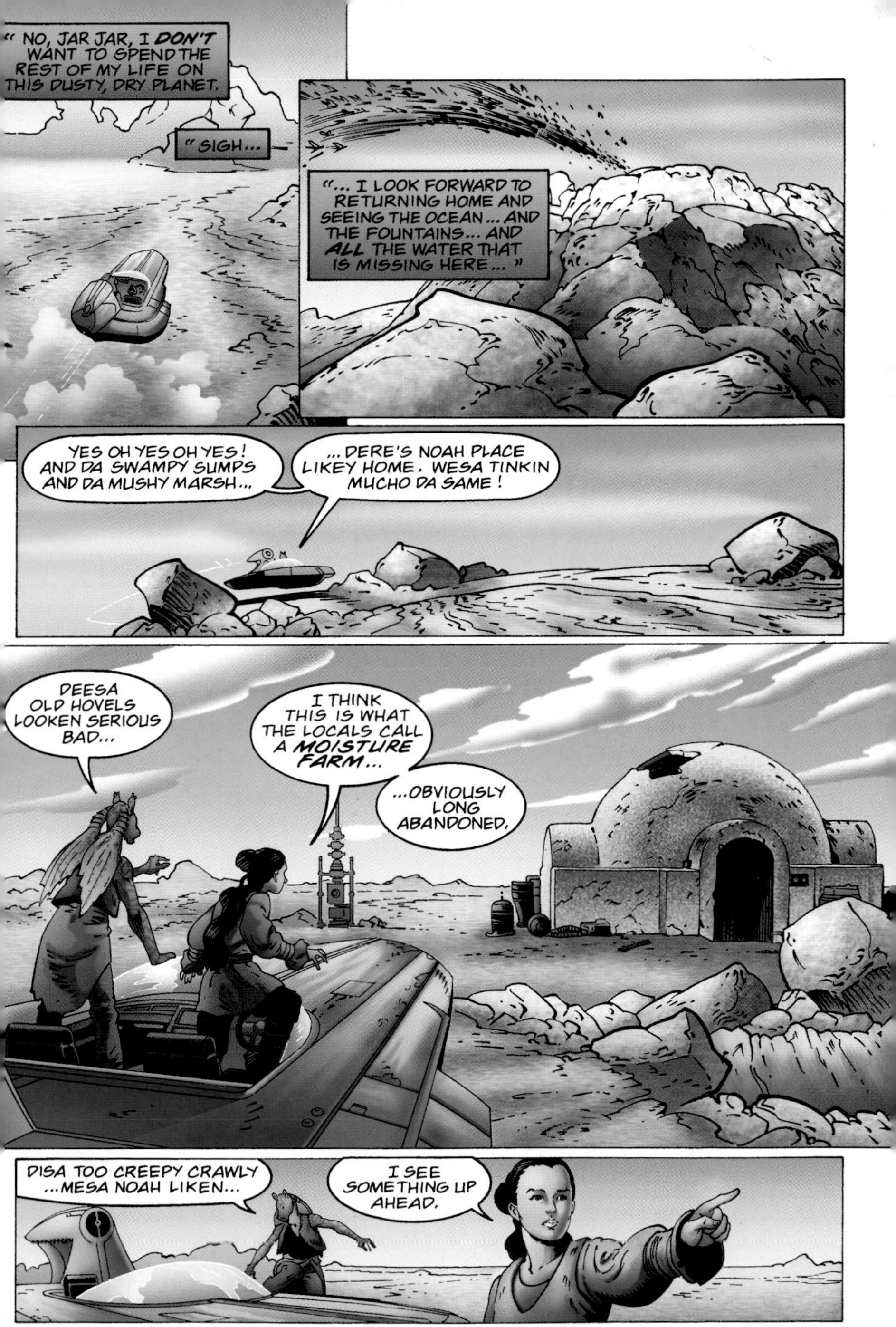
"NO, JAR JAR, I DON'T WANT TO SPEND THE REST OF MY LIFE ON THIS DUSTY, DRY PLANET.
"SIGH...
"... I LOOK FORWARD TO RETURNING HOME AND SEEING THE OCEAN... AND THE FOUNTAINS... AND ALL THE WATER THAT IS MISSING HERE..."
YES OH YES OH YES! AND DA SWAMPY SUMPS AND DA MUSHY MARSH...
...DERE'S NOAH PLACE LIKEY HOME, WESA TINKIN MUCHO DA SAME!
DEESA OLD HOVELS LOOKEN SERIOUS BAD...
I THINK THIS IS WHAT THE LOCALS CALL A MOISTURE FARM...
...OBVIOUSLY LONG ABANDONED.
DISA TOO CREEPY CRAWLY ...MESA NOAH LIKEN...
I SEE SOMETHING UP AHEAD.

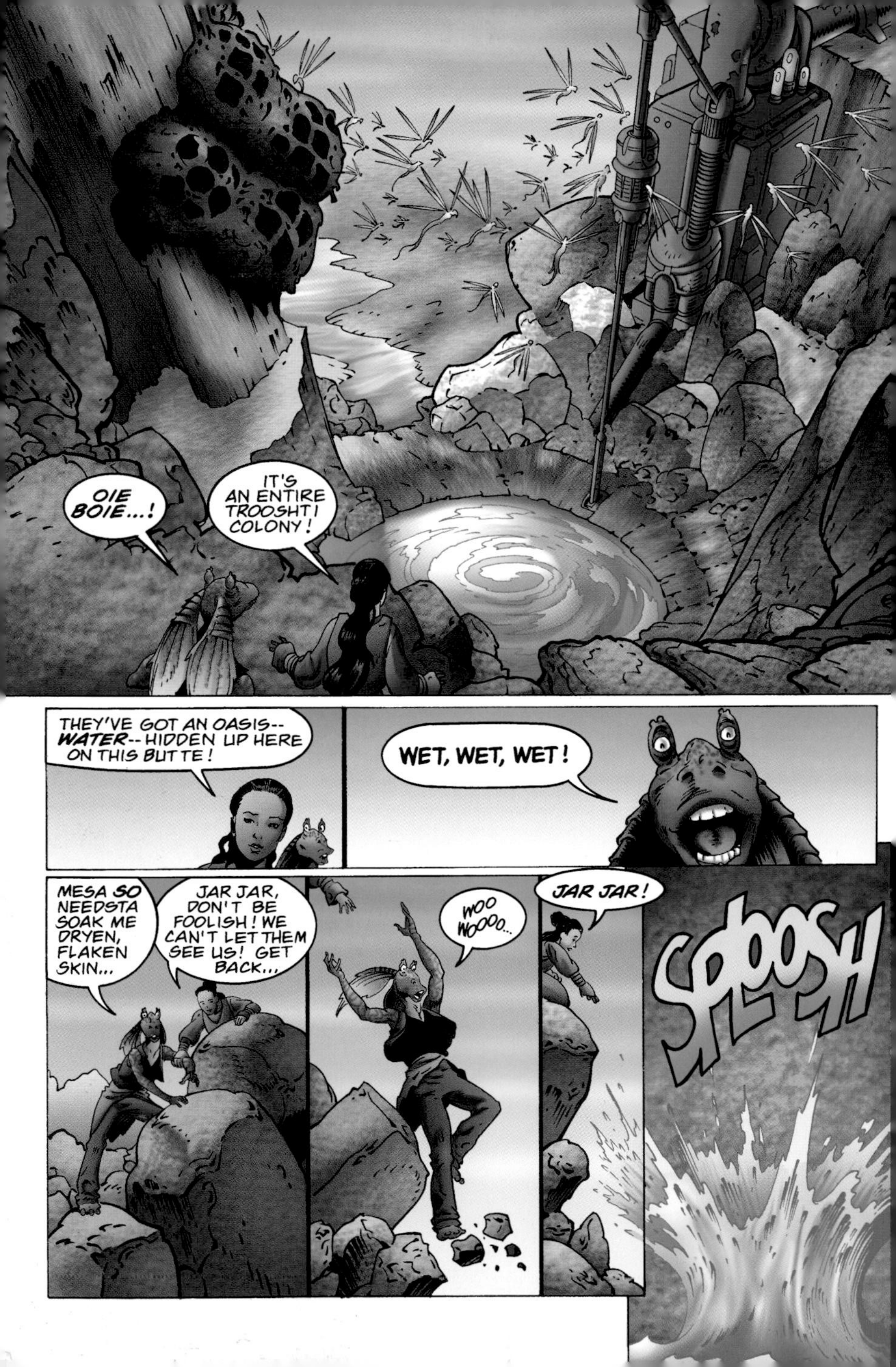
OIE BOIE...!
IT'S AN ENTIRE TROOSHT! COLONY!
THEY'VE GOT AN OASIS-- WATER-- HIDDEN UP HERE ON THIS BUTTE!
WET, WET, WET!
MESA SO NEEDSTA SOAK ME DRYEN, FLAKEN SKIN...
JAR JAR, DON'T BE FOOLISH! WE CAN'T LET THEM SEE US! GET BACK...,
WOO WOOOO...
JAR JAR!
SPLOOSH

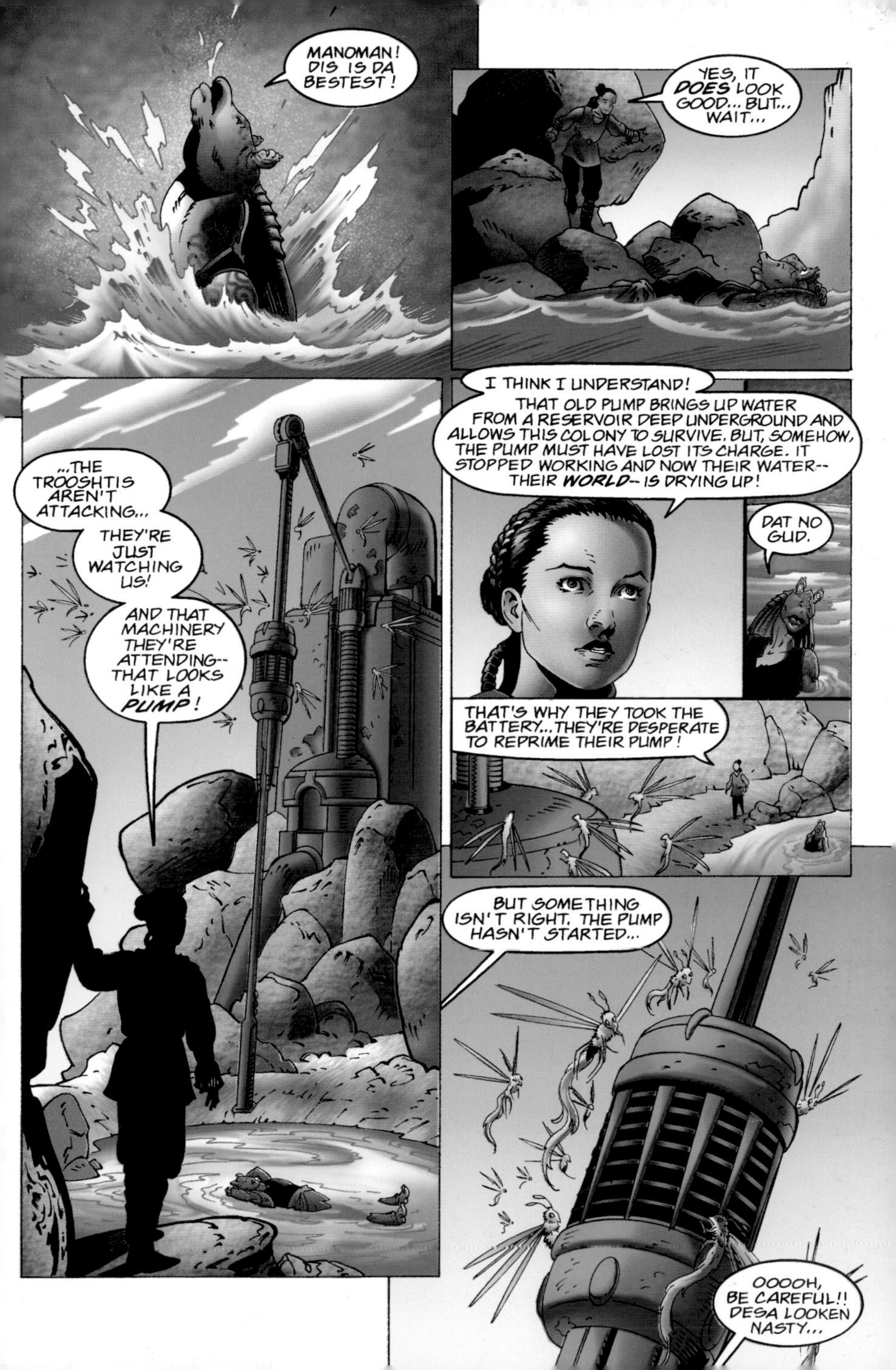
MANOMAN! DIS IS DA BESTEST!
YES, IT DOES LOOK GOOD... BUT... WAIT...
...THE TROOSHTIS AREN'T ATTACKING...
THEY'RE JUST WATCHING US!
AND THAT MACHINERY THEY'RE ATTENDING-- THAT LOOKS LIKE A PUMP!
I THINK I UNDERSTAND!
THAT OLD PUMP BRINGS UP WATER FROM A RESERVOIR DEEP UNDERGROUND AND ALLOWS THIS COLONY TO SURVIVE. BUT, SOMEHOW, THE PUMP MUST HAVE LOST ITS CHARGE. IT STOPPED WORKING AND NOW THEIR WATER-- THEIR WORLD-- IS DRYING UP!
DAT NO GUD.
THAT'S WHY THEY TOOK THE BATTERY... THEY'RE DESPERATE TO REPRIME THEIR PUMP!
BUT SOMETHING ISN'T RIGHT. THE PUMP HASN'T STARTED...
OOOOH, BE CAREFUL!! DESA LOOKEN NASTY...

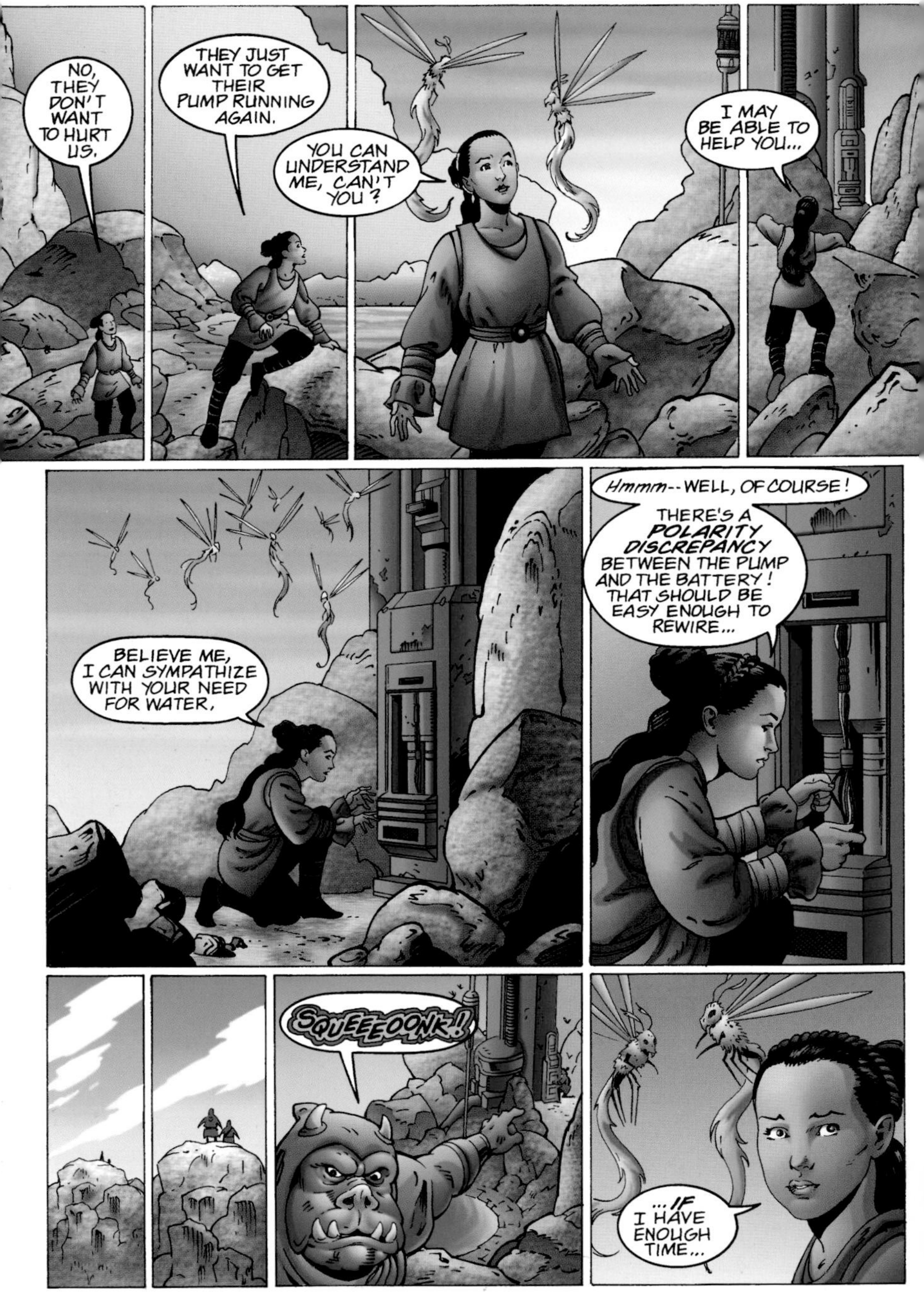
NO, THEY DON'T WANT TO HURT US.
THEY JUST WANT TO GET THEIR PUMP RUNNING AGAIN.
YOU CAN UNDERSTAND ME, CAN'T YOU?
I MAY BE ABLE TO HELP YOU...
BELIEVE ME, I CAN SYMPATHIZE WITH YOUR NEED FOR WATER.
Hmmm--WELL, OF COURSE!
THERE'S A POLARITY DISCREPANCY BETWEEN THE PUMP AND THE BATTERY! THAT SHOULD BE EASY ENOUGH TO REWIRE...
SQUEEEOONK!
...IF I HAVE ENOUGH TIME...

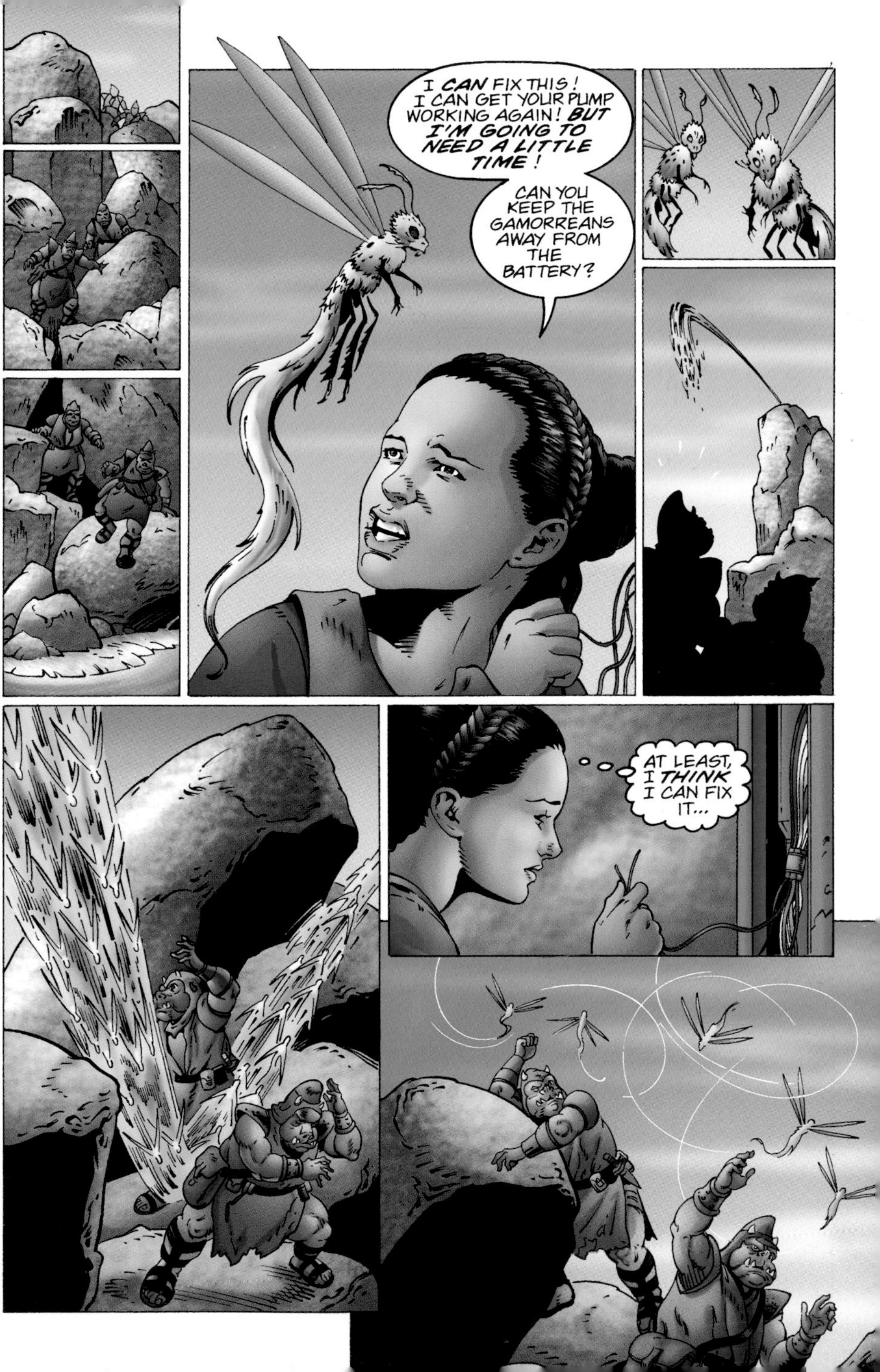
I CAN FIX THIS! I CAN GET YOUR PUMP WORKING AGAIN! BUT I'M GOING TO NEED A LITTLE TIME!
CAN YOU KEEP THE GAMORREANS AWAY FROM THE BATTERY?
AT LEAST, I THINK I CAN FIX IT...

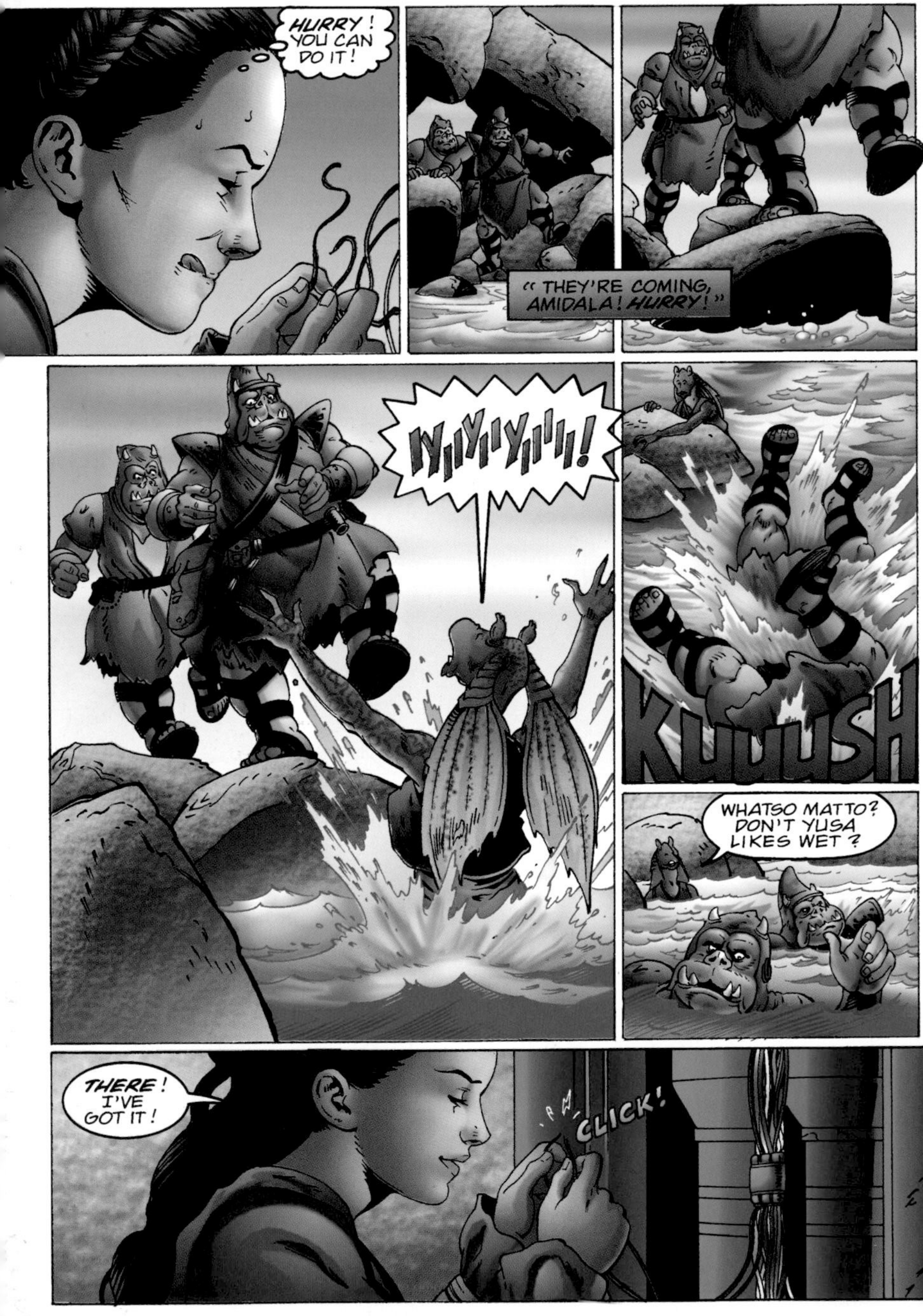
HURRY! YOU CAN DO IT!
"THEY'RE COMING, AMIDALA! HURRY!"
NYIYIYIII!
KUUUSH
WHATSO MATTO? DON'T YUSA LIKES WET?
THERE! I'VE GOT IT!
CLICK!

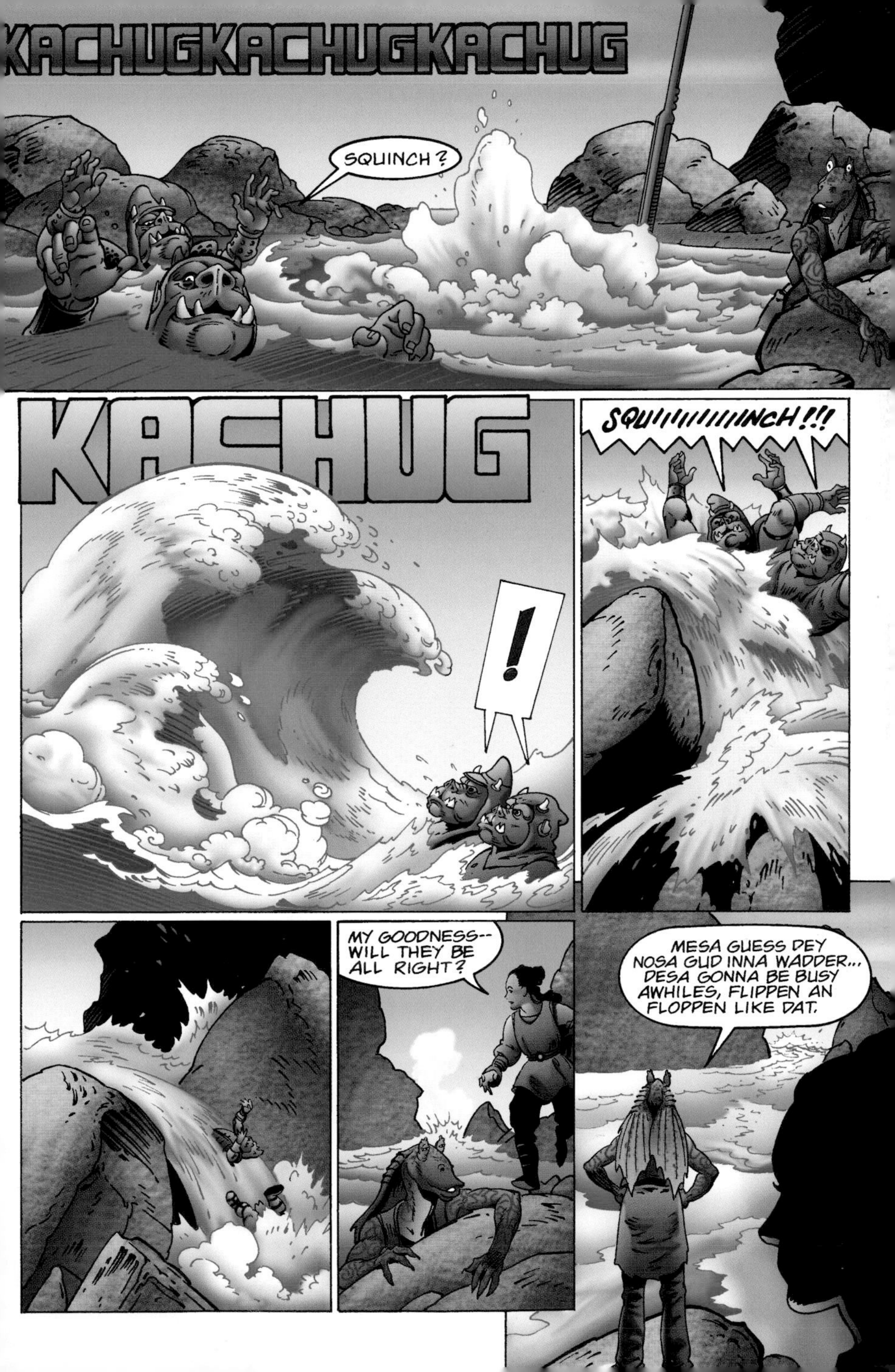
KACHUGKACHUGKACHUG
SQUINCH?
KACHUG
SQUIIIIIIIIINCH!!!
!
MY GOODNESS-- WILL THEY BE ALL RIGHT?
MESA GUESS DEY NOSA GUD INNA WADDER... DESA GONNA BE BUSY AWHILES, FLIPPEN AN FLOPPEN LIKE DAT.

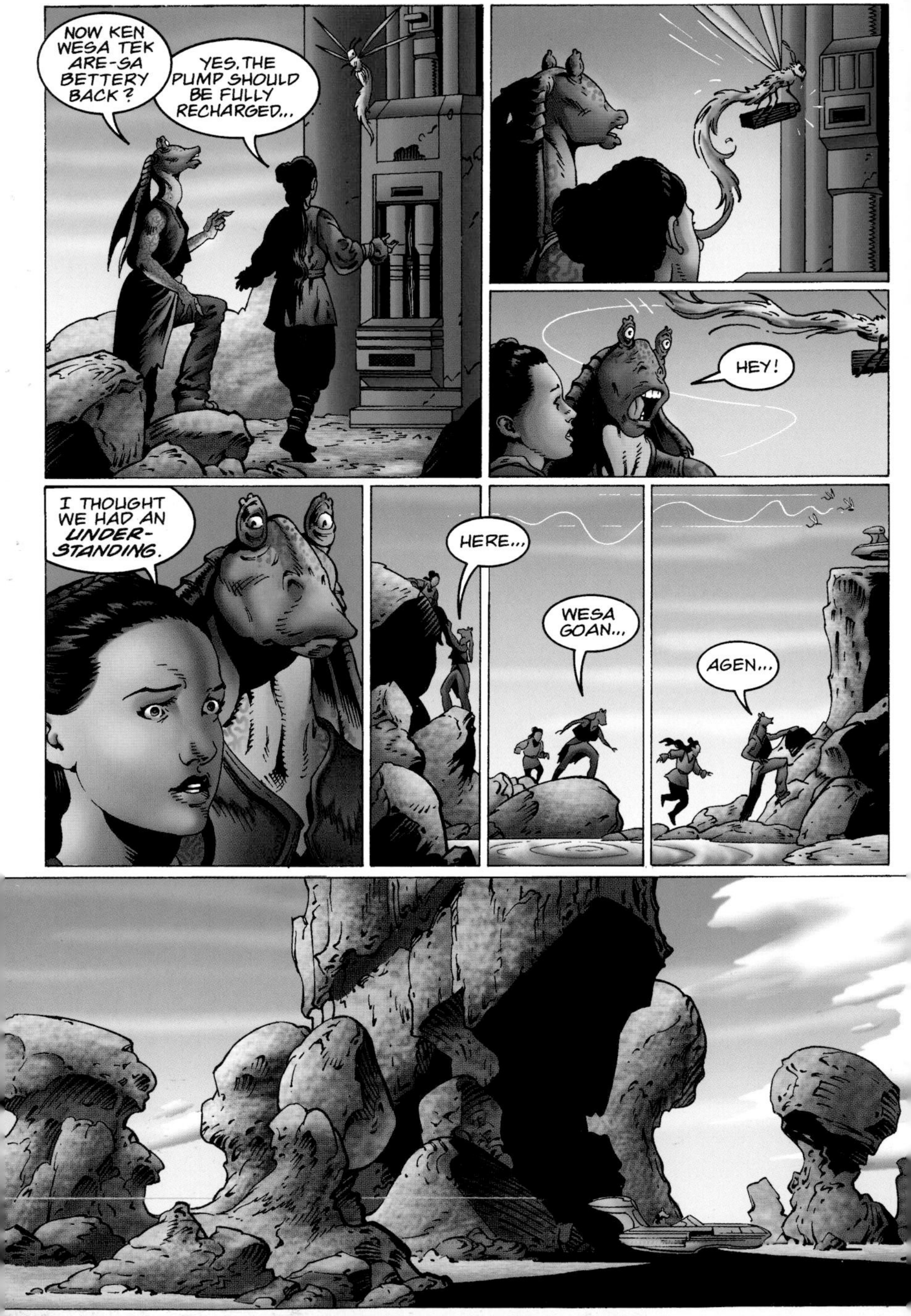
NOW KEN WESA TEK ARE-SA BETTERY BACK?
YES, THE PUMP SHOULD BE FULLY RECHARGED...
HEY!
I THOUGHT WE HAD AN *UNDER-STANDING*.
HERE...
WESA GOAN...
AGEN...

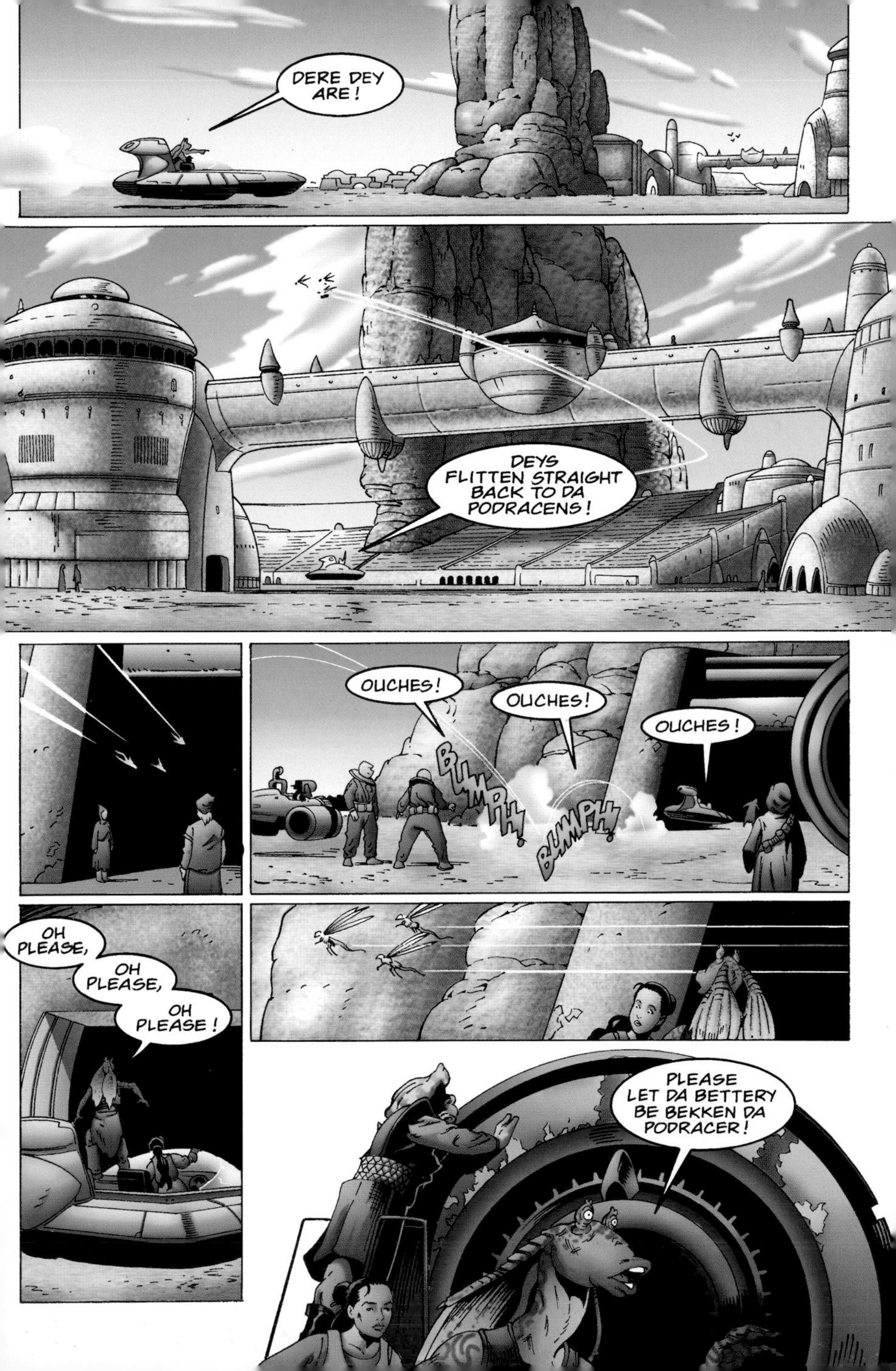
DERE DEY ARE!
DEYS FLITTEN STRAIGHT BACK TO DA PODRACENS!
OUCHES!
OUCHES!
OUCHES!
BUMPH!
BUMPH!
OH PLEASE,
OH PLEASE,
OH PLEASE!
PLEASE LET DA BETTERY BE BEKKEN DA PODRACER!

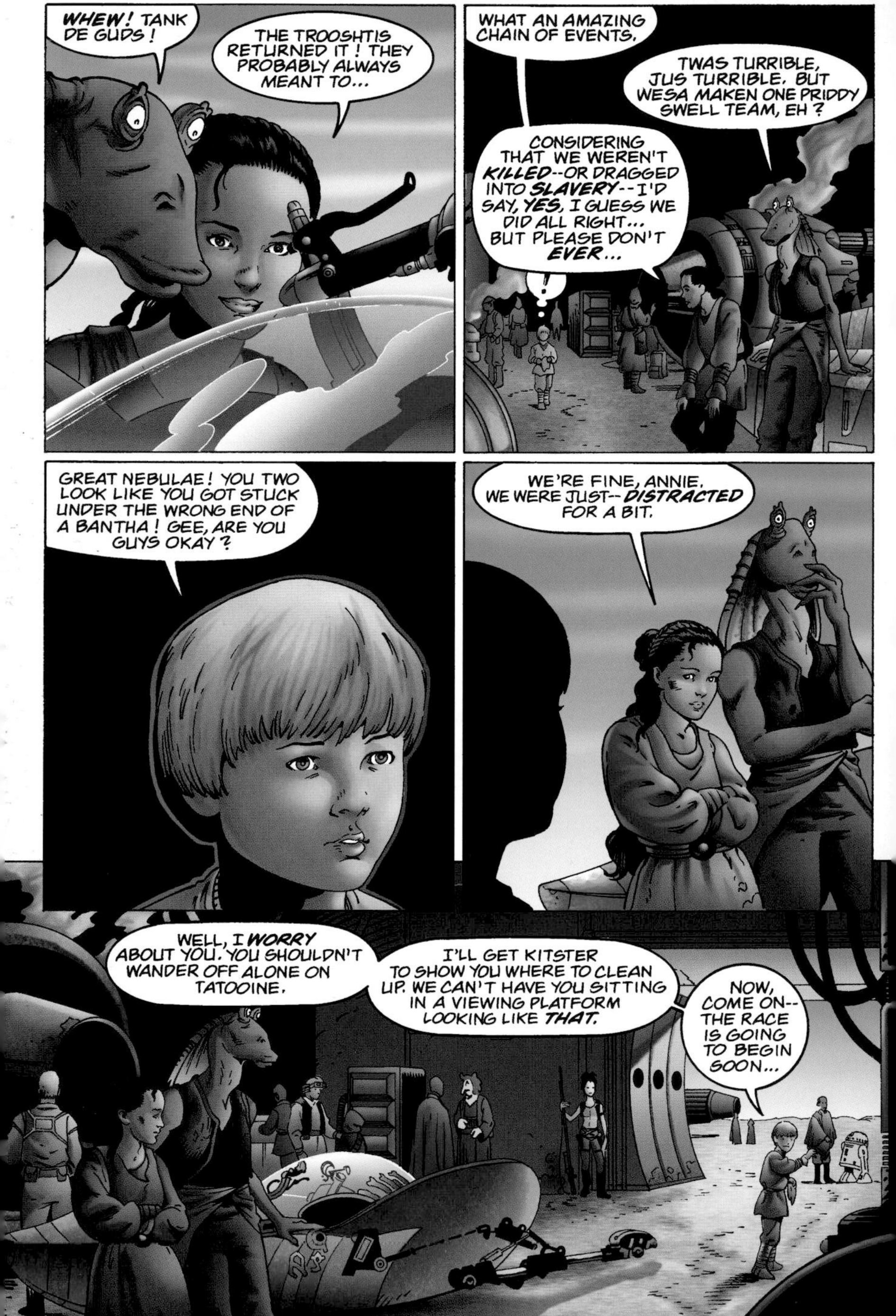
WHEW! TANK DE GUDS!
THE TROOSHTIS RETURNED IT! THEY PROBABLY ALWAYS MEANT TO...
WHAT AN AMAZING CHAIN OF EVENTS.
TWAS TURRIBLE, JUS TURRIBLE. BUT WESA MAKEN ONE PRIDDY SWELL TEAM, EH?
CONSIDERING THAT WE WEREN'T KILLED--OR DRAGGED INTO SLAVERY--I'D SAY, YES, I GUESS WE DID ALL RIGHT... BUT PLEASE DON'T EVER...
!
GREAT NEBULAE! YOU TWO LOOK LIKE YOU GOT STUCK UNDER THE WRONG END OF A BANTHA! GEE, ARE YOU GUYS OKAY?
WE'RE FINE, ANNIE. WE WERE JUST--DISTRACTED FOR A BIT.
WELL, I WORRY ABOUT YOU. YOU SHOULDN'T WANDER OFF ALONE ON TATOOINE.
I'LL GET KITSTER TO SHOW YOU WHERE TO CLEAN UP. WE CAN'T HAVE YOU SITTING IN A VIEWING PLATFORM LOOKING LIKE THAT.
NOW, COME ON--THE RACE IS GOING TO BEGIN SOON...

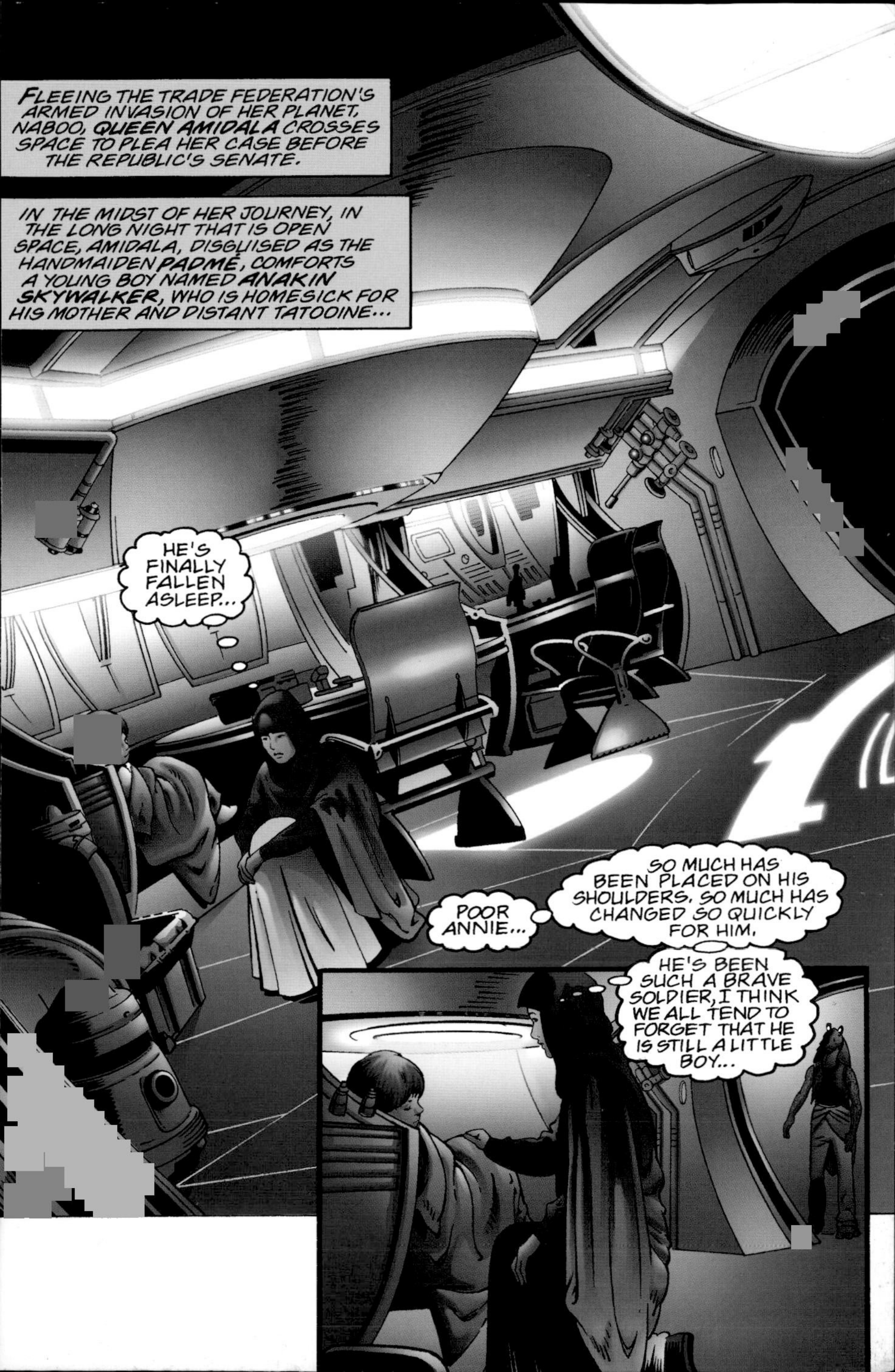
FLEEING THE TRADE FEDERATION'S ARMED INVASION OF HER PLANET, NABOO, QUEEN AMIDALA CROSSES SPACE TO PLEA HER CASE BEFORE THE REPUBLIC'S SENATE.
IN THE MIDST OF HER JOURNEY, IN THE LONG NIGHT THAT IS OPEN SPACE, AMIDALA, DISGUISED AS THE HANDMAIDEN PADMÉ, COMFORTS A YOUNG BOY NAMED ANAKIN SKYWALKER, WHO IS HOMESICK FOR HIS MOTHER AND DISTANT TATOOINE...
HE'S FINALLY FALLEN ASLEEP...
POOR ANNIE...
SO MUCH HAS BEEN PLACED ON HIS SHOULDERS. SO MUCH HAS CHANGED SO QUICKLY FOR HIM.
HE'S BEEN SUCH A BRAVE SOLDIER, I THINK WE ALL TEND TO FORGET THAT HE IS STILL A LITTLE BOY...

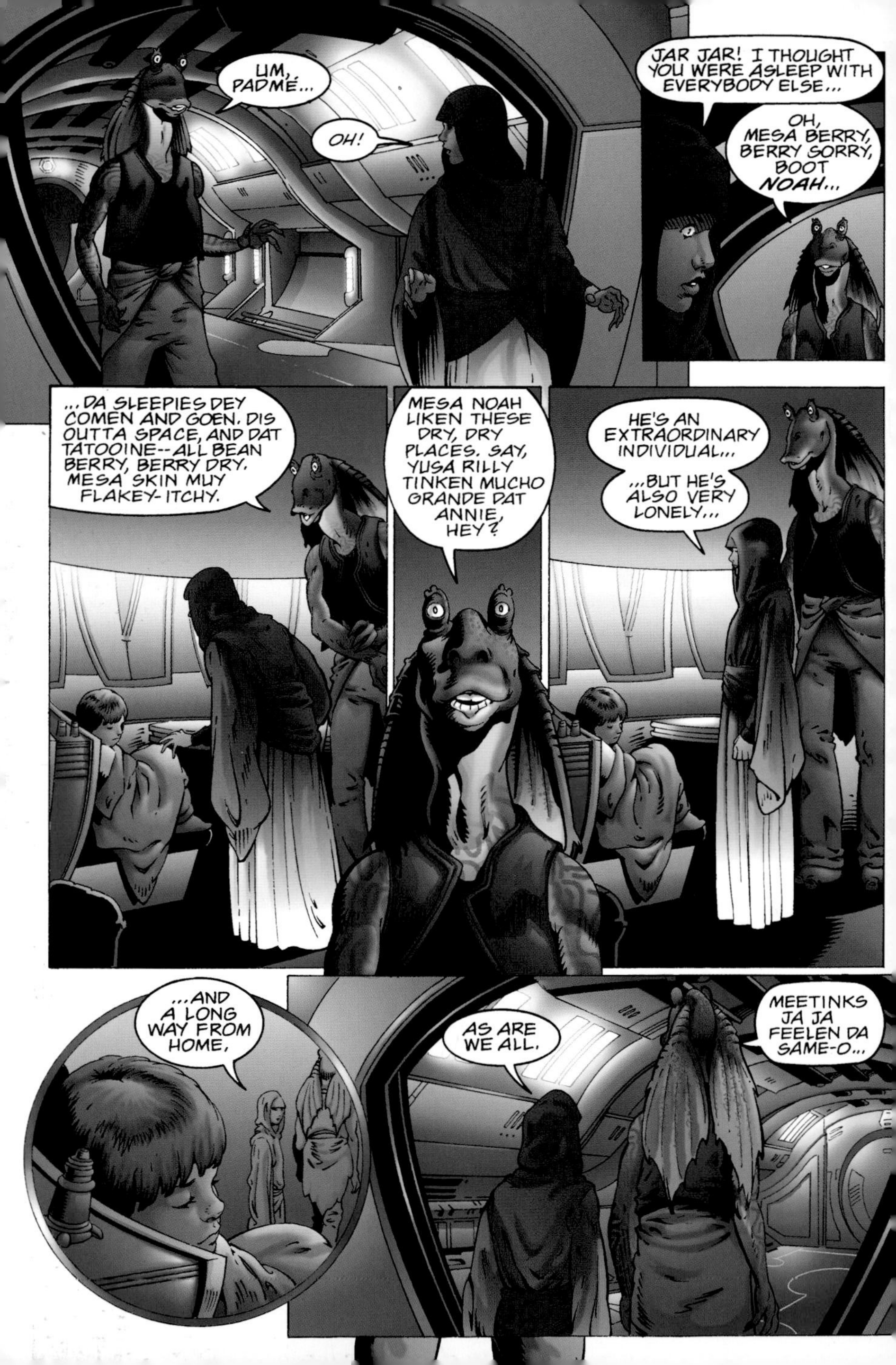
UM, PADMÉ...
OH!
JAR JAR! I THOUGHT YOU WERE ASLEEP WITH EVERYBODY ELSE...
OH, MESA BERRY, BERRY SORRY, BOOT NOAH...
...DA SLEEPIES DEY COMEN AND GOEN. DIS OUTTA SPACE, AND DAT TATOOINE--ALL BEAN BERRY, BERRY DRY. MESA SKIN MUY FLAKEY-ITCHY.
MESA NOAH LIKEN THESE DRY, DRY PLACES. SAY, YUSA RILLY TINKEN MUCHO GRANDE DAT ANNIE, HEY?
HE'S AN EXTRAORDINARY INDIVIDUAL...
...BUT HE'S ALSO VERY LONELY...
...AND A LONG WAY FROM HOME.
AS ARE WE ALL.
MEETINKS JA JA FEELEN DA SAME-O...

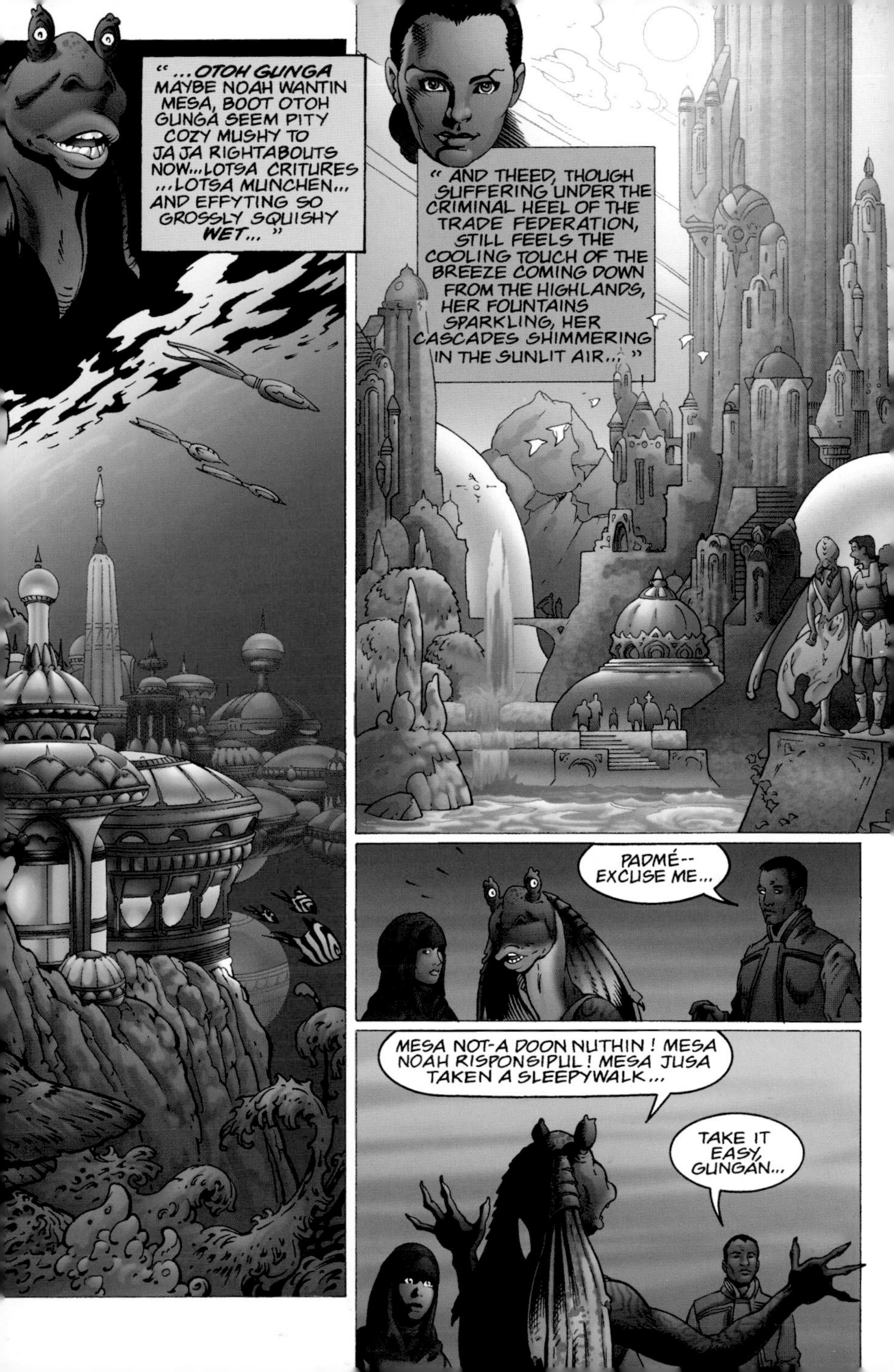
"...OTOH GUNGA MAYBE NOAH WANTIN MESA, BOOT OTOH GUNGA SEEM PITY COZY MUSHY TO JA JA RIGHTABOUTS NOW...LOTSA CRITURES ...LOTSA MUNCHEN... AND EFFYTING SO GROSSLY SQUISHY WET..."
"AND THEED, THOUGH SUFFERING UNDER THE CRIMINAL HEEL OF THE TRADE FEDERATION, STILL FEELS THE COOLING TOUCH OF THE BREEZE COMING DOWN FROM THE HIGHLANDS, HER FOUNTAINS SPARKLING, HER CASCADES SHIMMERING IN THE SUNLIT AIR..."
PADMÉ-- EXCUSE ME...
MESA NOT-A DOON NUTHIN! MESA NOAH RISPONSIPUL! MESA JUSA TAKEN A SLEEPYWALK...
TAKE IT EASY, GUNGAN...

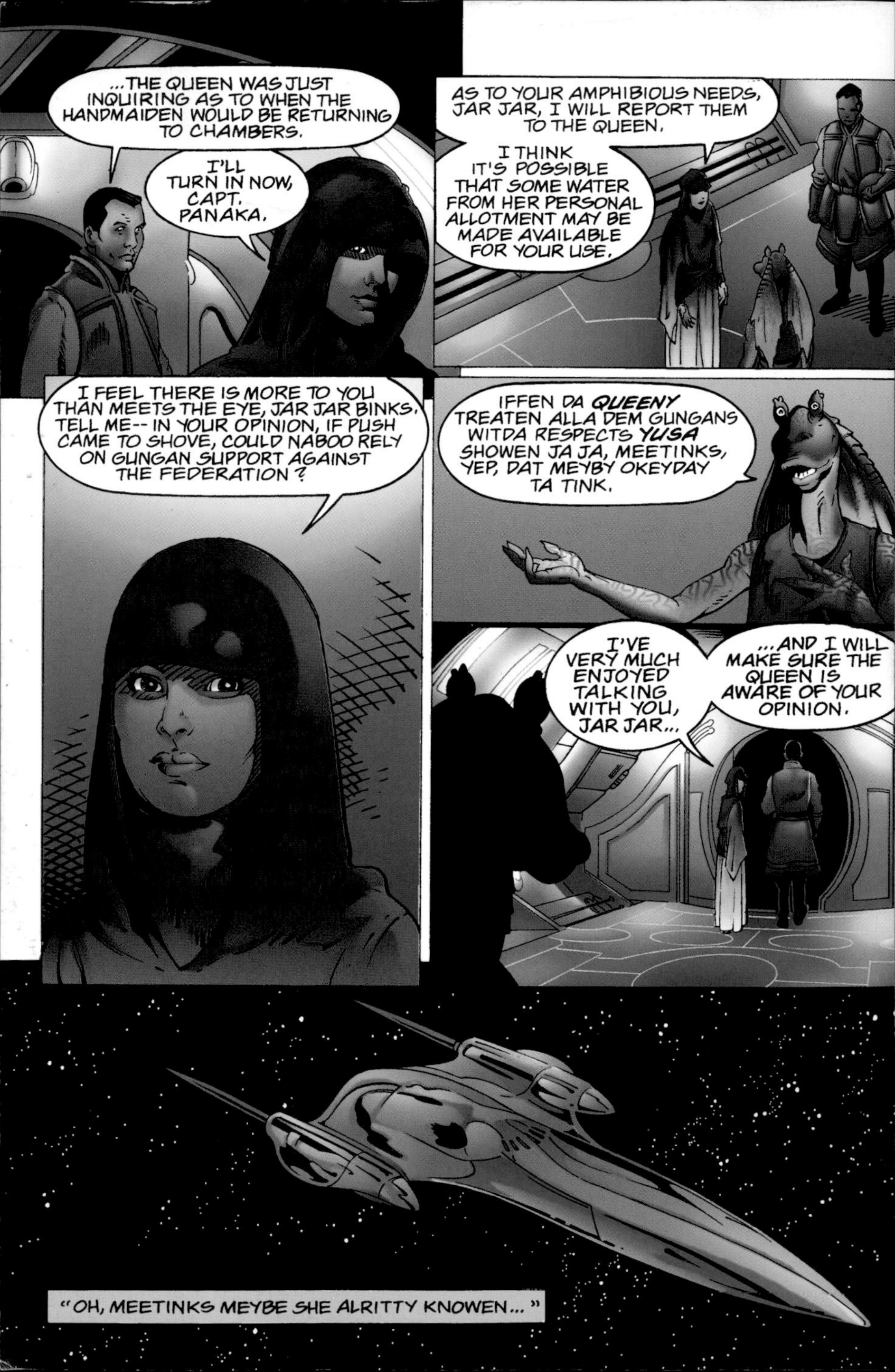
...THE QUEEN WAS JUST INQUIRING AS TO WHEN THE HANDMAIDEN WOULD BE RETURNING TO CHAMBERS.
I'LL TURN IN NOW, CAPT. PANAKA.
AS TO YOUR AMPHIBIOUS NEEDS, JAR JAR, I WILL REPORT THEM TO THE QUEEN.
I THINK IT'S POSSIBLE THAT SOME WATER FROM HER PERSONAL ALLOTMENT MAY BE MADE AVAILABLE FOR YOUR USE.
I FEEL THERE IS MORE TO YOU THAN MEETS THE EYE, JAR JAR BINKS. TELL ME-- IN YOUR OPINION, IF PUSH CAME TO SHOVE, COULD NABOO RELY ON GUNGAN SUPPORT AGAINST THE FEDERATION?
IFFEN DA QUEENY TREATEN ALLA DEM GUNGANS WITDA RESPECTS YUSA SHOWEN JA JA, MEETINKS, YEP, DAT MEYBY OKEYDAY TA TINK.
I'VE VERY MUCH ENJOYED TALKING WITH YOU, JAR JAR...
...AND I WILL MAKE SURE THE QUEEN IS AWARE OF YOUR OPINION.
"OH, MEETINKS MEYBE SHE ALRITTY KNOWEN..."

EPISODE I—QUI-GON JINN

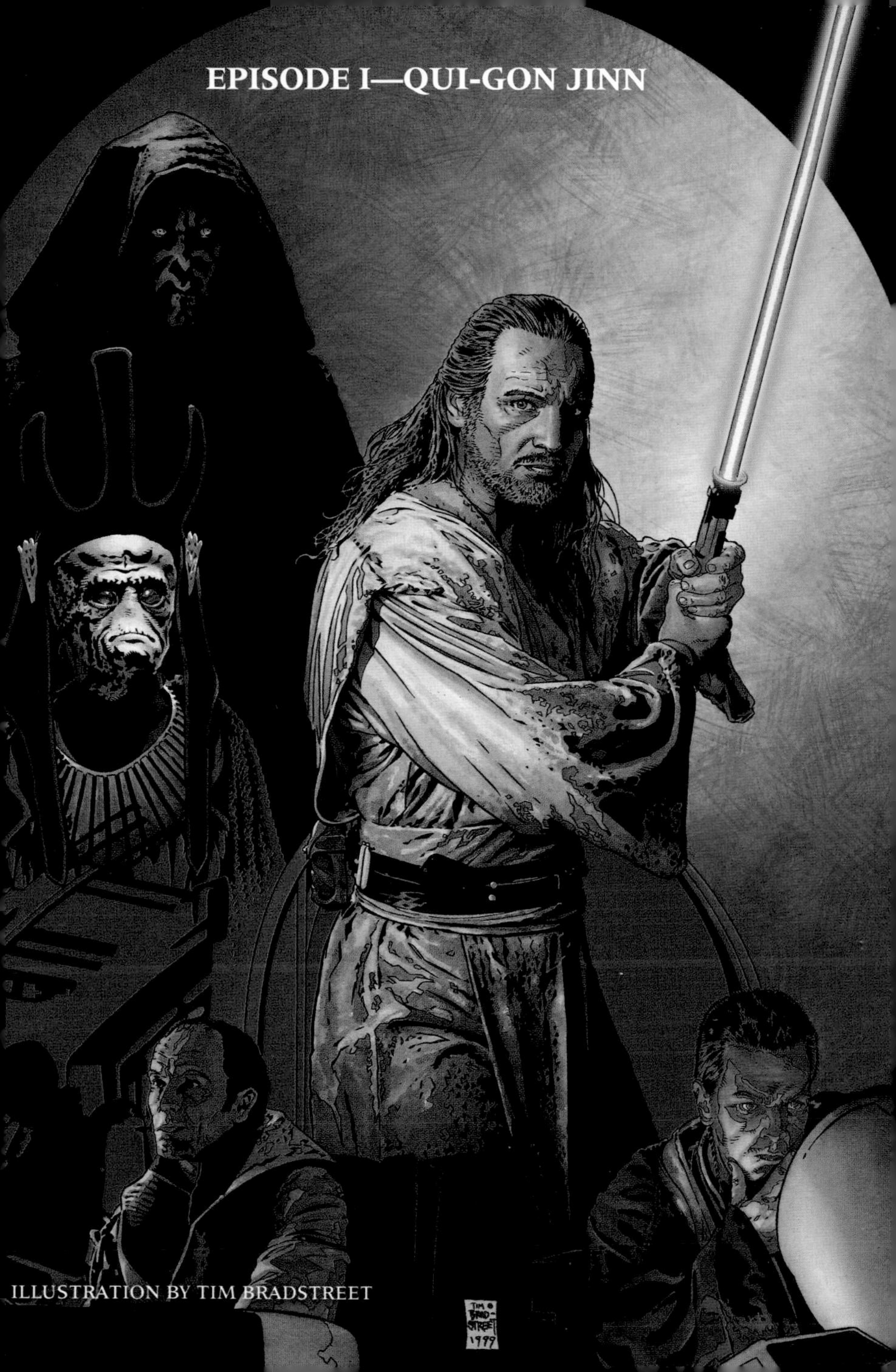
TIM BRAD-STREET 1999

ILLUSTRATION BY TIM BRADSTREET

Script
RYDER WINDHAM

Pencils
ROBERT TERANISHI

Inks and color rendering
CHRIS CHUCKRY

Lettering
VICKIE WILLIAMS

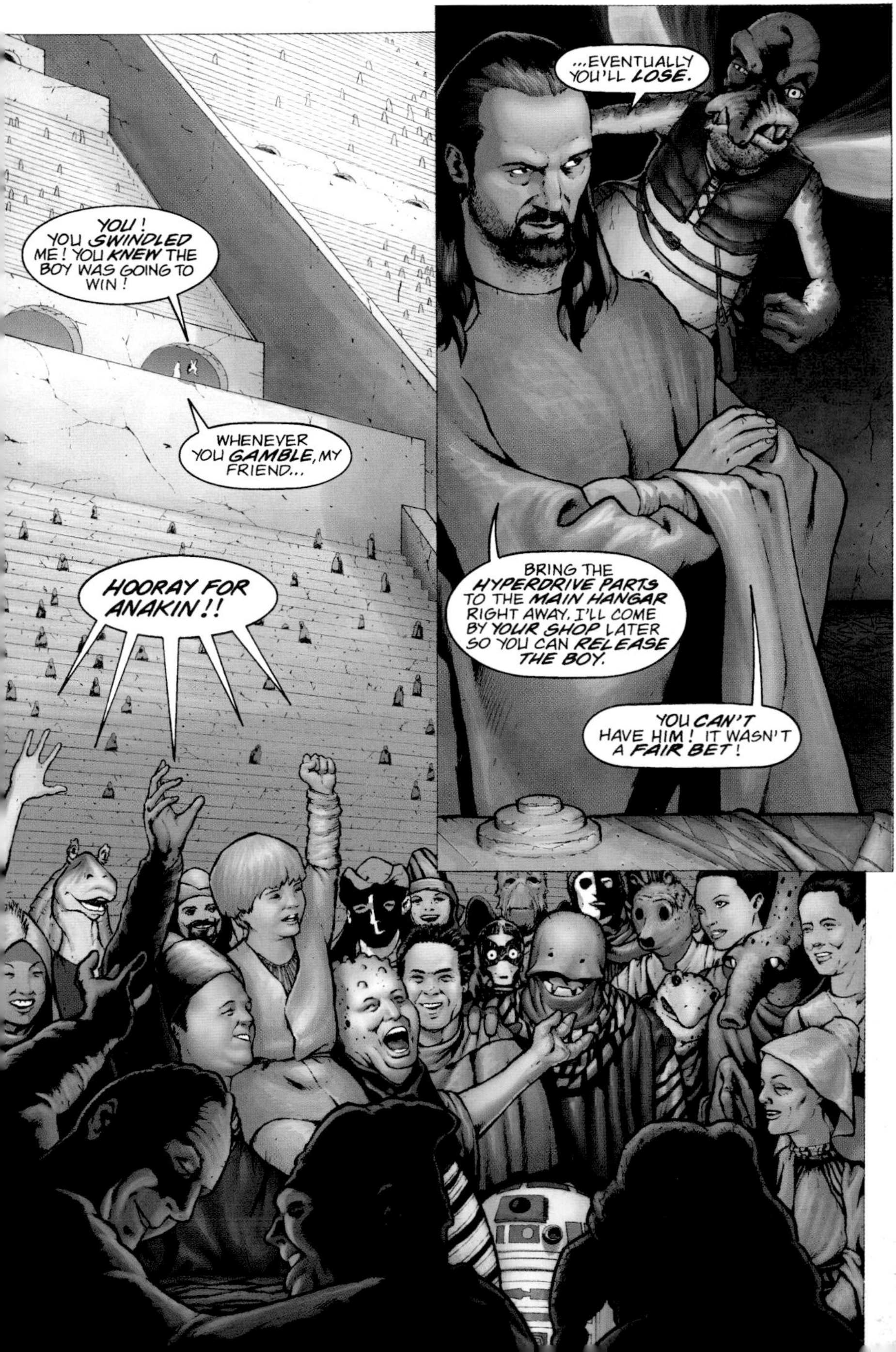
YOU! YOU SWINDLED ME! YOU KNEW THE BOY WAS GOING TO WIN!
WHENEVER YOU GAMBLE, MY FRIEND...
...EVENTUALLY YOU'LL LOSE.
BRING THE HYPERDRIVE PARTS TO THE MAIN HANGAR RIGHT AWAY. I'LL COME BY YOUR SHOP LATER SO YOU CAN RELEASE THE BOY.
YOU CAN'T HAVE HIM! IT WASN'T A FAIR BET!
HOORAY FOR ANAKIN!!

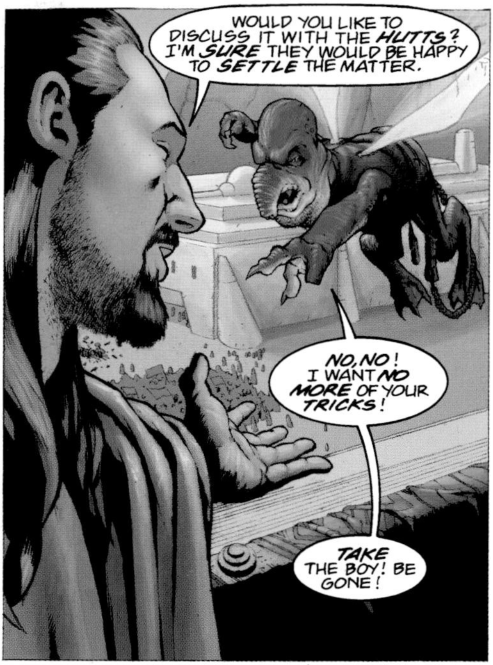
WOULD YOU LIKE TO DISCUSS IT WITH THE HUTTS? I'M SURE THEY WOULD BE HAPPY TO SETTLE THE MATTER.
NO, NO! I WANT NO MORE OF YOUR TRICKS!
TAKE THE BOY! BE GONE!
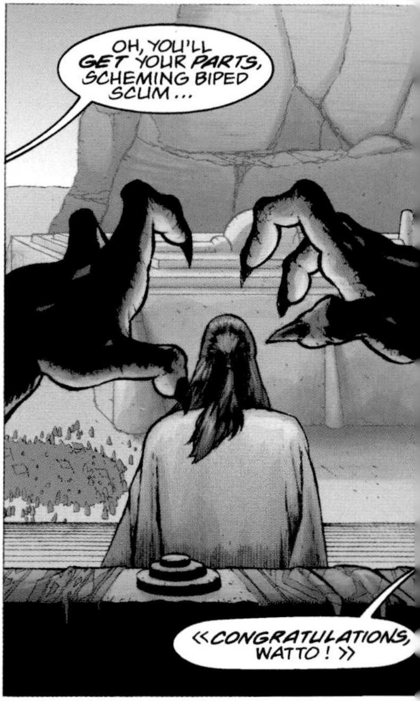
OH, YOU'LL GET YOUR PARTS, SCHEMING BIPED SCUM...
«CONGRATULATIONS, WATTO!»
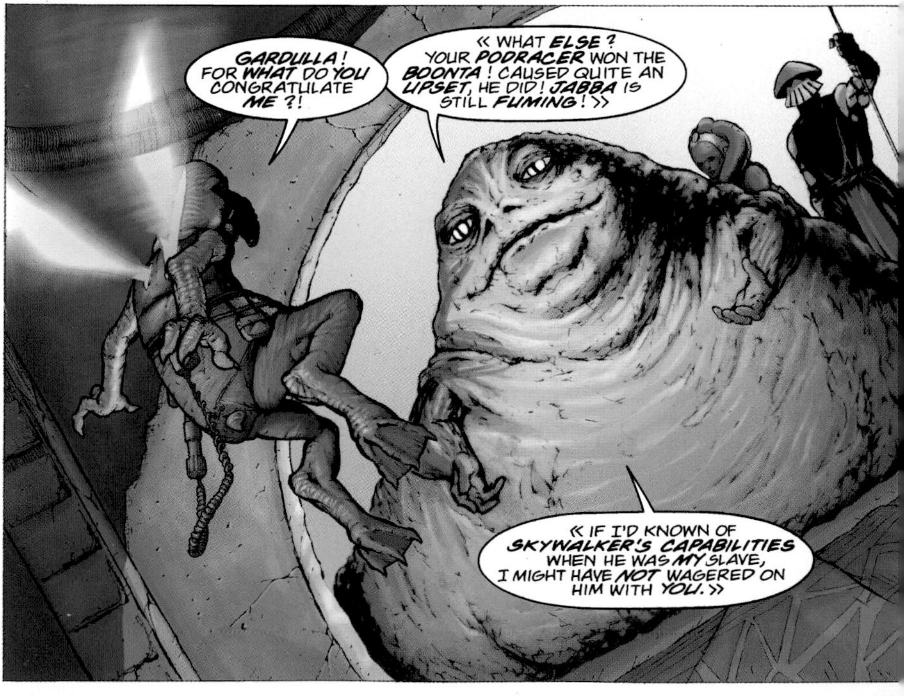
GARDULLA! FOR WHAT DO YOU CONGRATULATE ME?!
« WHAT ELSE? YOUR PODRACER WON THE BOONTA! CAUSED QUITE AN UPSET, HE DID! JABBA IS STILL FUMING!»
« IF I'D KNOWN OF SKYWALKER'S CAPABILITIES WHEN HE WAS MY SLAVE, I MIGHT HAVE NOT WAGERED ON HIM WITH YOU.»

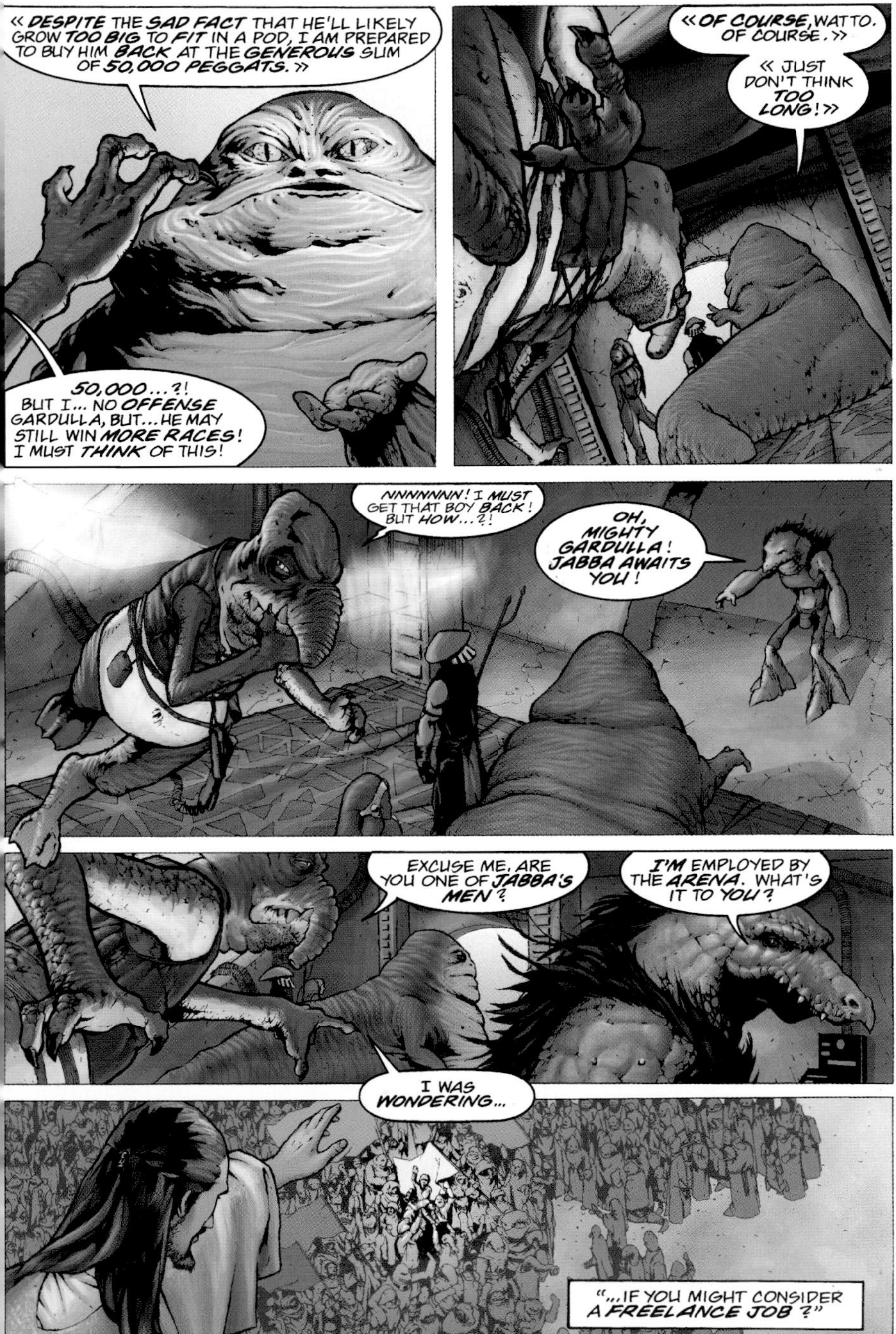
« DESPITE THE SAD FACT THAT HE'LL LIKELY GROW TOO BIG TO FIT IN A POD, I AM PREPARED TO BUY HIM BACK AT THE GENEROUS SUM OF 50,000 PEGGATS. »
50,000...?! BUT I... NO OFFENSE GARDULLA, BUT... HE MAY STILL WIN MORE RACES! I MUST THINK OF THIS!
« OF COURSE, WATTO. OF COURSE. »
« JUST DON'T THINK TOO LONG! »
NNNNNNN! I MUST GET THAT BOY BACK! BUT HOW...?!
OH, MIGHTY GARDULLA! JABBA AWAITS YOU!
EXCUSE ME, ARE YOU ONE OF JABBA'S MEN?
I'M EMPLOYED BY THE ARENA. WHAT'S IT TO YOU?
I WAS WONDERING...
"...IF YOU MIGHT CONSIDER A FREELANCE JOB?"

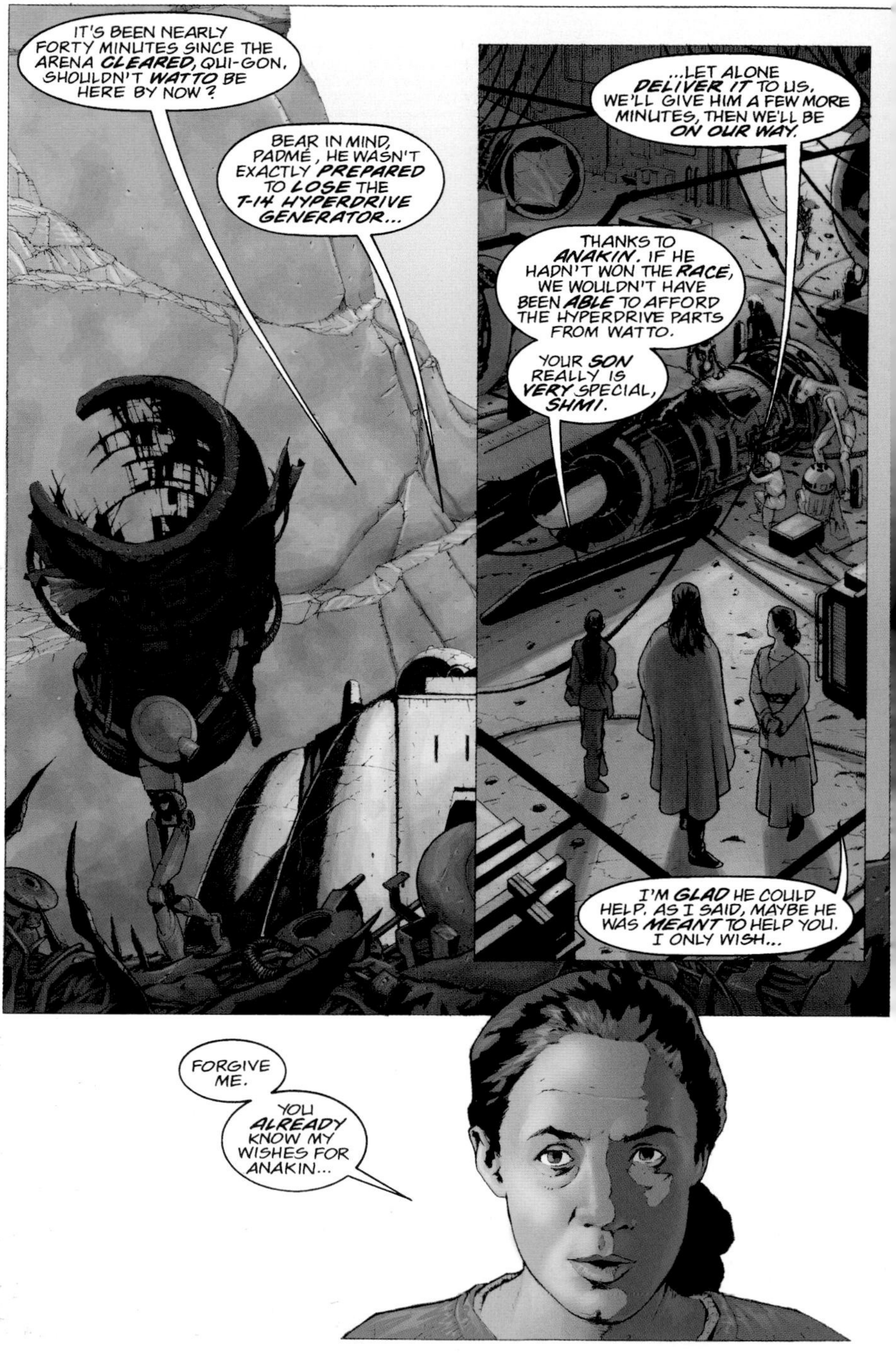
IT'S BEEN NEARLY FORTY MINUTES SINCE THE ARENA CLEARED, QUI-GON. SHOULDN'T WATTO BE HERE BY NOW?
BEAR IN MIND, PADMÉ, HE WASN'T EXACTLY PREPARED TO LOSE THE T-14 HYPERDRIVE GENERATOR...
...LET ALONE DELIVER IT TO US. WE'LL GIVE HIM A FEW MORE MINUTES, THEN WE'LL BE ON OUR WAY.
THANKS TO ANAKIN. IF HE HADN'T WON THE RACE, WE WOULDN'T HAVE BEEN ABLE TO AFFORD THE HYPERDRIVE PARTS FROM WATTO.
YOUR SON REALLY IS VERY SPECIAL, SHMI.
I'M GLAD HE COULD HELP. AS I SAID, MAYBE HE WAS MEANT TO HELP YOU. I ONLY WISH...
FORGIVE ME.
YOU ALREADY KNOW MY WISHES FOR ANAKIN...

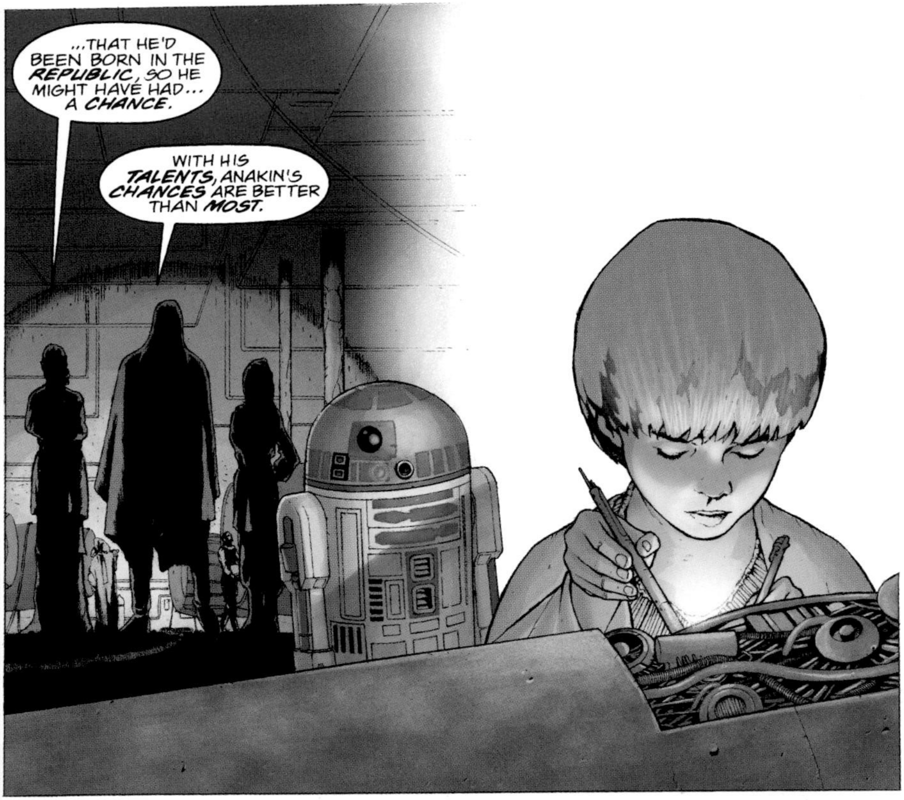
...THAT HE'D BEEN BORN IN THE REPUBLIC, SO HE MIGHT HAVE HAD... A CHANCE.
WITH HIS TALENTS, ANAKIN'S CHANCES ARE BETTER THAN MOST.

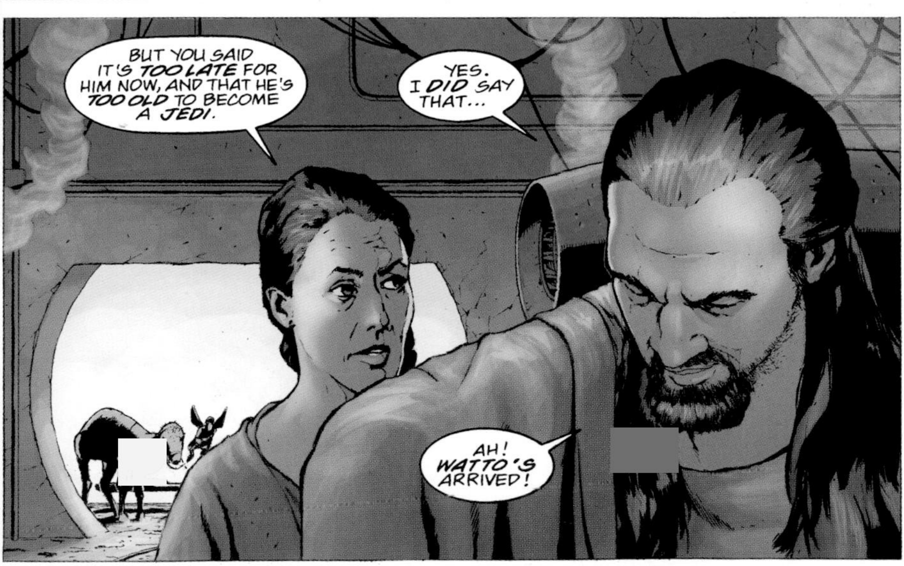
BUT YOU SAID IT'S TOO LATE FOR HIM NOW, AND THAT HE'S TOO OLD TO BECOME A JEDI.
YES. I DID SAY THAT...
AH! WATTO'S ARRIVED!

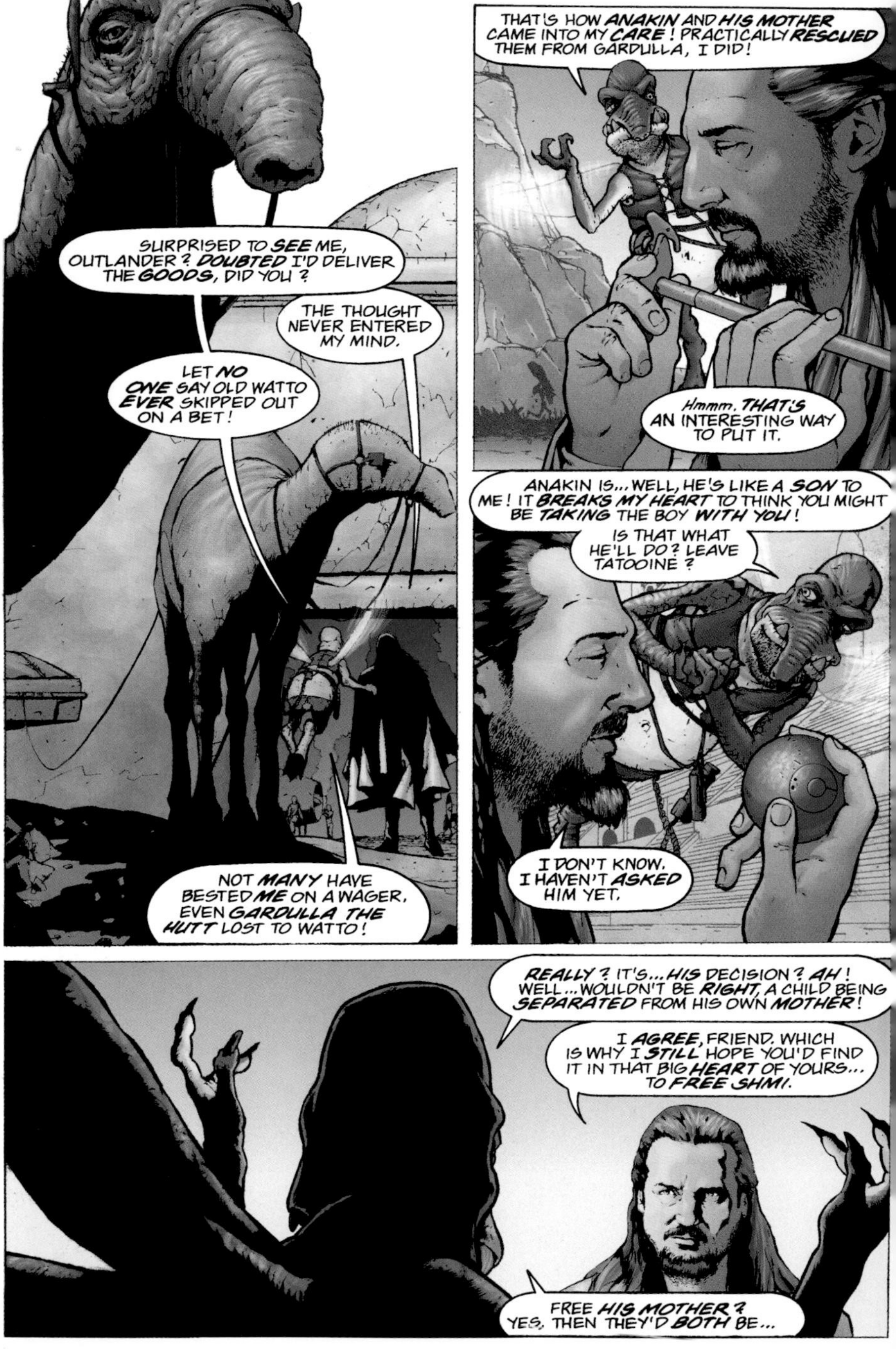
SURPRISED TO SEE ME, OUTLANDER? DOUBTED I'D DELIVER THE GOODS, DID YOU?
THE THOUGHT NEVER ENTERED MY MIND.
LET NO ONE SAY OLD WATTO EVER SKIPPED OUT ON A BET!
NOT MANY HAVE BESTED ME ON A WAGER. EVEN GARDULLA THE HUTT LOST TO WATTO!
THAT'S HOW ANAKIN AND HIS MOTHER CAME INTO MY CARE! PRACTICALLY RESCUED THEM FROM GARDULLA, I DID!
Hmmm. THAT'S AN INTERESTING WAY TO PUT IT.
ANAKIN IS... WELL, HE'S LIKE A SON TO ME! IT BREAKS MY HEART TO THINK YOU MIGHT BE TAKING THE BOY WITH YOU!
IS THAT WHAT HE'LL DO? LEAVE TATOOINE?
I DON'T KNOW. I HAVEN'T ASKED HIM YET.
REALLY? IT'S... HIS DECISION? AH! WELL... WOULDN'T BE RIGHT, A CHILD BEING SEPARATED FROM HIS OWN MOTHER!
I AGREE, FRIEND. WHICH IS WHY I STILL HOPE YOU'D FIND IT IN THAT BIG HEART OF YOURS... TO FREE SHMI.
FREE HIS MOTHER? YES. THEN THEY'D BOTH BE...

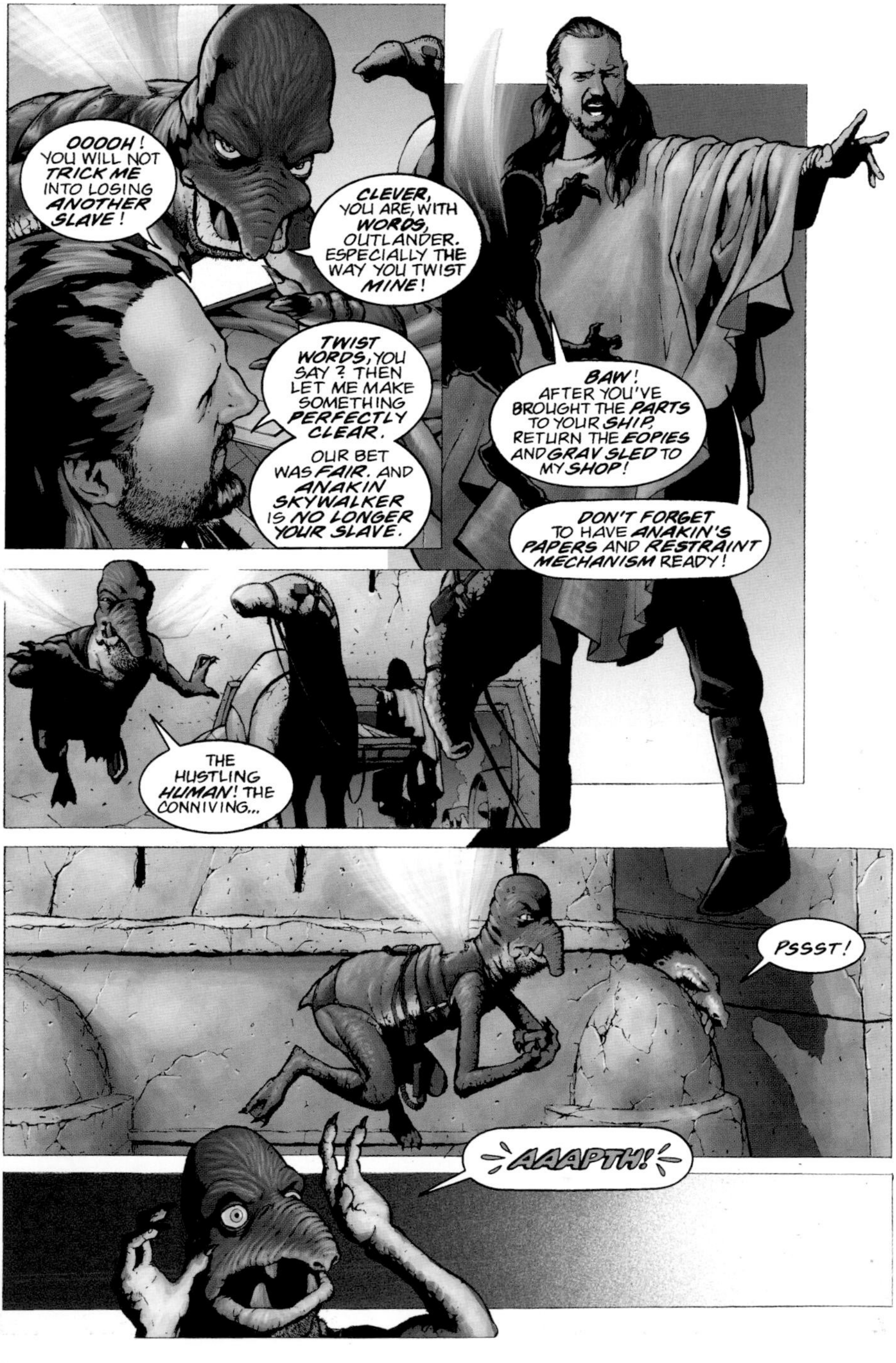
OOOOH! YOU WILL NOT TRICK ME INTO LOSING ANOTHER SLAVE!
CLEVER, YOU ARE, WITH WORDS, OUTLANDER. ESPECIALLY THE WAY YOU TWIST MINE!
TWIST WORDS, YOU SAY? THEN LET ME MAKE SOMETHING PERFECTLY CLEAR.
OUR BET WAS FAIR. AND ANAKIN SKYWALKER IS NO LONGER YOUR SLAVE.
BAW! AFTER YOU'VE BROUGHT THE PARTS TO YOUR SHIP, RETURN THE EOPIES AND GRAV SLED TO MY SHOP!
DON'T FORGET TO HAVE ANAKIN'S PAPERS AND RESTRAINT MECHANISM READY!
THE HUSTLING HUMAN! THE CONNIVING...
PSSST!
AAAPTH!

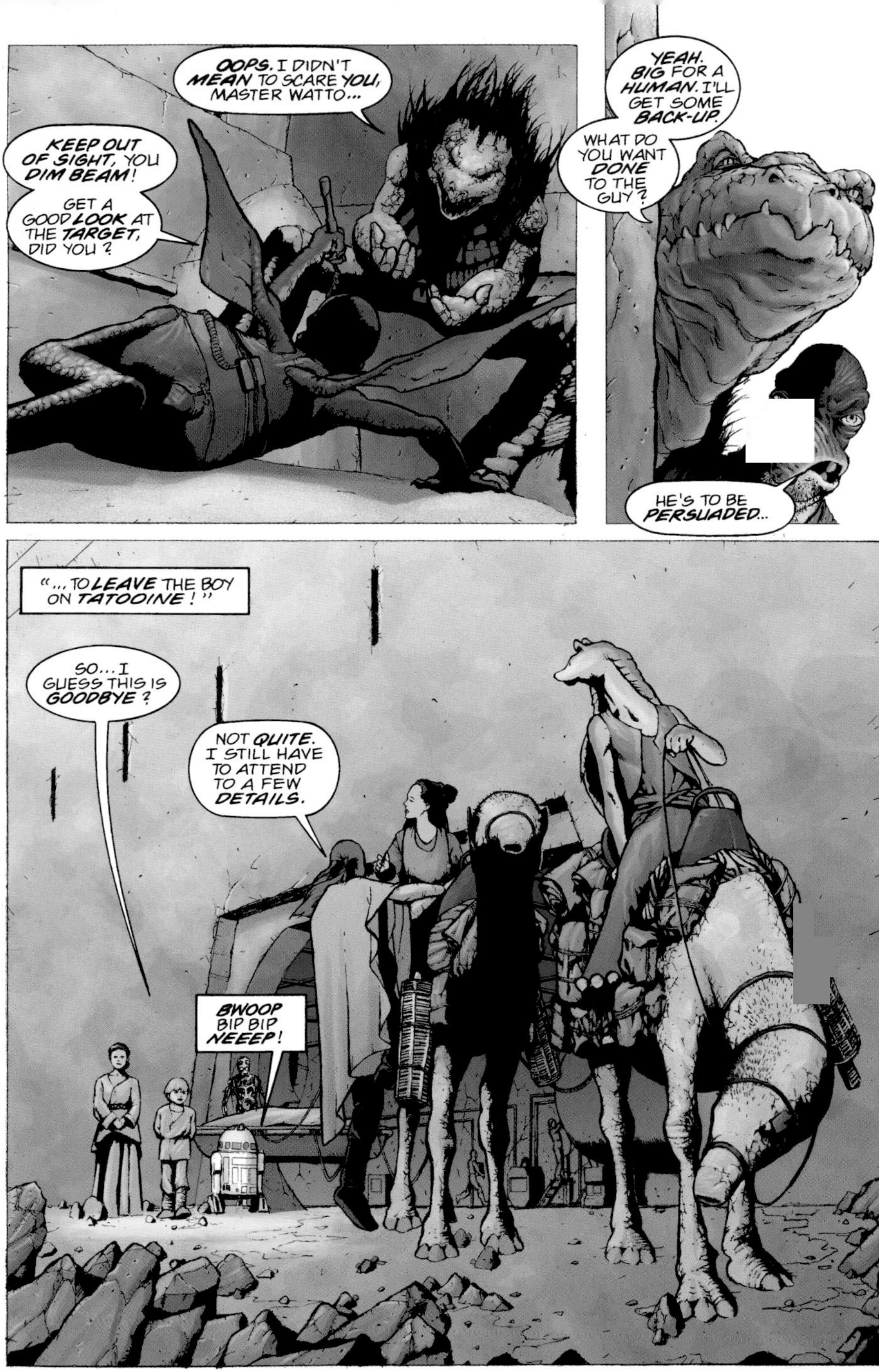
OOPS. I DIDN'T MEAN TO SCARE YOU, MASTER WATTO...
KEEP OUT OF SIGHT, YOU DIM BEAM!
GET A GOOD LOOK AT THE TARGET, DID YOU?
YEAH. BIG FOR A HUMAN. I'LL GET SOME BACK-UP.
WHAT DO YOU WANT DONE TO THE GUY?
HE'S TO BE PERSUADED...
"...TO LEAVE THE BOY ON TATOOINE!"
SO... I GUESS THIS IS GOODBYE?
NOT QUITE. I STILL HAVE TO ATTEND TO A FEW DETAILS.
BWOOP BIP BIP NEEEP!

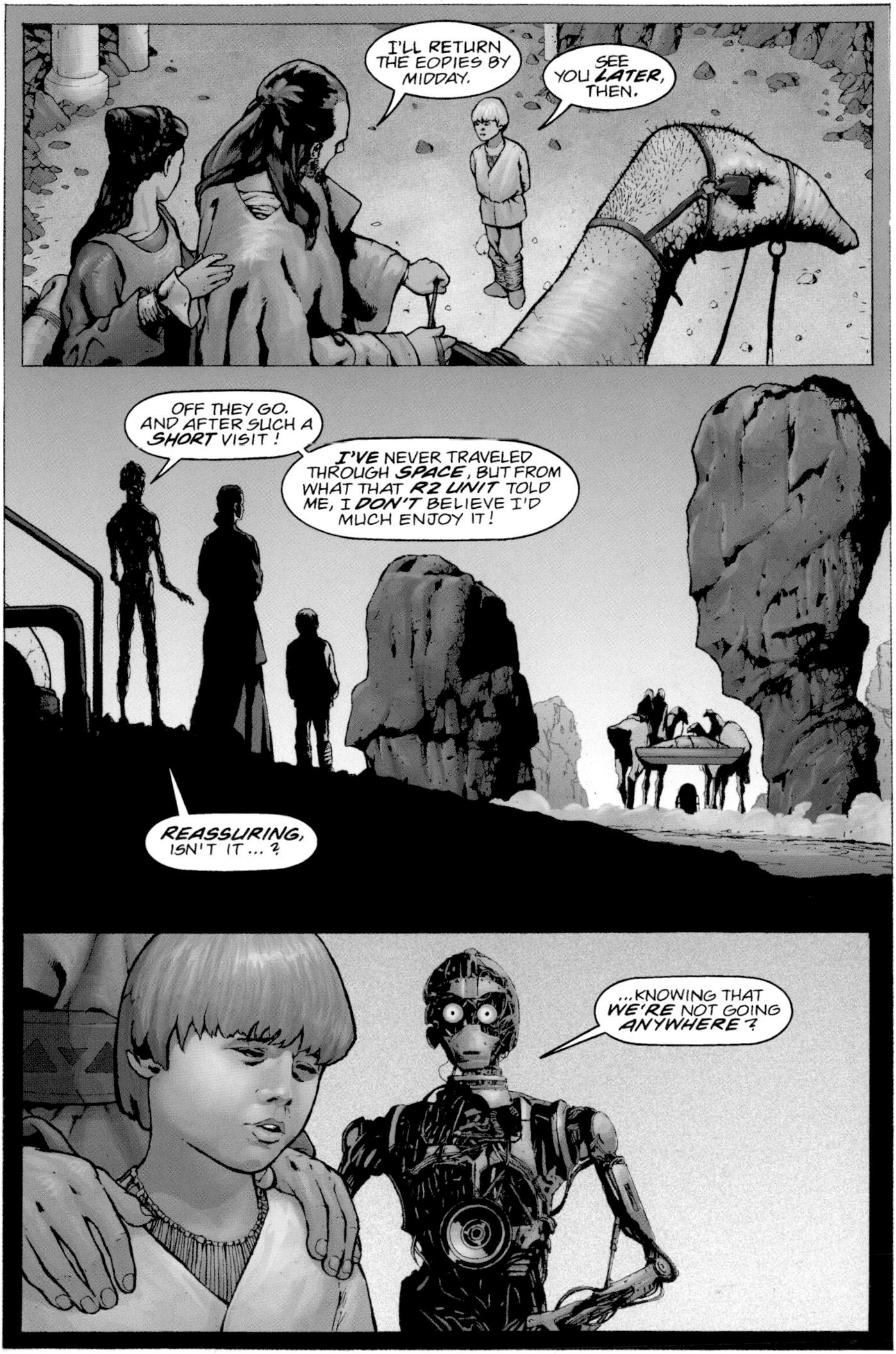
I'LL RETURN THE EOPIES BY MIDDAY.
SEE YOU LATER, THEN.
OFF THEY GO. AND AFTER SUCH A SHORT VISIT!
I'VE NEVER TRAVELED THROUGH SPACE, BUT FROM WHAT THAT R2 UNIT TOLD ME, I DON'T BELIEVE I'D MUCH ENJOY IT!
REASSURING, ISN'T IT...?
...KNOWING THAT WE'RE NOT GOING ANYWHERE?

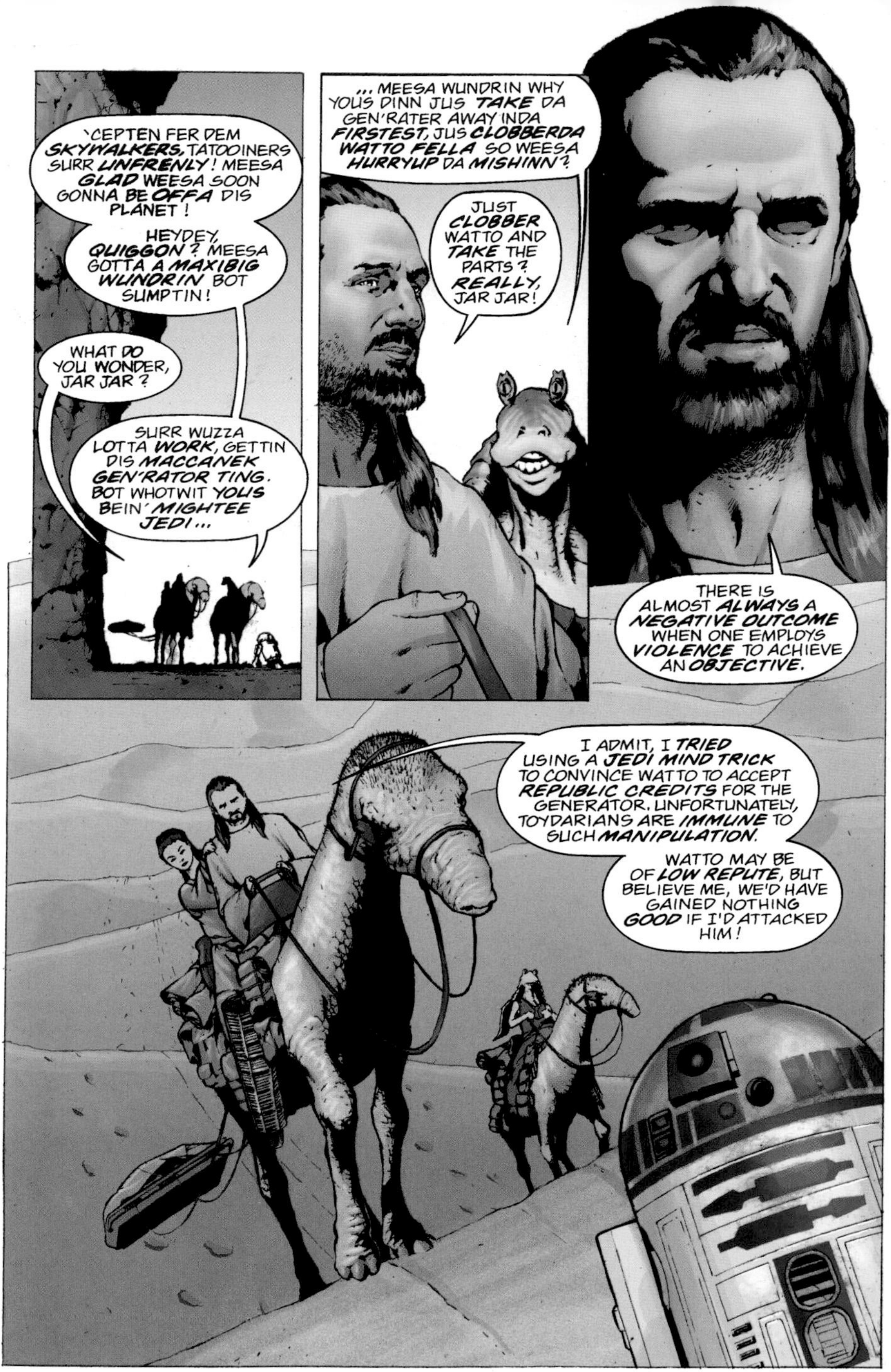
`CEPTEN FER DEM SKYWALKERS, TATOOINERS SURR UNFRENLY! MEESA GLAD WEESA SOON GONNA BE OFFA DIS PLANET!
HEYDEY, QUIGGON? MEESA GOTTA A MAXIBIG WUNDRIN BOT SUMPTIN!
WHAT DO YOU WONDER, JAR JAR?
SURR WUZZA LOTTA WORK, GETTIN DIS MACCANEK GEN'RATOR TING. BOT WHOTWIT YOUS BEIN' MIGHTEE JEDI...
...MEESA WUNDRIN WHY YOUS DINN JUS TAKE DA GEN'RATER AWAY INDA FIRSTEST, JUS CLOBBERDA WATTO FELLA SO WEESA HURRYUP DA MISHINN?
JUST CLOBBER WATTO AND TAKE THE PARTS? REALLY, JAR JAR!
THERE IS ALMOST ALWAYS A NEGATIVE OUTCOME WHEN ONE EMPLOYS VIOLENCE TO ACHIEVE AN OBJECTIVE.
I ADMIT, I TRIED USING A JEDI MIND TRICK TO CONVINCE WATTO TO ACCEPT REPUBLIC CREDITS FOR THE GENERATOR. UNFORTUNATELY, TOYDARIANS ARE IMMUNE TO SUCH MANIPULATION.
WATTO MAY BE OF LOW REPUTE, BUT BELIEVE ME, WE'D HAVE GAINED NOTHING GOOD IF I'D ATTACKED HIM!

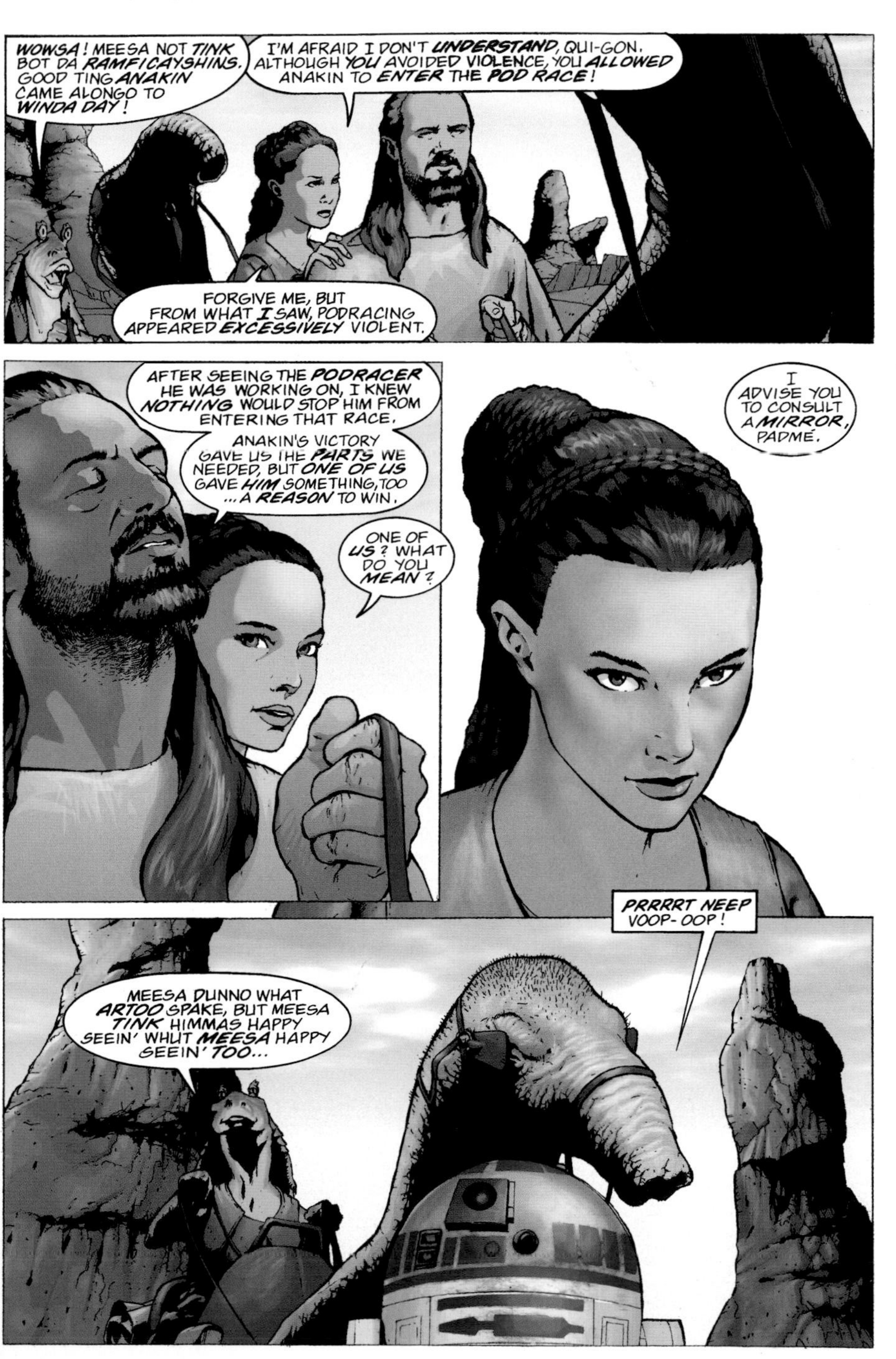

WOWSA! MEESA NOT TINK BOT DA RAMFICAYSHINS. GOOD TING ANAKIN CAME ALONGO TO WINDA DAY!
I'M AFRAID I DON'T UNDERSTAND, QUI-GON. ALTHOUGH YOU AVOIDED VIOLENCE, YOU ALLOWED ANAKIN TO ENTER THE POD RACE!
FORGIVE ME, BUT FROM WHAT I SAW, PODRACING APPEARED EXCESSIVELY VIOLENT.
AFTER SEEING THE PODRACER HE WAS WORKING ON, I KNEW NOTHING WOULD STOP HIM FROM ENTERING THAT RACE.
ANAKIN'S VICTORY GAVE US THE PARTS WE NEEDED, BUT ONE OF US GAVE HIM SOMETHING, TOO ...A REASON TO WIN.
ONE OF US? WHAT DO YOU MEAN?
I ADVISE YOU TO CONSULT A MIRROR, PADMÉ.
MEESA DUNNO WHAT ARTOO SPAKE, BUT MEESA TINK HIMMAS HAPPY SEEIN' WHUT MEESA HAPPY SEEIN' TOO...
PRRRRT NEEP VOOP-OOP!

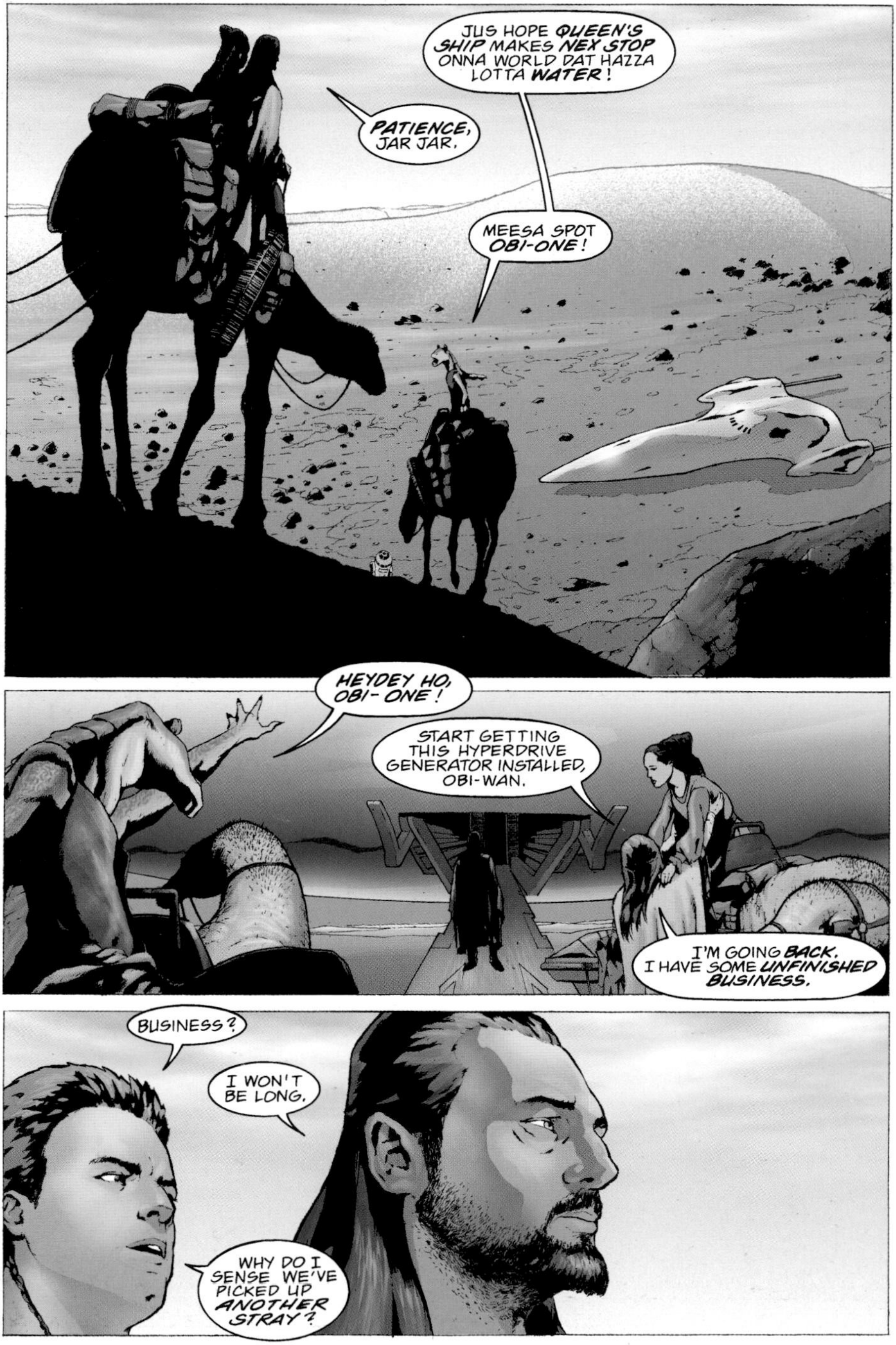
JUS HOPE QUEEN'S SHIP MAKES NEX STOP ONNA WORLD DAT HAZZA LOTTA WATER!
PATIENCE, JAR JAR.
MEESA SPOT OBI-ONE!
HEYDEY HO, OBI-ONE!
START GETTING THIS HYPERDRIVE GENERATOR INSTALLED, OBI-WAN.
I'M GOING BACK. I HAVE SOME UNFINISHED BUSINESS.
BUSINESS?
I WON'T BE LONG.
WHY DO I SENSE WE'VE PICKED UP ANOTHER STRAY?

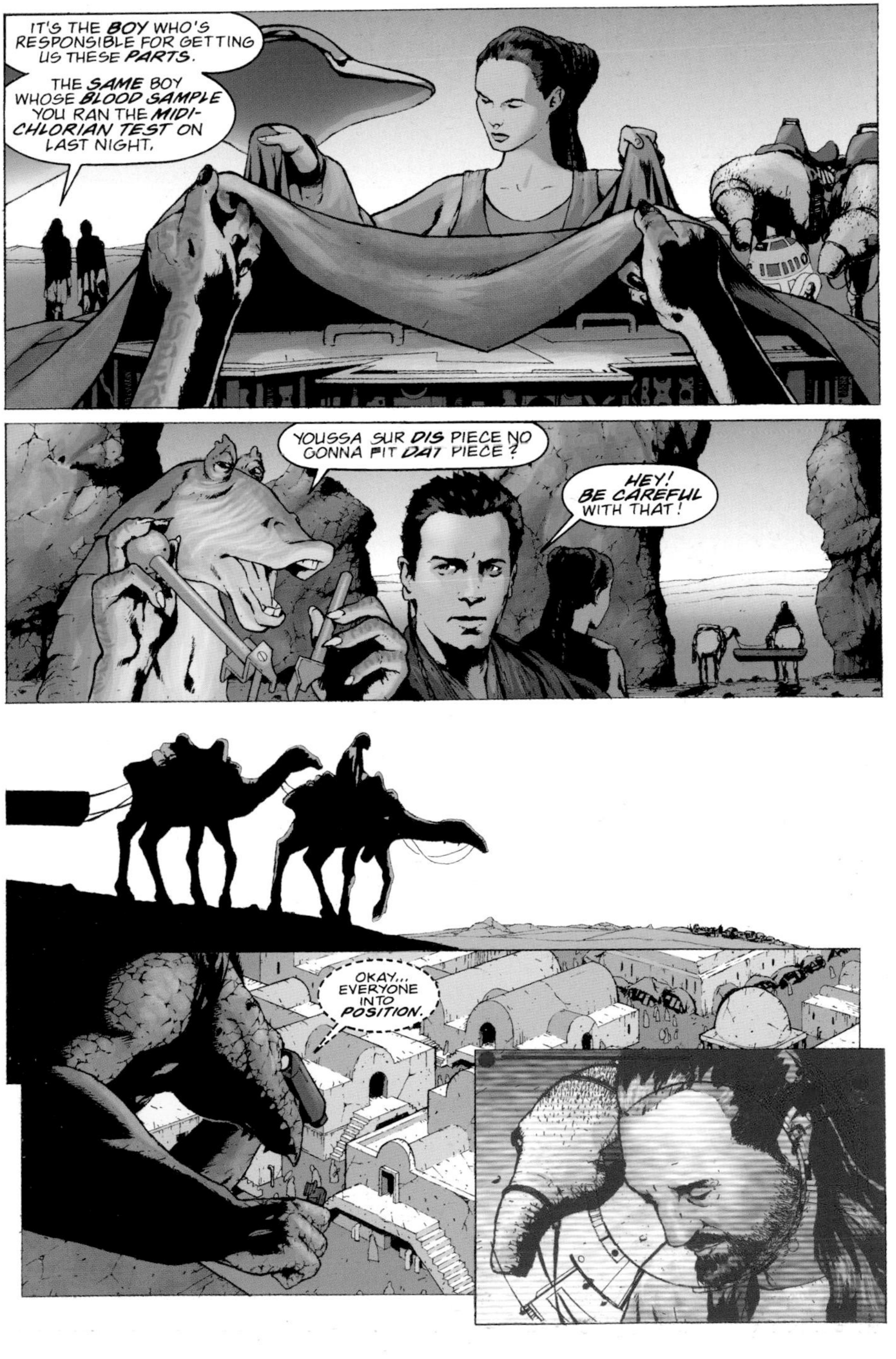
IT'S THE BOY WHO'S RESPONSIBLE FOR GETTING US THESE PARTS.
THE SAME BOY WHOSE BLOOD SAMPLE YOU RAN THE MIDI-CHLORIAN TEST ON LAST NIGHT.
YOUSSA SUR DIS PIECE NO GONNA FIT DAT PIECE?
HEY! BE CAREFUL WITH THAT!
OKAY... EVERYONE INTO POSITION.

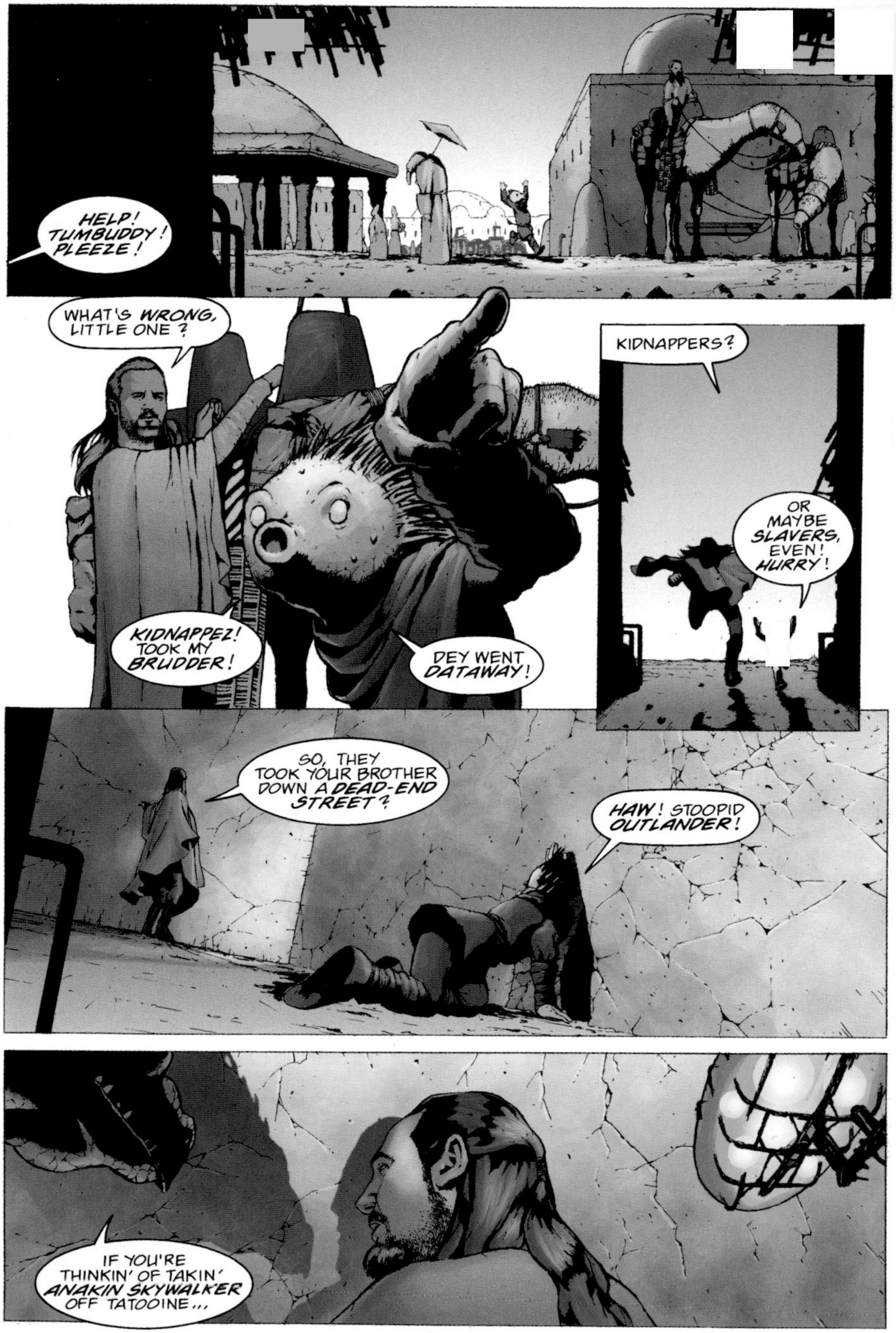
HELP! TUMBUDDY! PLEEZE!
WHAT'S WRONG, LITTLE ONE?
KIDNAPPEZ! TOOK MY BRUDDER!
DEY WENT DATAWAY!
KIDNAPPERS?
OR MAYBE SLAVERS, EVEN! HURRY!
SO, THEY TOOK YOUR BROTHER DOWN A DEAD-END STREET?
HAW! STOOPID OUTLANDER!
IF YOU'RE THINKIN' OF TAKIN' ANAKIN SKYWALKER OFF TATOOINE...

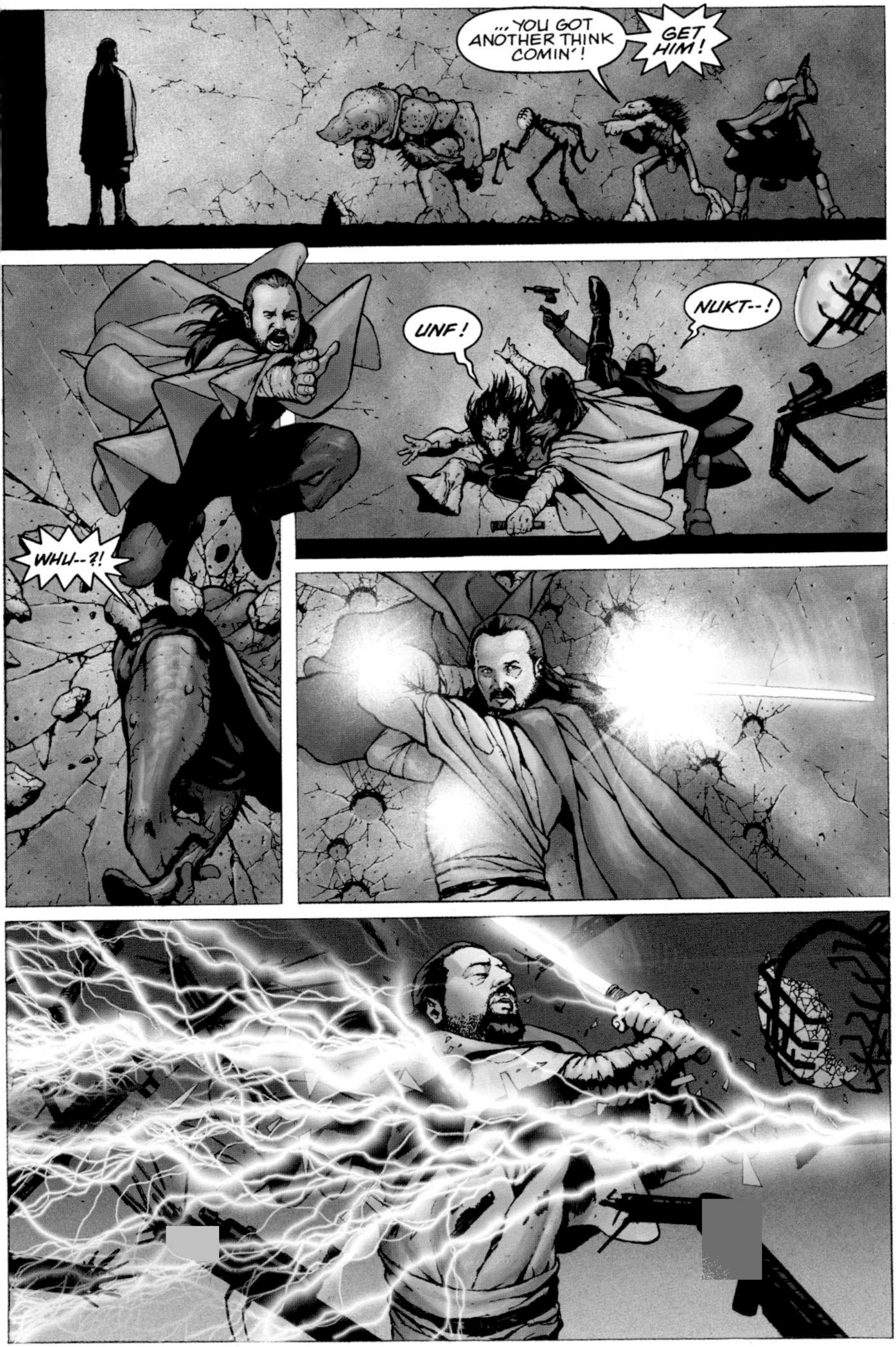
...YOU GOT ANOTHER THINK COMIN'!
GET HIM!
UNF!
NUKT--!
WHU--?!

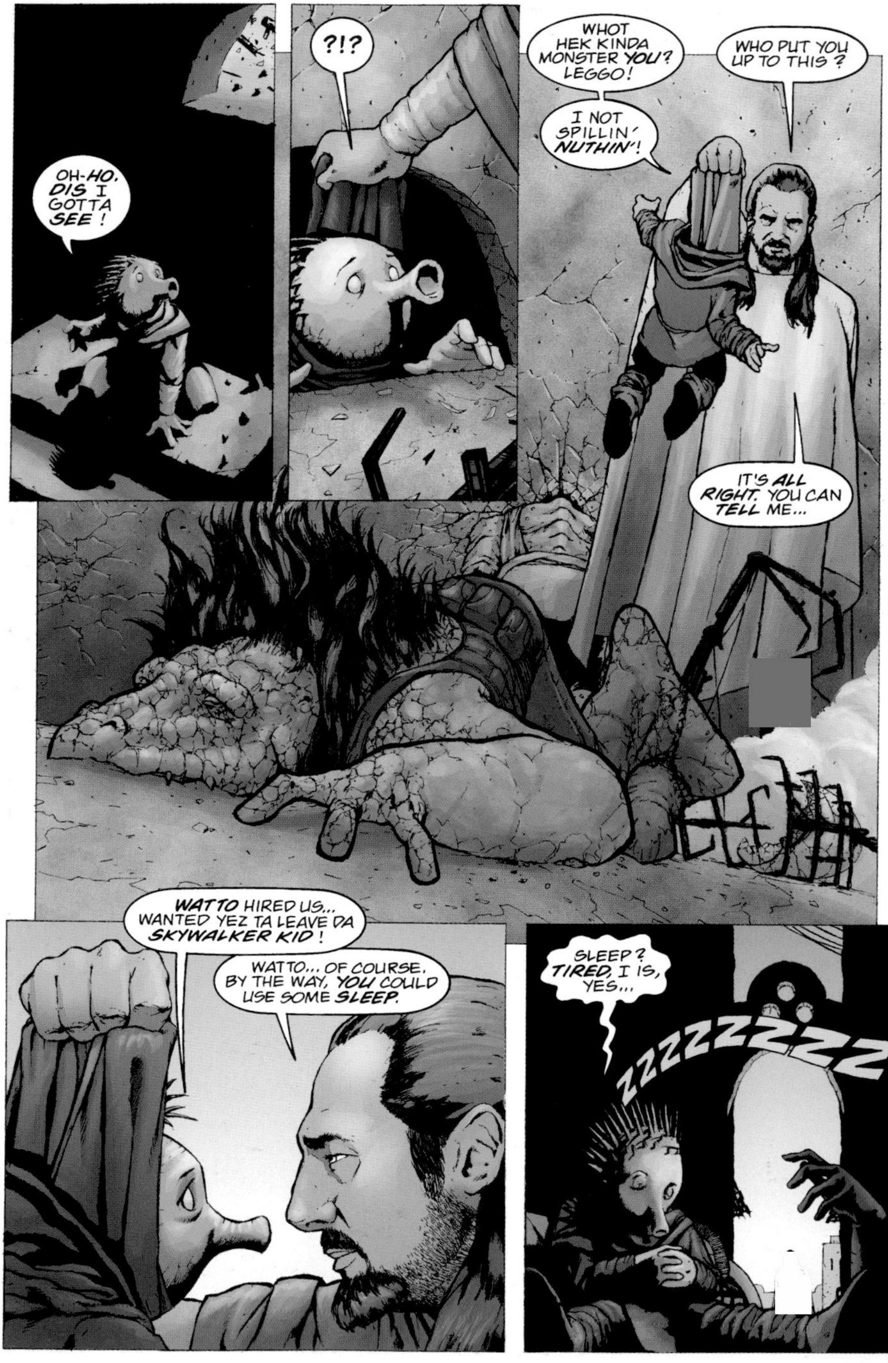
OH-HO. DIS I GOTTA SEE!
?!?
WHOT HEK KINDA MONSTER YOU? LEGGO!
I NOT SPILLIN' NUTHIN'!
WHO PUT YOU UP TO THIS?
IT'S ALL RIGHT. YOU CAN TELL ME...
WATTO HIRED US... WANTED YEZ TA LEAVE DA SKYWALKER KID!
WATTO... OF COURSE. BY THE WAY, YOU COULD USE SOME SLEEP.
SLEEP? TIRED, I IS, YES...
ZZZZZZZZZ

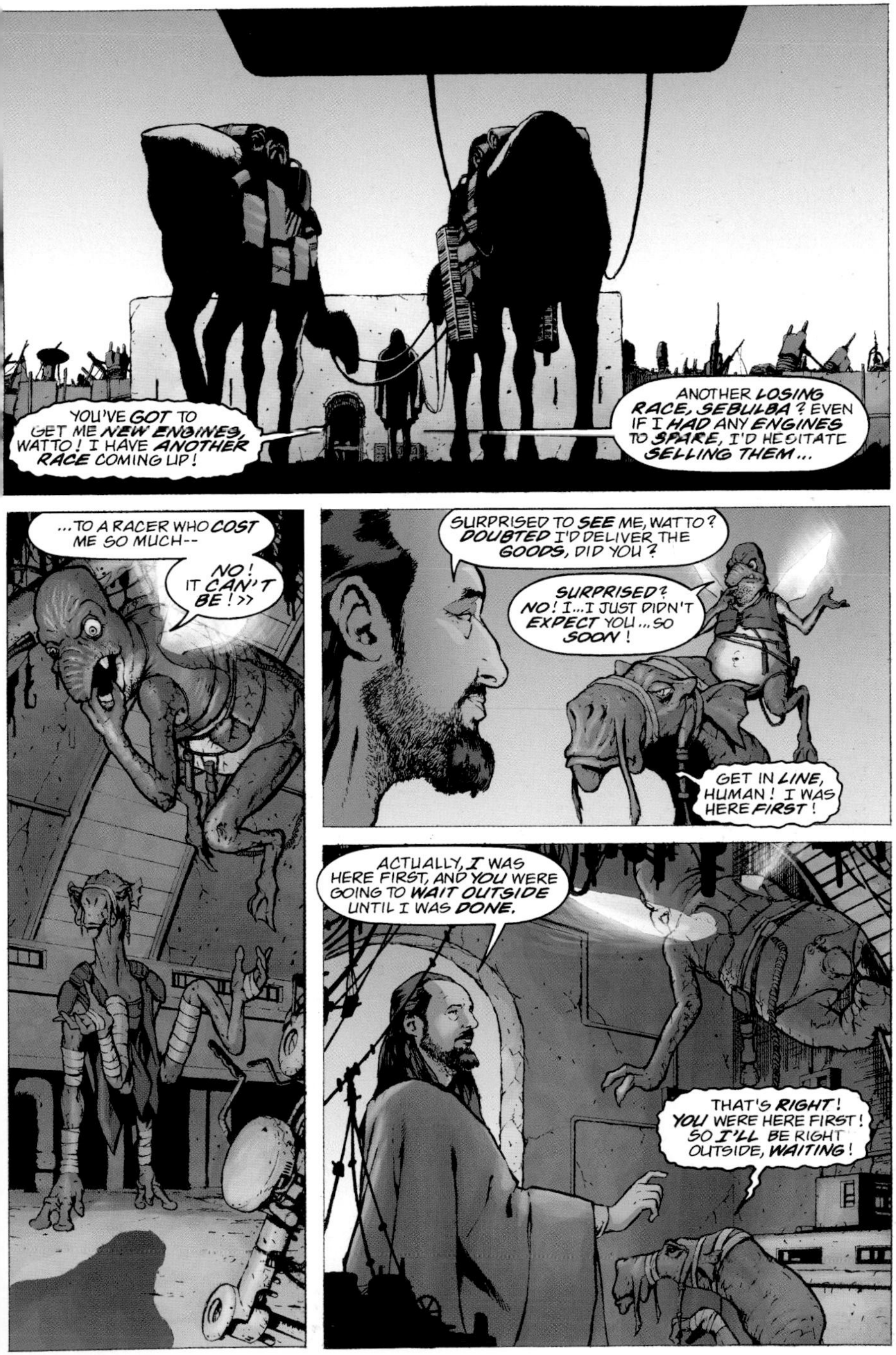
YOU'VE GOT TO GET ME NEW ENGINES, WATTO! I HAVE ANOTHER RACE COMING UP!
ANOTHER LOSING RACE, SEBULBA? EVEN IF I HAD ANY ENGINES TO SPARE, I'D HESITATE SELLING THEM...
...TO A RACER WHO COST ME SO MUCH--
NO! IT CAN'T BE! >>
SURPRISED TO SEE ME, WATTO? DOUBTED I'D DELIVER THE GOODS, DID YOU?
SURPRISED? NO! I...I JUST DIDN'T EXPECT YOU...SO SOON!
GET IN LINE, HUMAN! I WAS HERE FIRST!
ACTUALLY, I WAS HERE FIRST, AND YOU WERE GOING TO WAIT OUTSIDE UNTIL I WAS DONE.
THAT'S RIGHT! YOU WERE HERE FIRST! SO I'LL BE RIGHT OUTSIDE, WAITING!

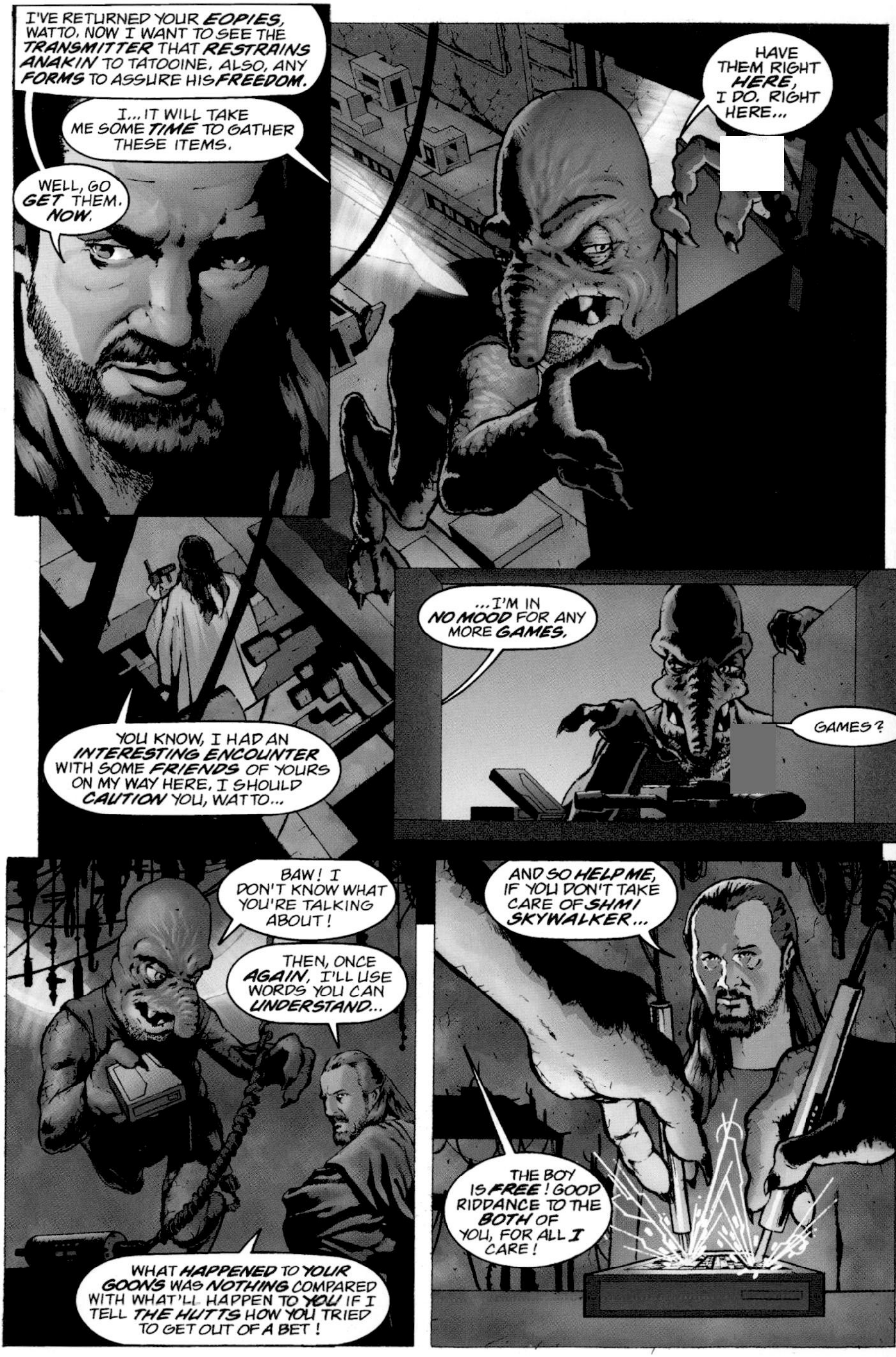
I'VE RETURNED YOUR EOPIES, WATTO. NOW I WANT TO SEE THE TRANSMITTER THAT RESTRAINS ANAKIN TO TATOOINE. ALSO, ANY FORMS TO ASSURE HIS FREEDOM.
I... IT WILL TAKE ME SOME TIME TO GATHER THESE ITEMS.
WELL, GO GET THEM. NOW.
HAVE THEM RIGHT HERE, I DO. RIGHT HERE...
YOU KNOW, I HAD AN INTERESTING ENCOUNTER WITH SOME FRIENDS OF YOURS ON MY WAY HERE. I SHOULD CAUTION YOU, WATTO...
...I'M IN NO MOOD FOR ANY MORE GAMES.
GAMES?
BAW! I DON'T KNOW WHAT YOU'RE TALKING ABOUT!
THEN, ONCE AGAIN, I'LL USE WORDS YOU CAN UNDERSTAND...
WHAT HAPPENED TO YOUR GOONS WAS NOTHING COMPARED WITH WHAT'LL HAPPEN TO YOU! IF I TELL THE HUTTS HOW YOU TRIED TO GET OUT OF A BET!
AND SO HELP ME, IF YOU DON'T TAKE CARE OF SHMI SKYWALKER...
THE BOY IS FREE! GOOD RIDDANCE TO THE BOTH OF YOU, FOR ALL I CARE!

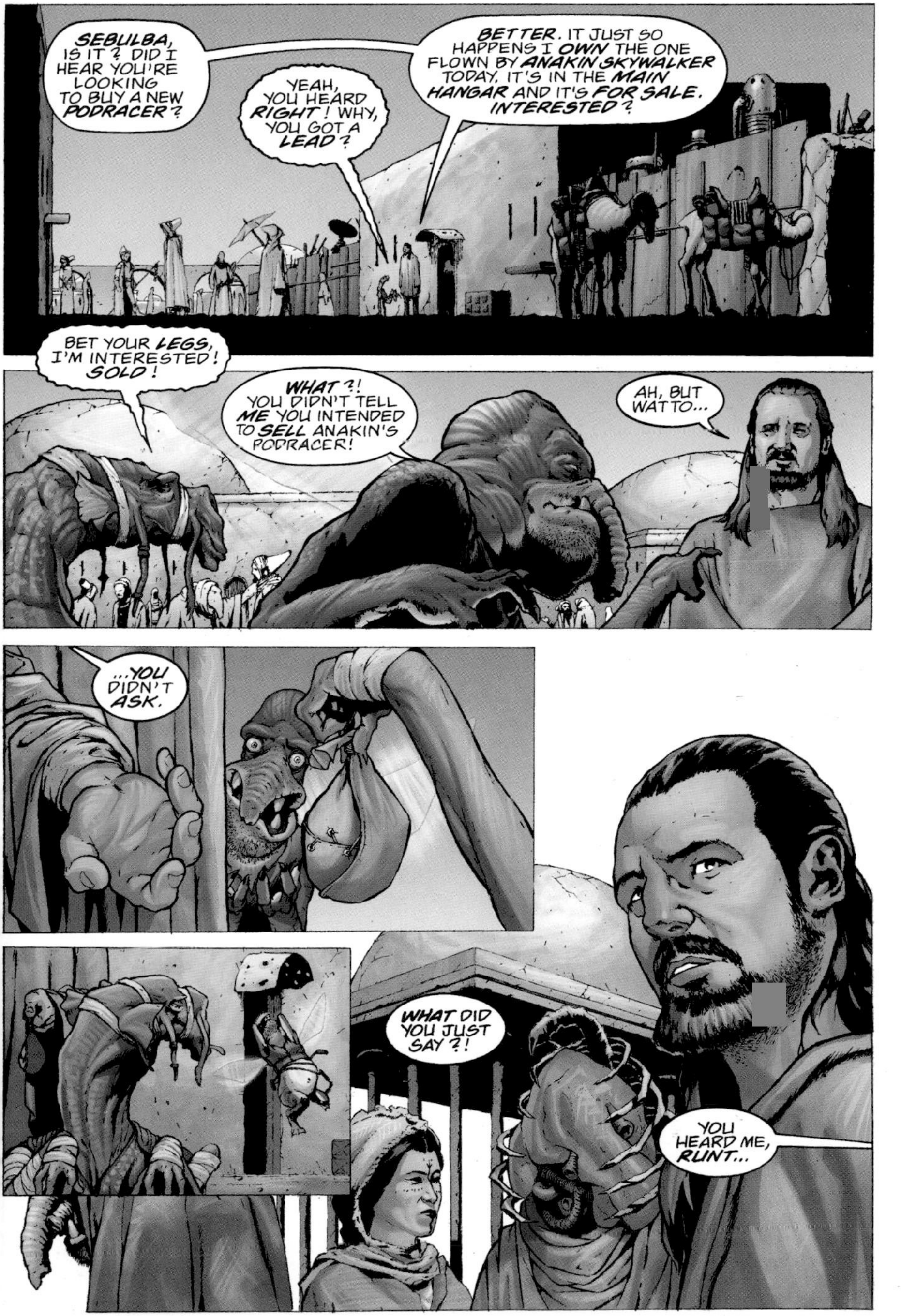
SEBULBA, IS IT? DID I HEAR YOU'RE LOOKING TO BUY A NEW PODRACER?
YEAH, YOU HEARD RIGHT! WHY, YOU GOT A LEAD?
BETTER. IT JUST SO HAPPENS I OWN THE ONE FLOWN BY ANAKIN SKYWALKER TODAY. IT'S IN THE MAIN HANGAR AND IT'S FOR SALE. INTERESTED?
BET YOUR LEGS, I'M INTERESTED! SOLD!
WHAT?! YOU DIDN'T TELL ME YOU INTENDED TO SELL ANAKIN'S PODRACER!
AH, BUT WATTO...
...YOU DIDN'T ASK.
WHAT DID YOU JUST SAY?!
YOU HEARD ME, RUNT...

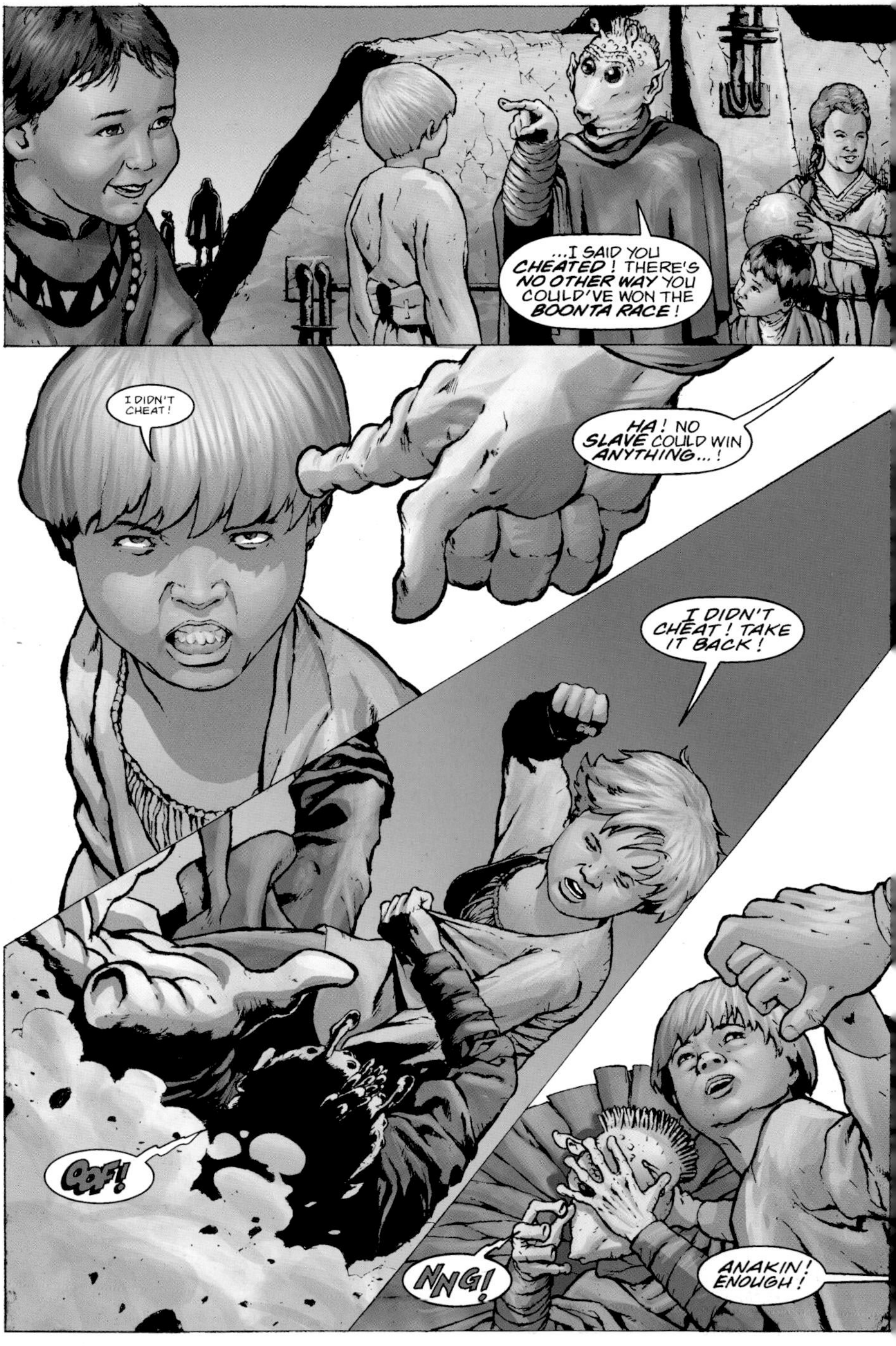
...I SAID YOU CHEATED! THERE'S NO OTHER WAY YOU COULD'VE WON THE BOONTA RACE!
I DIDN'T CHEAT!
HA! NO SLAVE COULD WIN ANYTHING...!
I DIDN'T CHEAT! TAKE IT BACK!
OOF!
NNG!
ANAKIN! ENOUGH!

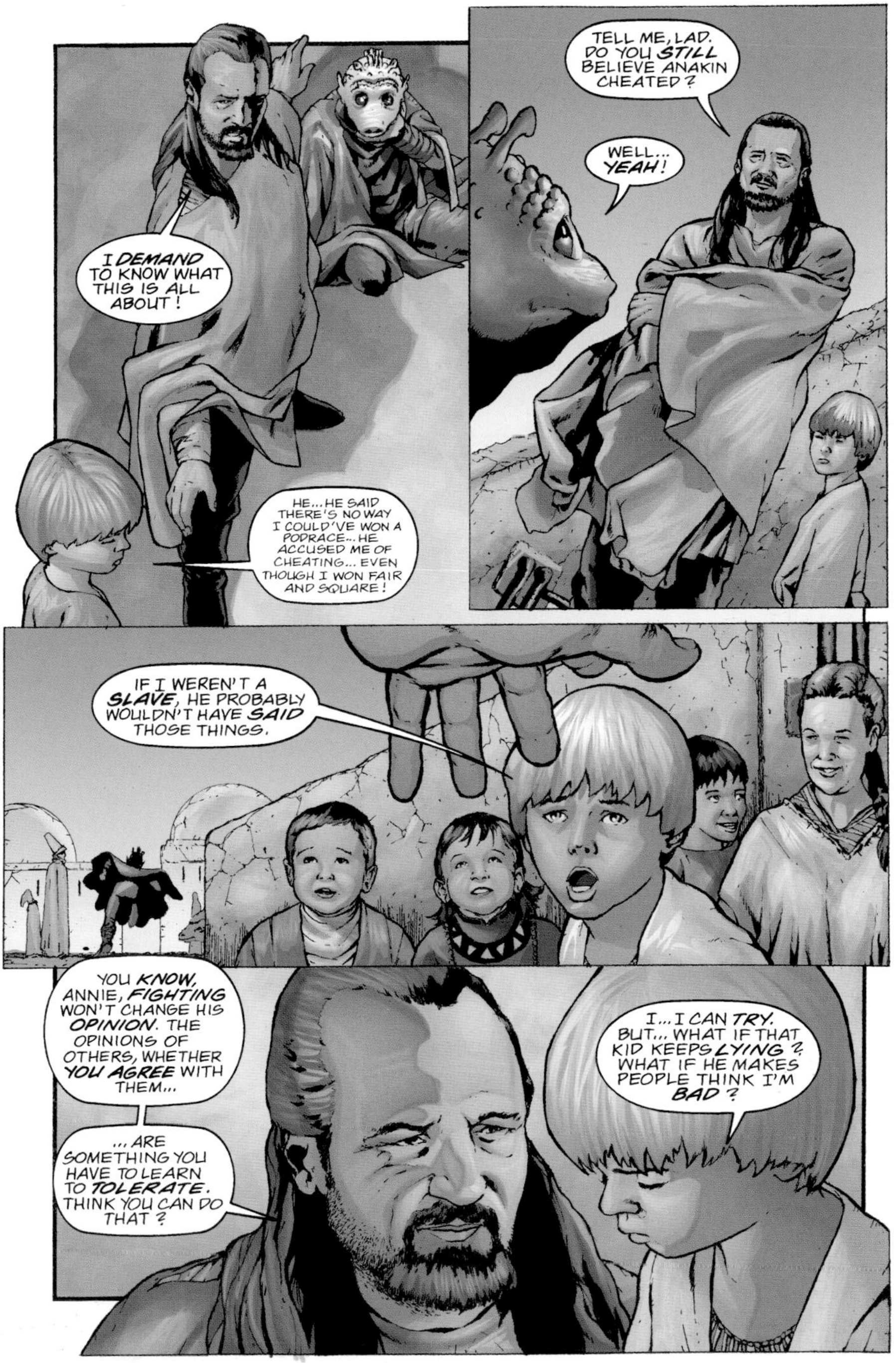
I DEMAND TO KNOW WHAT THIS IS ALL ABOUT!
HE... HE SAID THERE'S NO WAY I COULD'VE WON A PODRACE... HE ACCUSED ME OF CHEATING... EVEN THOUGH I WON FAIR AND SQUARE!
TELL ME, LAD. DO YOU STILL BELIEVE ANAKIN CHEATED?
WELL... YEAH!
IF I WEREN'T A SLAVE, HE PROBABLY WOULDN'T HAVE SAID THOSE THINGS.
YOU KNOW, ANNIE, FIGHTING WON'T CHANGE HIS OPINION. THE OPINIONS OF OTHERS, WHETHER YOU AGREE WITH THEM...
...ARE SOMETHING YOU HAVE TO LEARN TO TOLERATE. THINK YOU CAN DO THAT?
I... I CAN TRY. BUT... WHAT IF THAT KID KEEPS LYING? WHAT IF HE MAKES PEOPLE THINK I'M BAD?

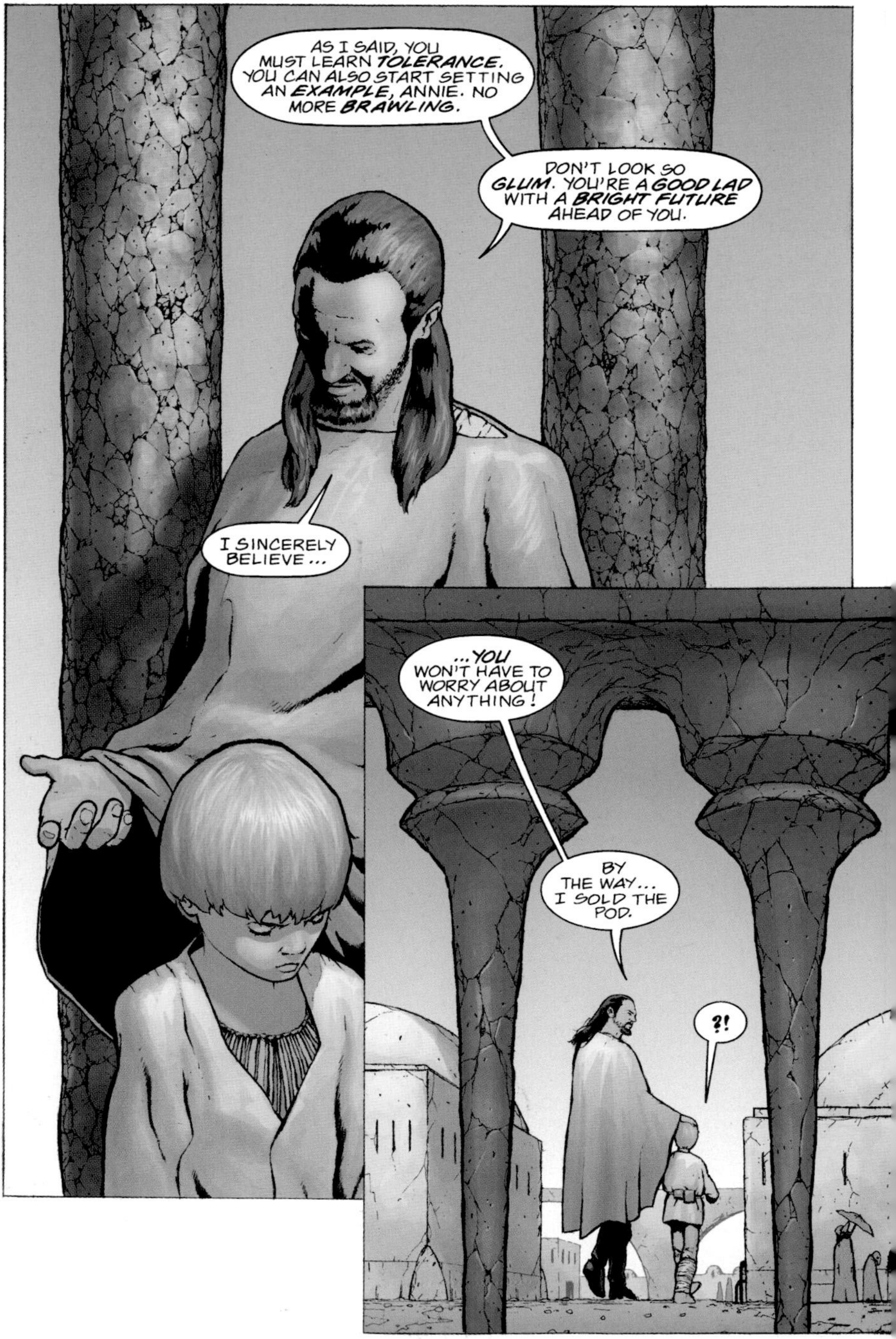
AS I SAID, YOU MUST LEARN TOLERANCE. YOU CAN ALSO START SETTING AN EXAMPLE, ANNIE. NO MORE BRAWLING.
DON'T LOOK SO GLUM. YOU'RE A GOOD LAD WITH A BRIGHT FUTURE AHEAD OF YOU.
I SINCERELY BELIEVE ...
...YOU WON'T HAVE TO WORRY ABOUT ANYTHING!
BY THE WAY... I SOLD THE POD.
?!

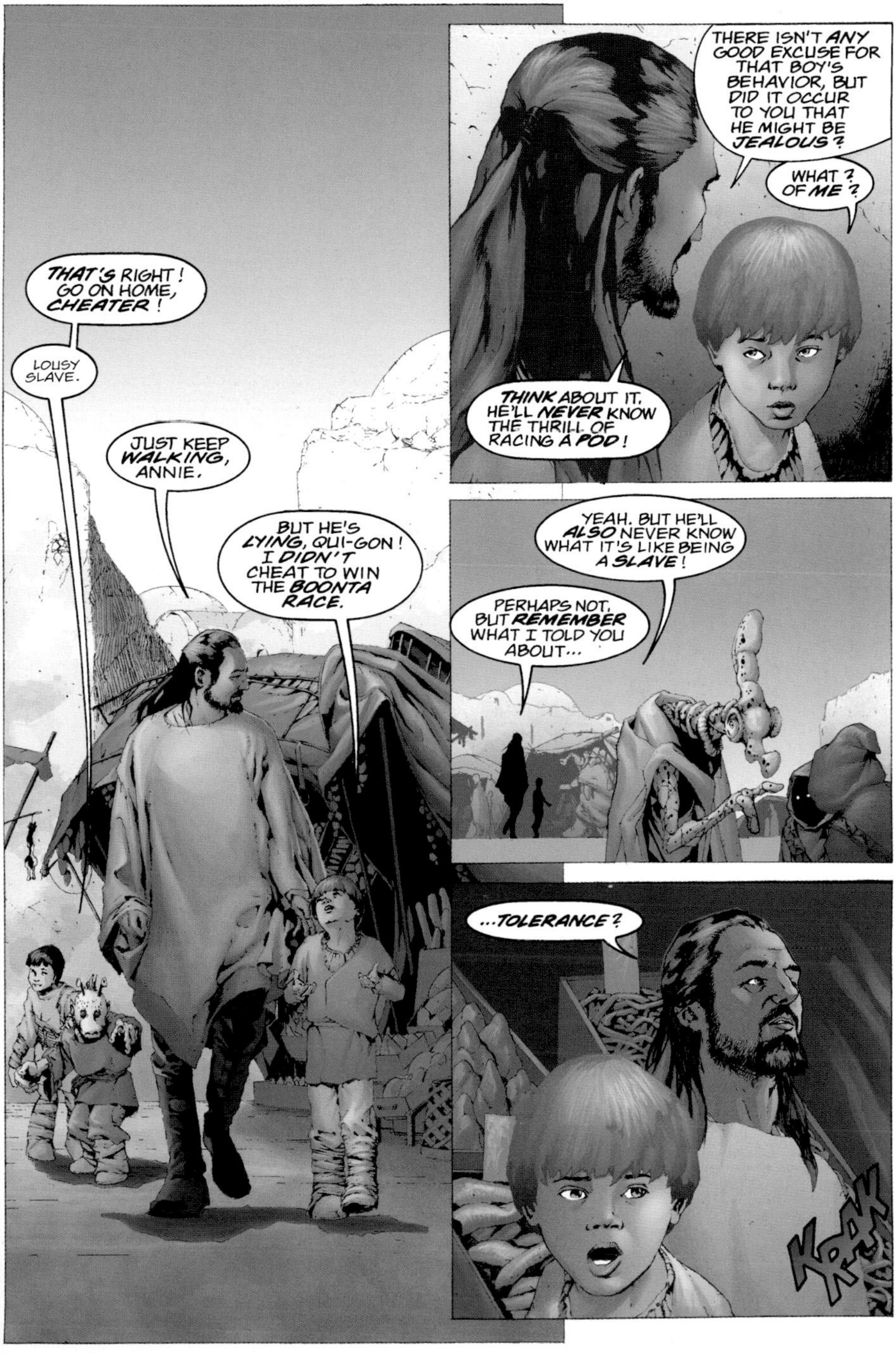

THAT'S RIGHT! GO ON HOME, CHEATER!
LOUSY SLAVE.
JUST KEEP WALKING, ANNIE.
BUT HE'S LYING, QUI-GON! I DIDN'T CHEAT TO WIN THE BOONTA RACE.
THERE ISN'T ANY GOOD EXCUSE FOR THAT BOY'S BEHAVIOR, BUT DID IT OCCUR TO YOU THAT HE MIGHT BE JEALOUS?
WHAT? OF ME?
THINK ABOUT IT. HE'LL NEVER KNOW THE THRILL OF RACING A POD!
YEAH. BUT HE'LL ALSO NEVER KNOW WHAT IT'S LIKE BEING A SLAVE!
PERHAPS NOT, BUT REMEMBER WHAT I TOLD YOU ABOUT...
...TOLERANCE?
KRAK

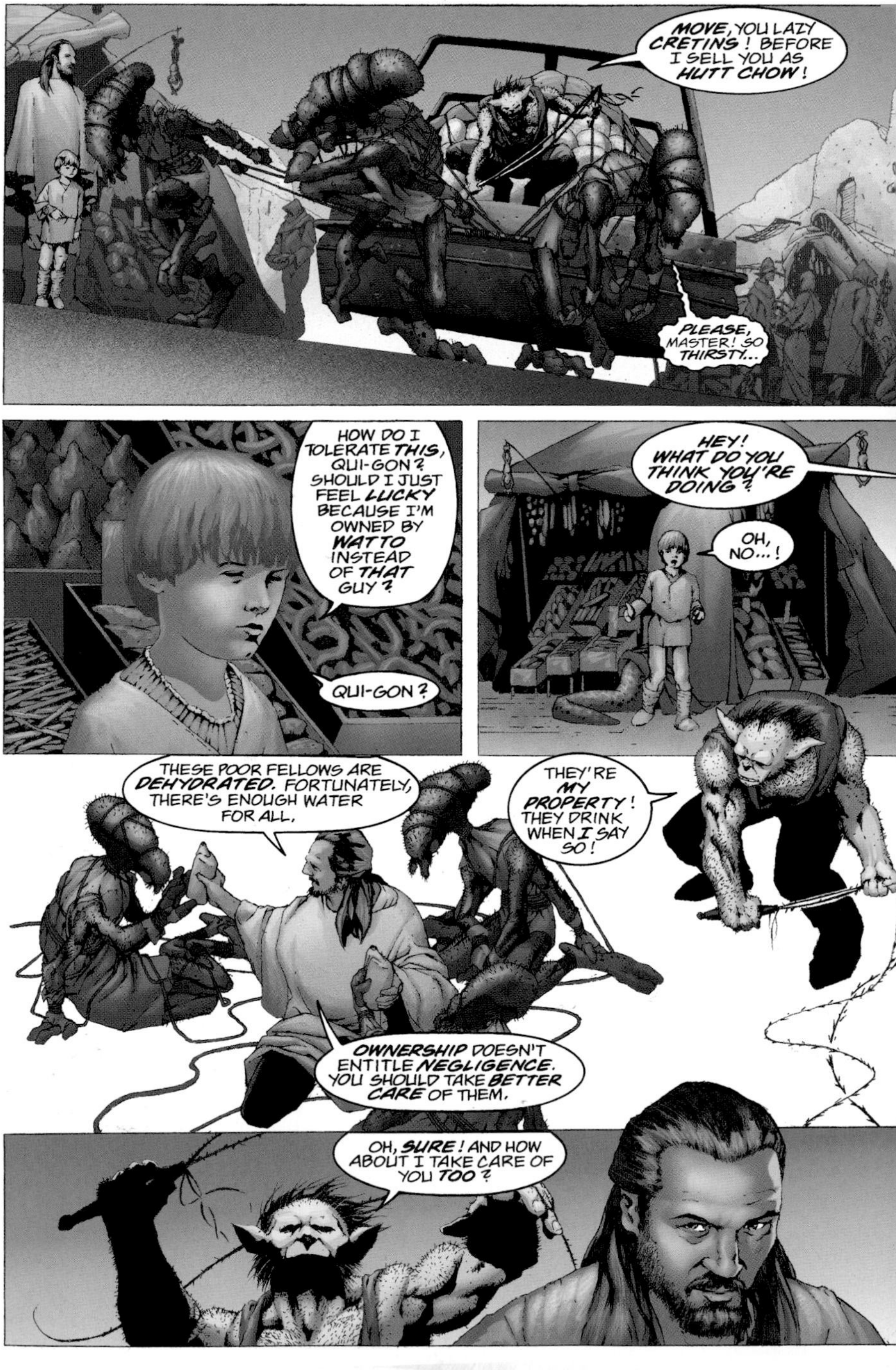
MOVE, YOU LAZY CRETINS! BEFORE I SELL YOU AS HUTT CHOW!
PLEASE, MASTER! SO THIRSTY...
HOW DO I TOLERATE THIS, QUI-GON? SHOULD I JUST FEEL LUCKY BECAUSE I'M OWNED BY WATTO INSTEAD OF THAT GUY?
QUI-GON?
HEY! WHAT DO YOU THINK YOU'RE DOING?
OH, NO...!
THESE POOR FELLOWS ARE DEHYDRATED. FORTUNATELY, THERE'S ENOUGH WATER FOR ALL.
THEY'RE MY PROPERTY! THEY DRINK WHEN I SAY SO!
OWNERSHIP DOESN'T ENTITLE NEGLIGENCE. YOU SHOULD TAKE BETTER CARE OF THEM.
OH, SURE! AND HOW ABOUT I TAKE CARE OF YOU TOO?

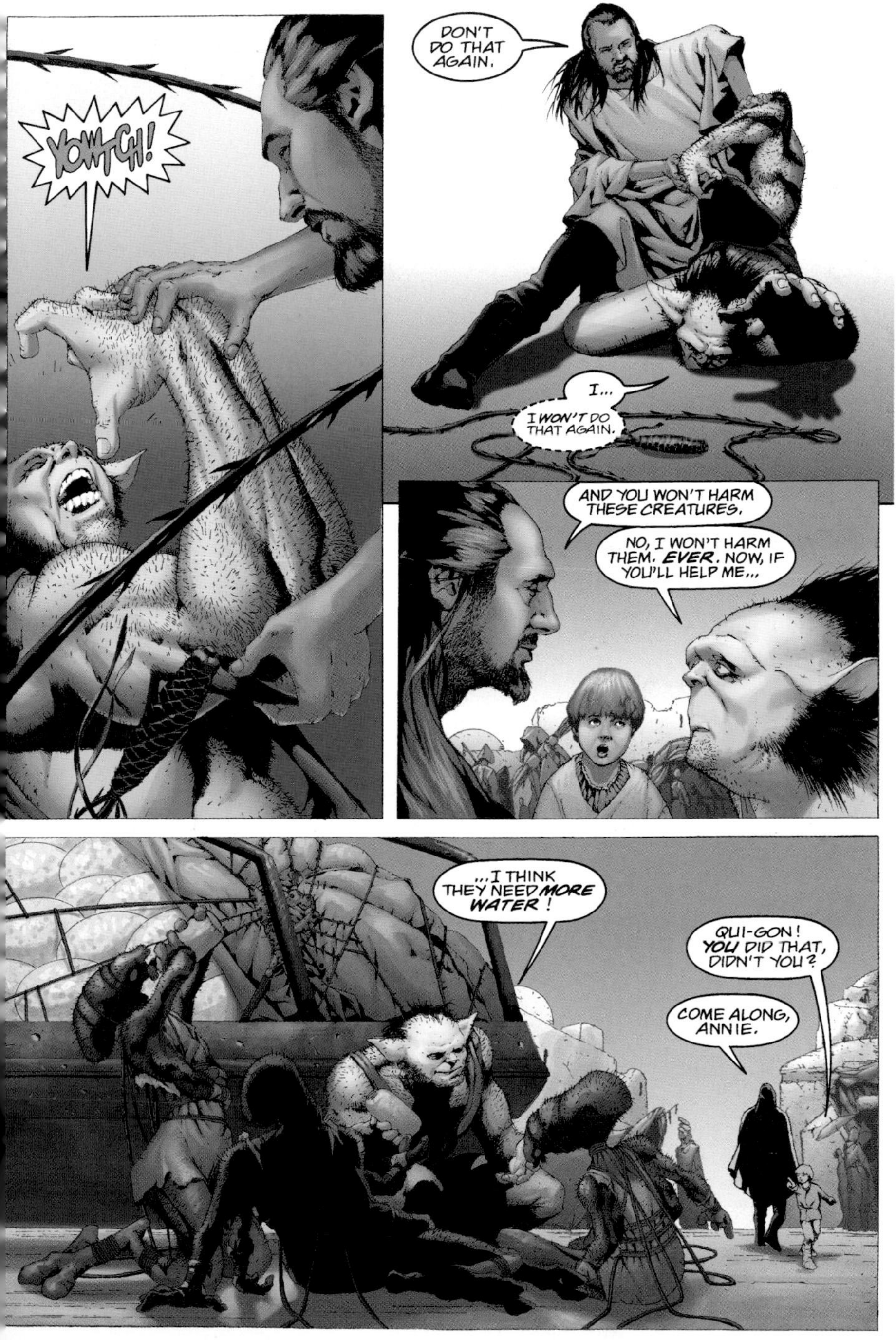
YOWTCH!
DON'T DO THAT AGAIN.
I...
I WON'T DO THAT AGAIN.
AND YOU WON'T HARM THESE CREATURES.
NO, I WON'T HARM THEM. EVER. NOW, IF YOU'LL HELP ME...
...I THINK THEY NEED MORE WATER!
QUI-GON! YOU DID THAT, DIDN'T YOU?
COME ALONG, ANNIE.

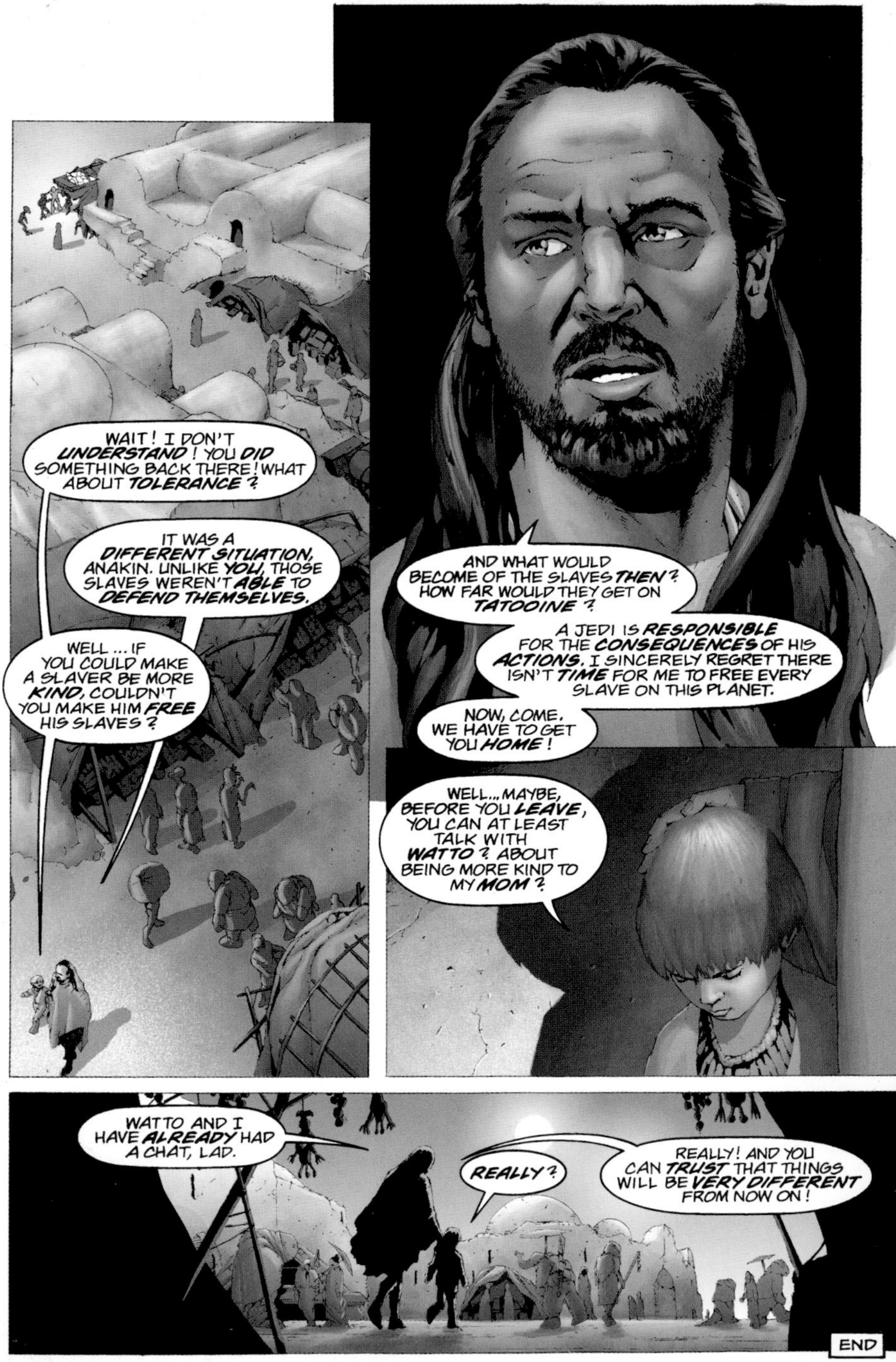
WAIT! I DON'T UNDERSTAND! YOU DID SOMETHING BACK THERE! WHAT ABOUT TOLERANCE?
IT WAS A DIFFERENT SITUATION, ANAKIN. UNLIKE YOU, THOSE SLAVES WEREN'T ABLE TO DEFEND THEMSELVES.
WELL ... IF YOU COULD MAKE A SLAVER BE MORE KIND, COULDN'T YOU MAKE HIM FREE HIS SLAVES?
AND WHAT WOULD BECOME OF THE SLAVES THEN? HOW FAR WOULD THEY GET ON TATOOINE?
A JEDI IS RESPONSIBLE FOR THE CONSEQUENCES OF HIS ACTIONS. I SINCERELY REGRET THERE ISN'T TIME FOR ME TO FREE EVERY SLAVE ON THIS PLANET.
NOW, COME. WE HAVE TO GET YOU HOME!
WELL... MAYBE, BEFORE YOU LEAVE, YOU CAN AT LEAST TALK WITH WATTO? ABOUT BEING MORE KIND TO MY MOM?
WATTO AND I HAVE ALREADY HAD A CHAT, LAD.
REALLY?
REALLY! AND YOU CAN TRUST THAT THINGS WILL BE VERY DIFFERENT FROM NOW ON!
END

EPISODE I—OBI-WAN KENOBI

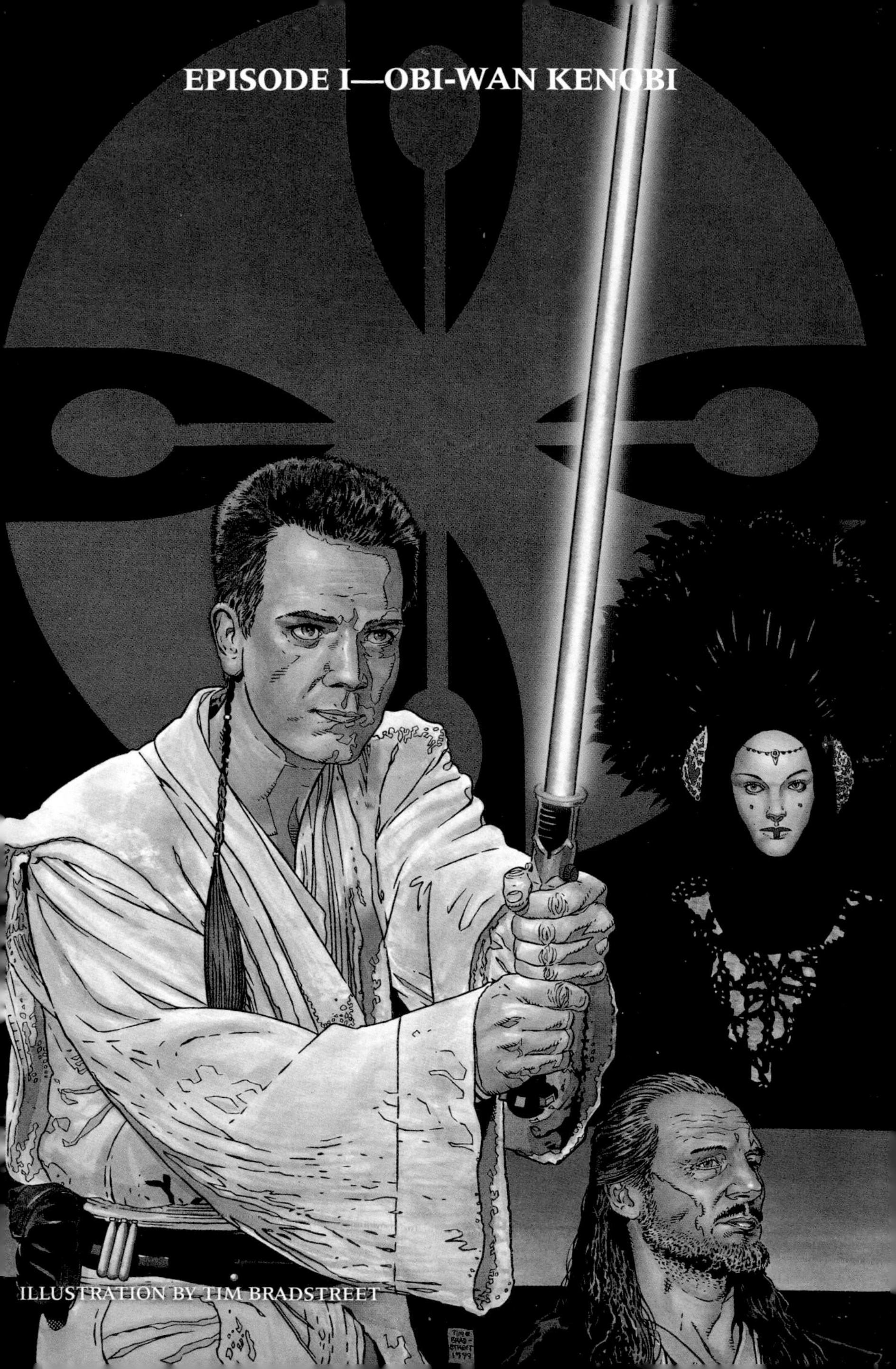

ILLUSTRATION BY TIM BRADSTREET

Script
HENRY GILROY

Pencils
MARTIN EGELAND

Inks
HOWARD M. SHUM

Colors
HAROLD MACKINNON

Lettering
VICKIE WILLIAMS

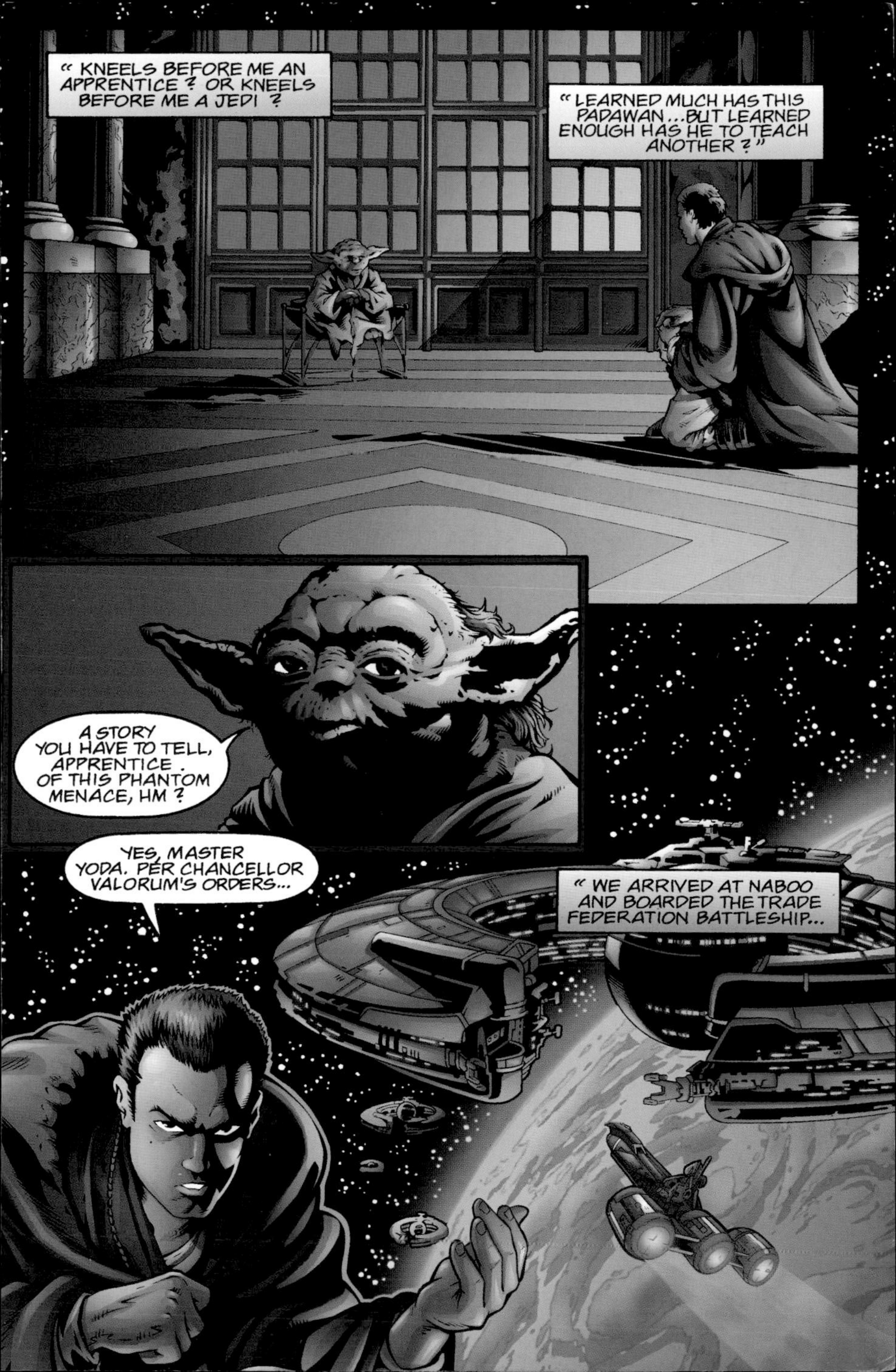

" KNEELS BEFORE ME AN APPRENTICE ? OR KNEELS BEFORE ME A JEDI ?
" LEARNED MUCH HAS THIS PADAWAN ... BUT LEARNED ENOUGH HAS HE TO TEACH ANOTHER ?"
A STORY YOU HAVE TO TELL, APPRENTICE . OF THIS PHANTOM MENACE, HM ?
YES, MASTER YODA. PER CHANCELLOR VALORUM'S ORDERS...
" WE ARRIVED AT NABOO AND BOARDED THE TRADE FEDERATION BATTLESHIP...

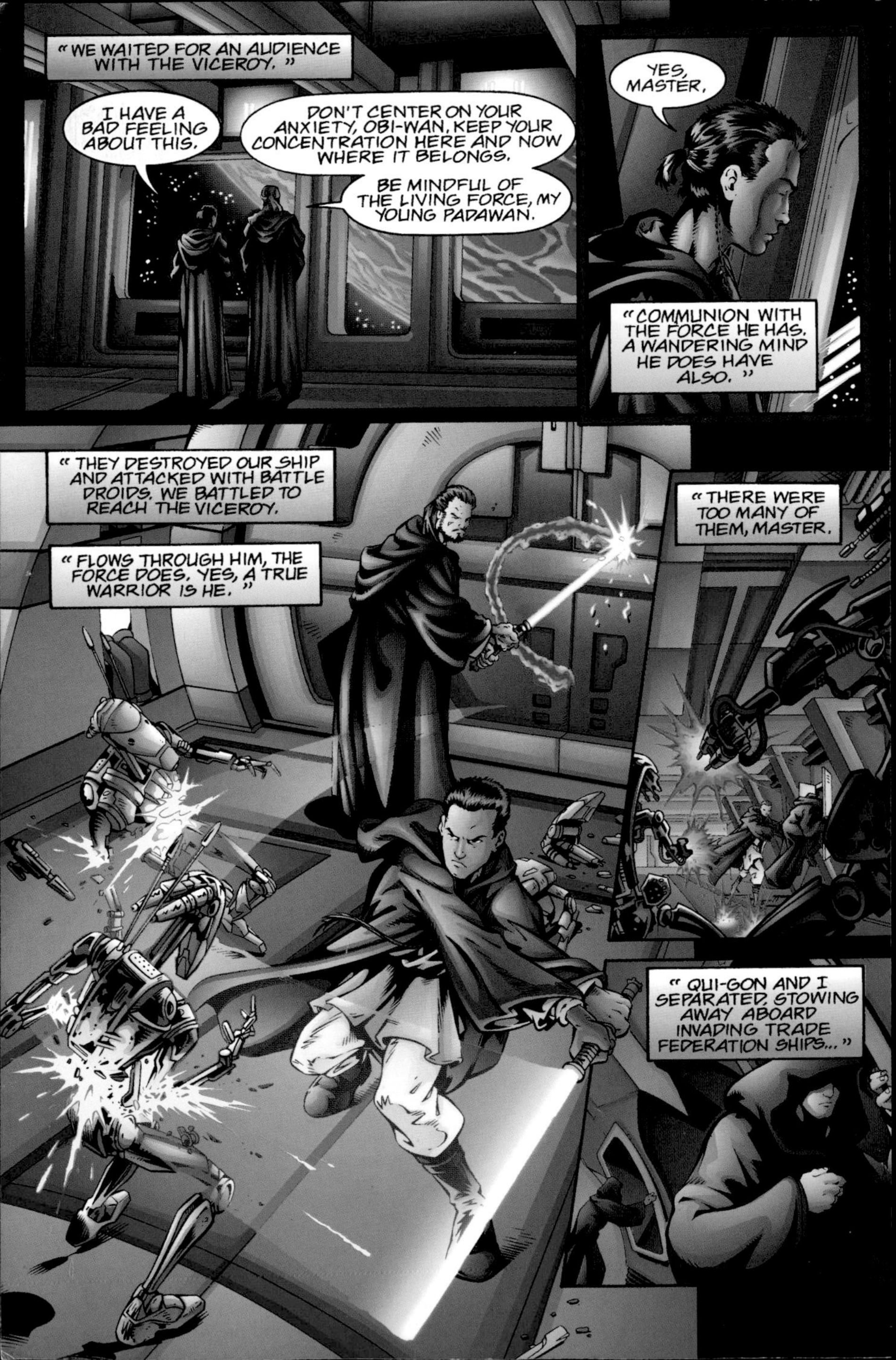
"WE WAITED FOR AN AUDIENCE WITH THE VICEROY."
I HAVE A BAD FEELING ABOUT THIS.
DON'T CENTER ON YOUR ANXIETY, OBI-WAN. KEEP YOUR CONCENTRATION HERE AND NOW WHERE IT BELONGS.
BE MINDFUL OF THE LIVING FORCE, MY YOUNG PADAWAN.
YES, MASTER.
"COMMUNION WITH THE FORCE HE HAS. A WANDERING MIND HE DOES HAVE ALSO."
"THEY DESTROYED OUR SHIP AND ATTACKED WITH BATTLE DROIDS. WE BATTLED TO REACH THE VICEROY.
"FLOWS THROUGH HIM, THE FORCE DOES. YES, A TRUE WARRIOR IS HE."
"THERE WERE TOO MANY OF THEM, MASTER.
"QUI-GON AND I SEPARATED, STOWING AWAY ABOARD INVADING TRADE FEDERATION SHIPS..."

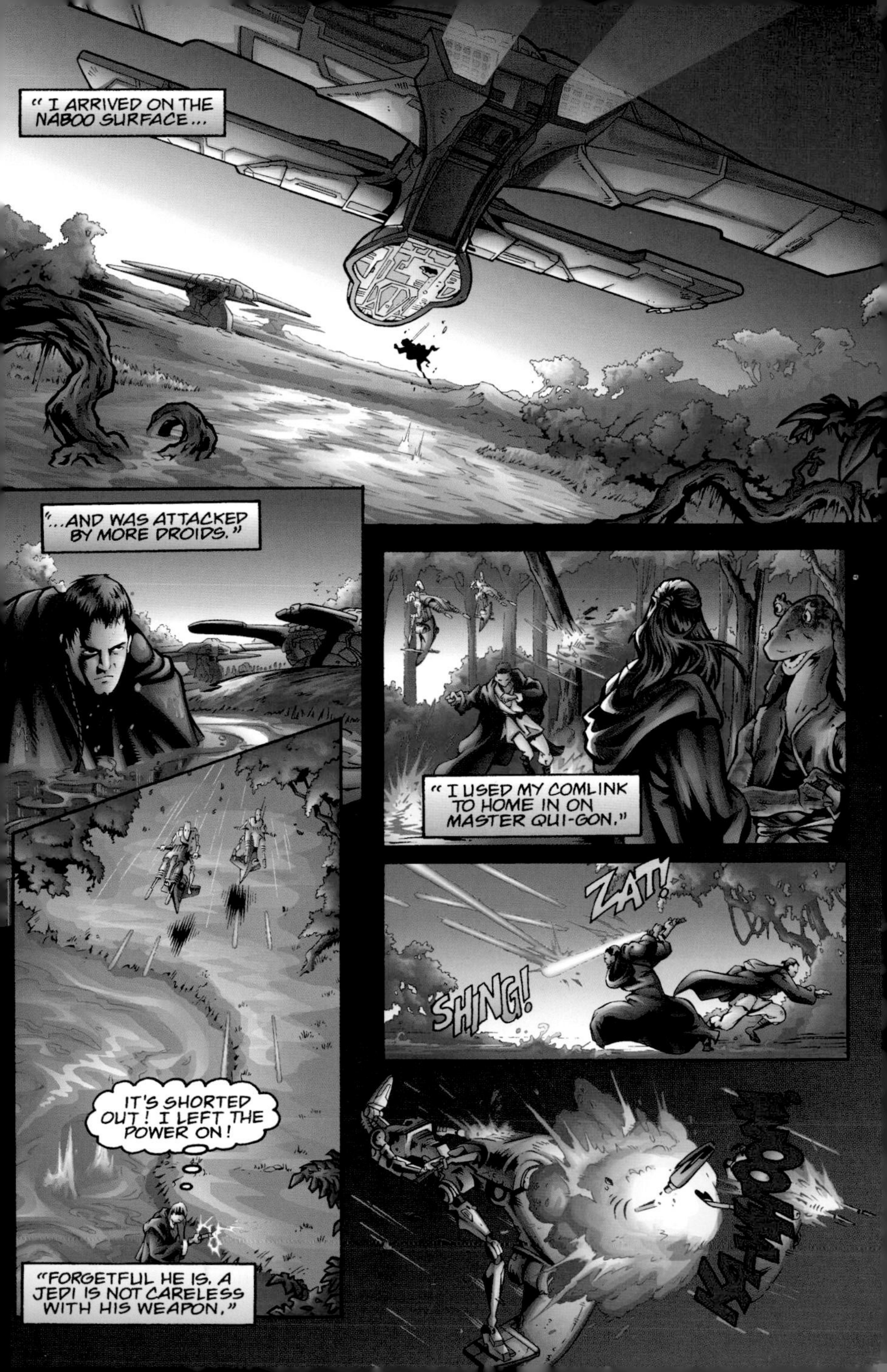
"I ARRIVED ON THE NABOO SURFACE...
"...AND WAS ATTACKED BY MORE DROIDS."
"I USED MY COMLINK TO HOME IN ON MASTER QUI-GON."
ZAT!
SHING!
IT'S SHORTED OUT! I LEFT THE POWER ON!
"FORGETFUL HE IS. A JEDI IS NOT CARELESS WITH HIS WEAPON."

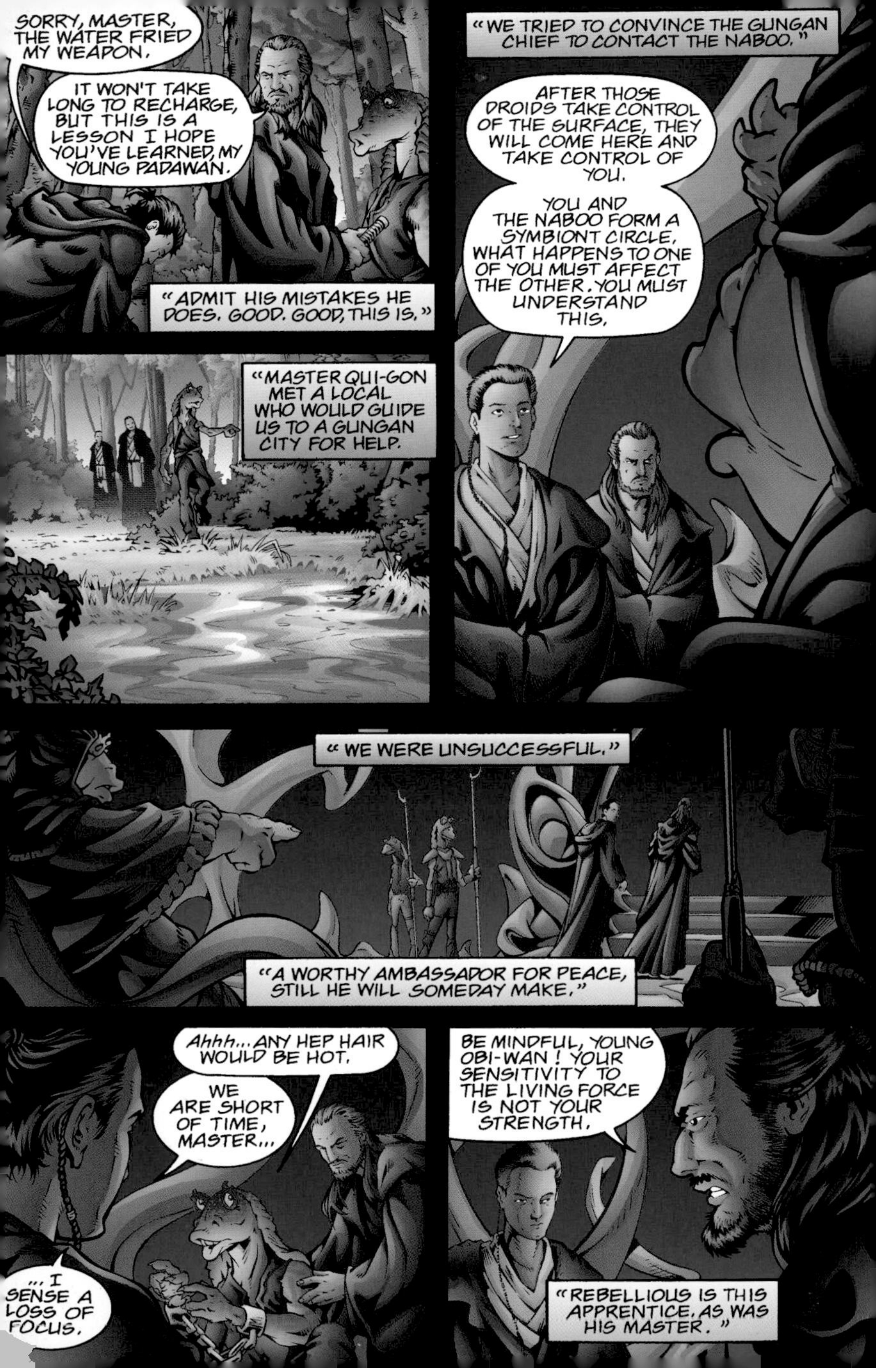
SORRY, MASTER, THE WATER FRIED MY WEAPON.
IT WON'T TAKE LONG TO RECHARGE, BUT THIS IS A LESSON I HOPE YOU'VE LEARNED, MY YOUNG PADAWAN.
"ADMIT HIS MISTAKES HE DOES. GOOD. GOOD, THIS IS."
"MASTER QUI-GON MET A LOCAL WHO WOULD GUIDE US TO A GUNGAN CITY FOR HELP.
"WE TRIED TO CONVINCE THE GUNGAN CHIEF TO CONTACT THE NABOO."
AFTER THOSE DROIDS TAKE CONTROL OF THE SURFACE, THEY WILL COME HERE AND TAKE CONTROL OF YOU.
YOU AND THE NABOO FORM A SYMBIONT CIRCLE. WHAT HAPPENS TO ONE OF YOU MUST AFFECT THE OTHER. YOU MUST UNDERSTAND THIS.
"WE WERE UNSUCCESSFUL."
"A WORTHY AMBASSADOR FOR PEACE, STILL HE WILL SOMEDAY MAKE."
Ahhh... ANY HEP HAIR WOULD BE HOT.
WE ARE SHORT OF TIME, MASTER...
...I SENSE A LOSS OF FOCUS.
BE MINDFUL, YOUNG OBI-WAN! YOUR SENSITIVITY TO THE LIVING FORCE IS NOT YOUR STRENGTH.
"REBELLIOUS IS THIS APPRENTICE, AS WAS HIS MASTER."

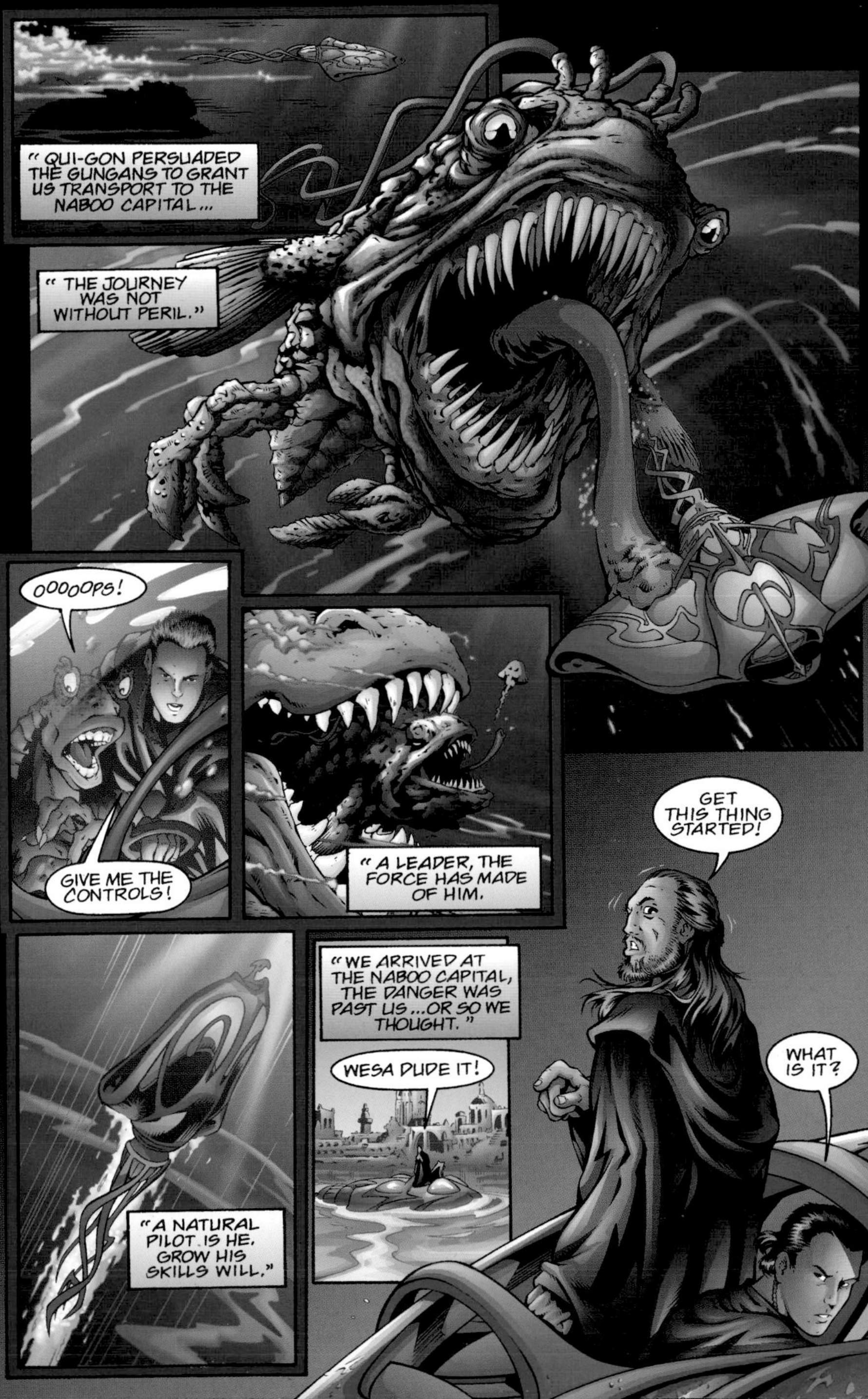
"QUI-GON PERSUADED THE GUNGANS TO GRANT US TRANSPORT TO THE NABOO CAPITAL...
"THE JOURNEY WAS NOT WITHOUT PERIL."
OOOOOPS!
GIVE ME THE CONTROLS!
"A LEADER, THE FORCE HAS MADE OF HIM.
GET THIS THING STARTED!
"A NATURAL PILOT IS HE. GROW HIS SKILLS WILL."
"WE ARRIVED AT THE NABOO CAPITAL, THE DANGER WAS PAST US...OR SO WE THOUGHT."
WESA DUDE IT!
WHAT IS IT?

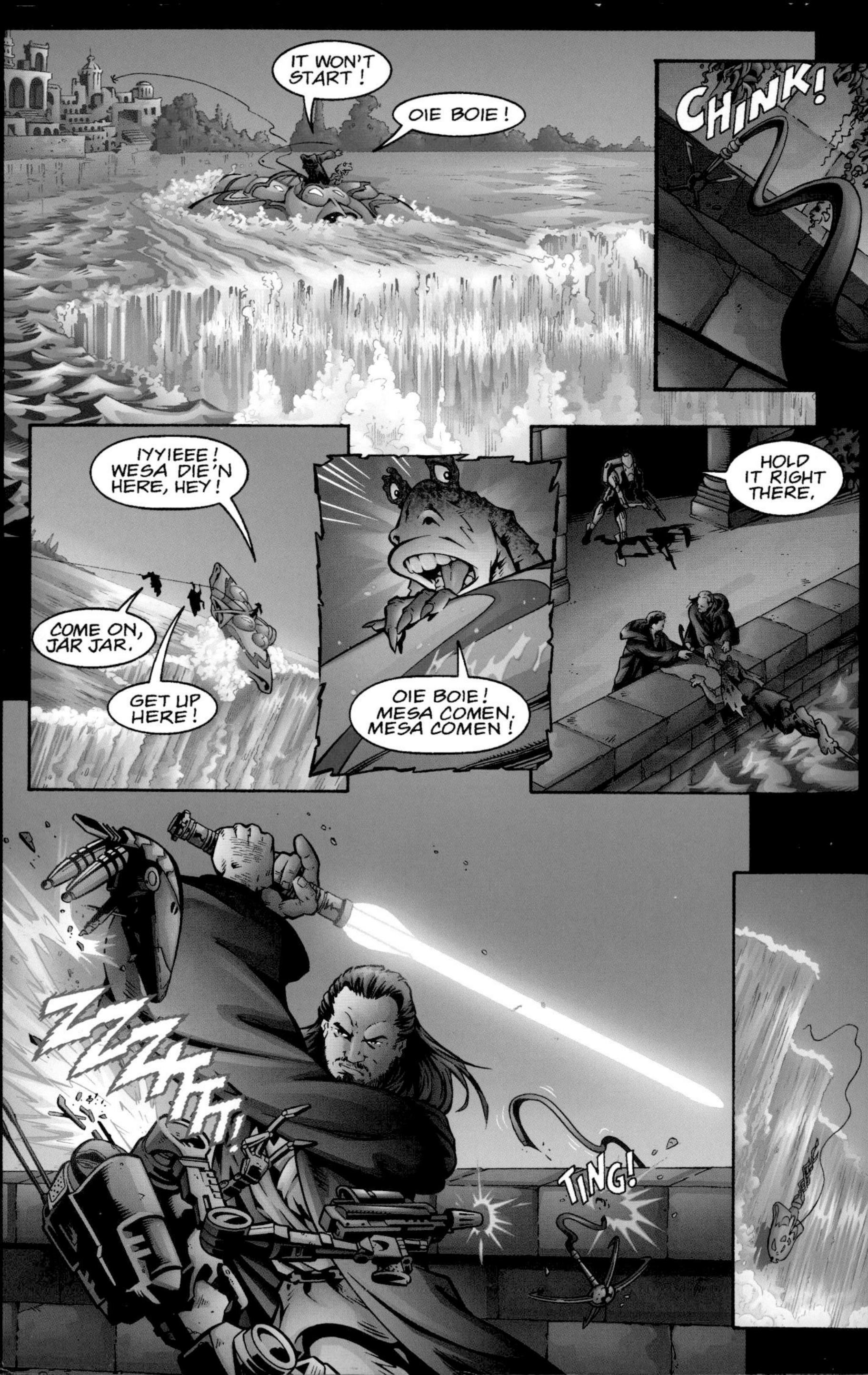
IT WON'T START!
OIE BOIE!
CHINK!
IYYIEEE! WESA DIE'N HERE, HEY!
COME ON, JAR JAR.
GET UP HERE!
OIE BOIE! MESA COMEN. MESA COMEN!
HOLD IT RIGHT THERE.
ZZZKKT!
TING!

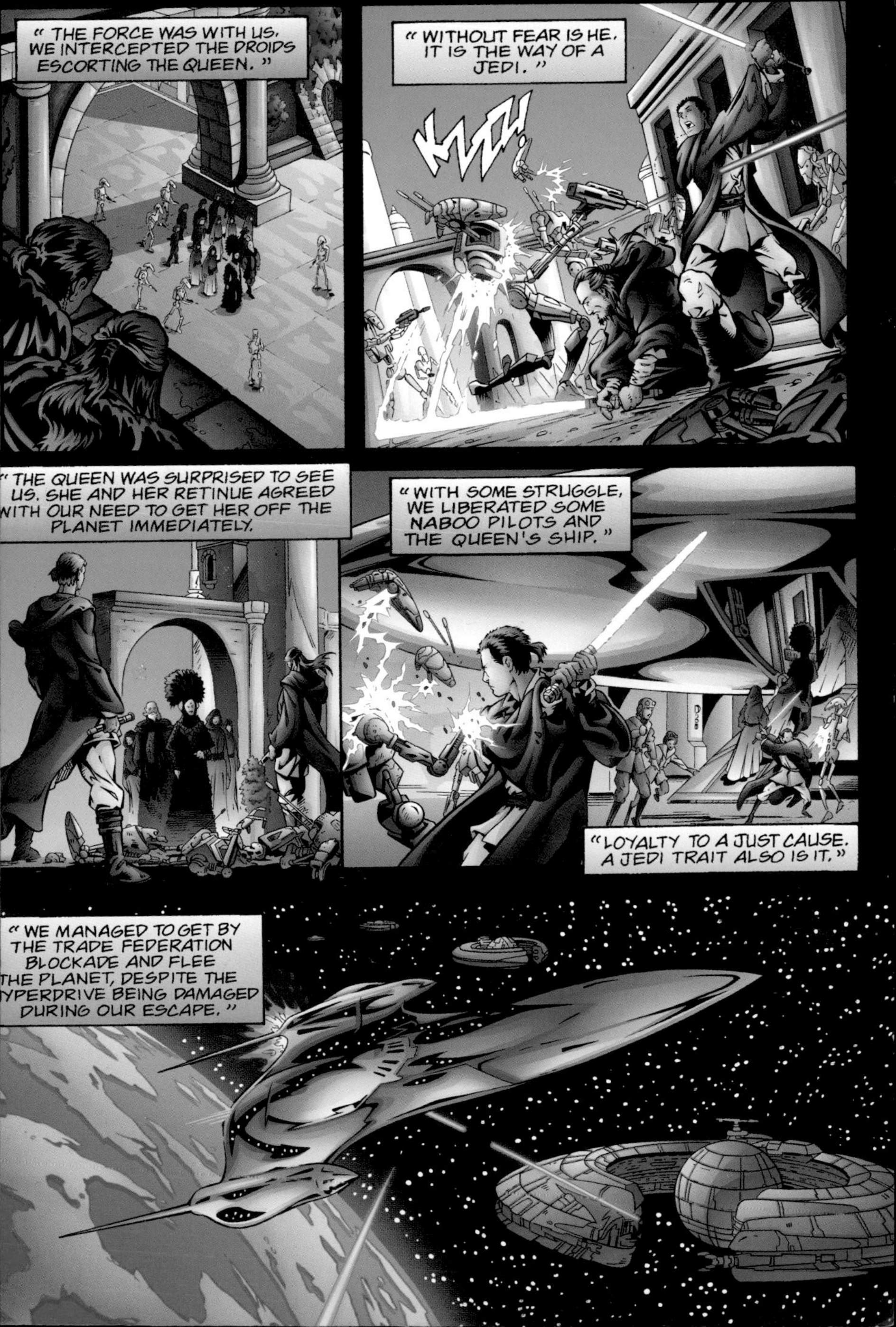
" THE FORCE WAS WITH US. WE INTERCEPTED THE DROIDS ESCORTING THE QUEEN. "
" WITHOUT FEAR IS HE. IT IS THE WAY OF A JEDI. "
KZZT!
" THE QUEEN WAS SURPRISED TO SEE US. SHE AND HER RETINUE AGREED WITH OUR NEED TO GET HER OFF THE PLANET IMMEDIATELY.
" WITH SOME STRUGGLE, WE LIBERATED SOME NABOO PILOTS AND THE QUEEN'S SHIP. "
" LOYALTY TO A JUST CAUSE. A JEDI TRAIT ALSO IS IT. "
" WE MANAGED TO GET BY THE TRADE FEDERATION BLOCKADE AND FLEE THE PLANET, DESPITE THE HYPERDRIVE BEING DAMAGED DURING OUR ESCAPE. "

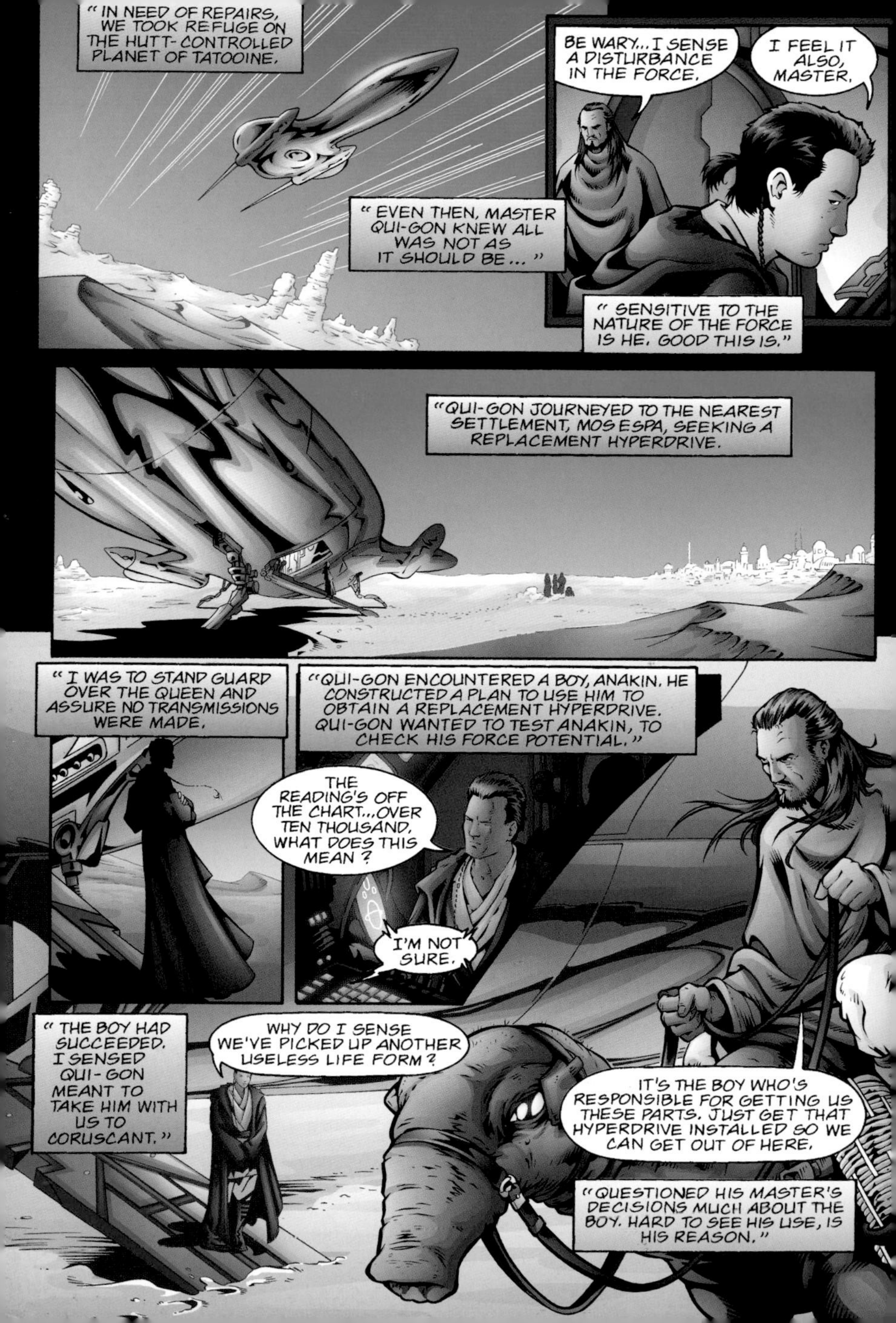
"IN NEED OF REPAIRS, WE TOOK REFUGE ON THE HUTT-CONTROLLED PLANET OF TATOOINE.
BE WARY... I SENSE A DISTURBANCE IN THE FORCE.
I FEEL IT ALSO, MASTER.
"EVEN THEN, MASTER QUI-GON KNEW ALL WAS NOT AS IT SHOULD BE..."
"SENSITIVE TO THE NATURE OF THE FORCE IS HE. GOOD THIS IS."
"QUI-GON JOURNEYED TO THE NEAREST SETTLEMENT, MOS ESPA, SEEKING A REPLACEMENT HYPERDRIVE.
"I WAS TO STAND GUARD OVER THE QUEEN AND ASSURE NO TRANSMISSIONS WERE MADE.
"QUI-GON ENCOUNTERED A BOY, ANAKIN. HE CONSTRUCTED A PLAN TO USE HIM TO OBTAIN A REPLACEMENT HYPERDRIVE. QUI-GON WANTED TO TEST ANAKIN, TO CHECK HIS FORCE POTENTIAL."
THE READING'S OFF THE CHART... OVER TEN THOUSAND. WHAT DOES THIS MEAN?
I'M NOT SURE.
"THE BOY HAD SUCCEEDED. I SENSED QUI-GON MEANT TO TAKE HIM WITH US TO CORUSCANT."
WHY DO I SENSE WE'VE PICKED UP ANOTHER USELESS LIFE FORM?
IT'S THE BOY WHO'S RESPONSIBLE FOR GETTING US THESE PARTS. JUST GET THAT HYPERDRIVE INSTALLED SO WE CAN GET OUT OF HERE.
"QUESTIONED HIS MASTER'S DECISIONS MUCH ABOUT THE BOY. HARD TO SEE HIS USE, IS HIS REASON."

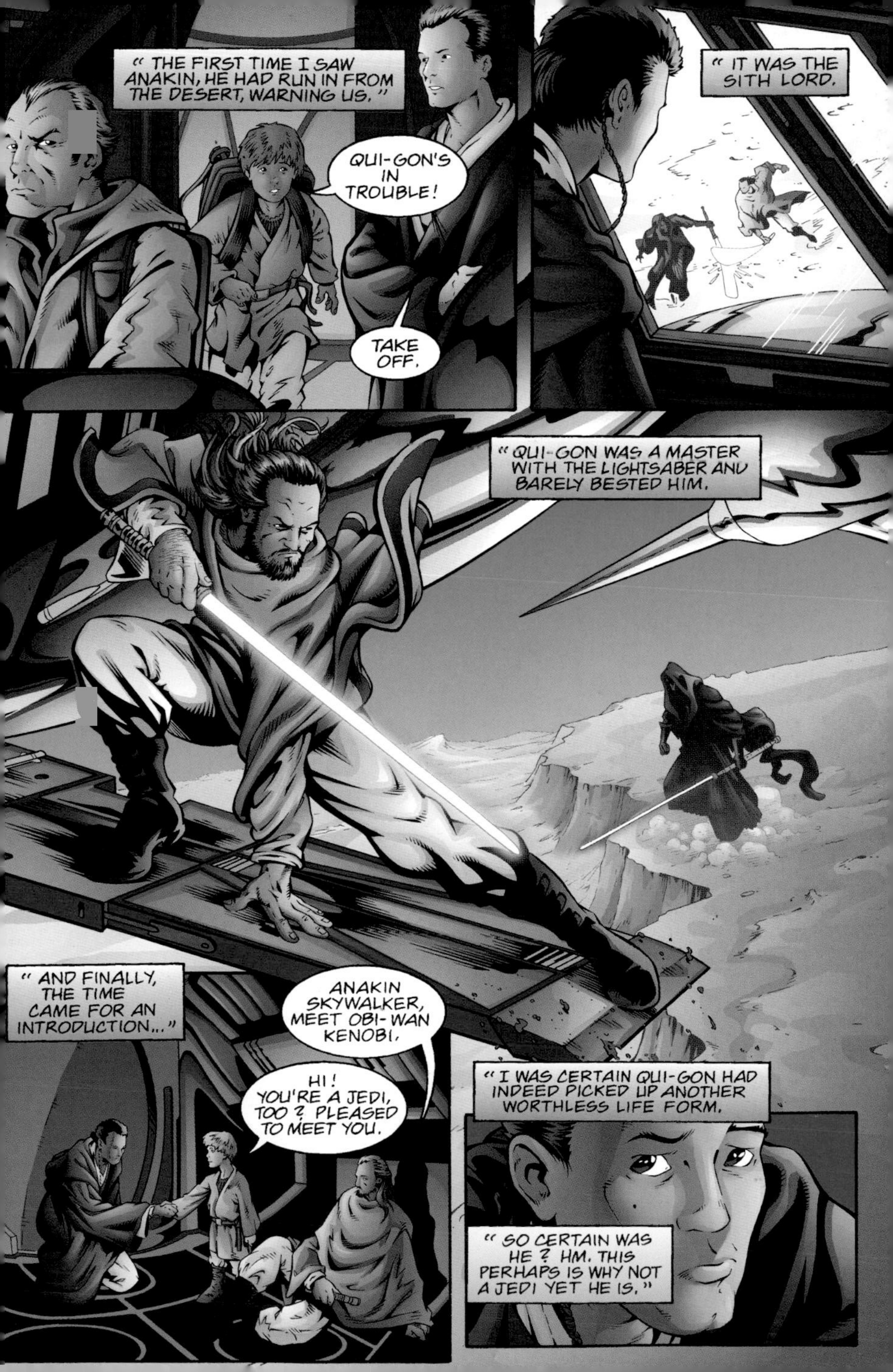
"THE FIRST TIME I SAW ANAKIN, HE HAD RUN IN FROM THE DESERT, WARNING US."
QUI-GON'S IN TROUBLE!
TAKE OFF.
"IT WAS THE SITH LORD.
"QUI-GON WAS A MASTER WITH THE LIGHTSABER AND BARELY BESTED HIM.
"AND FINALLY, THE TIME CAME FOR AN INTRODUCTION..."
ANAKIN SKYWALKER, MEET OBI-WAN KENOBI.
HI! YOU'RE A JEDI, TOO? PLEASED TO MEET YOU.
"I WAS CERTAIN QUI-GON HAD INDEED PICKED UP ANOTHER WORTHLESS LIFE FORM.
"SO CERTAIN WAS HE? HM. THIS PERHAPS IS WHY NOT A JEDI YET HE IS."

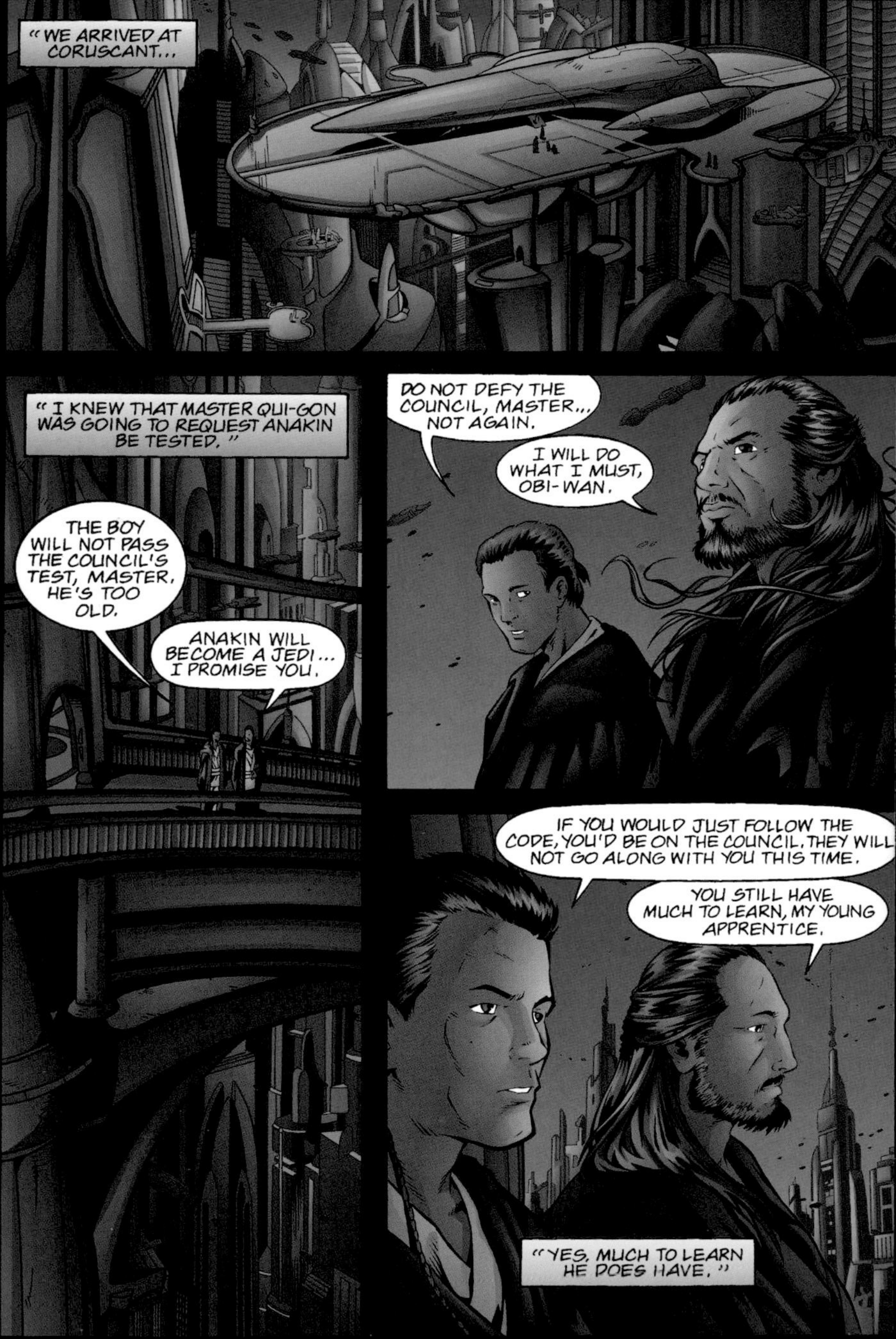
"WE ARRIVED AT CORUSCANT...
"I KNEW THAT MASTER QUI-GON WAS GOING TO REQUEST ANAKIN BE TESTED."
THE BOY WILL NOT PASS THE COUNCIL'S TEST, MASTER. HE'S TOO OLD.
ANAKIN WILL BECOME A JEDI... I PROMISE YOU.
DO NOT DEFY THE COUNCIL, MASTER... NOT AGAIN.
I WILL DO WHAT I MUST, OBI-WAN.
IF YOU WOULD JUST FOLLOW THE CODE, YOU'D BE ON THE COUNCIL. THEY WILL NOT GO ALONG WITH YOU THIS TIME.
YOU STILL HAVE MUCH TO LEARN, MY YOUNG APPRENTICE.
"YES, MUCH TO LEARN HE DOES HAVE."

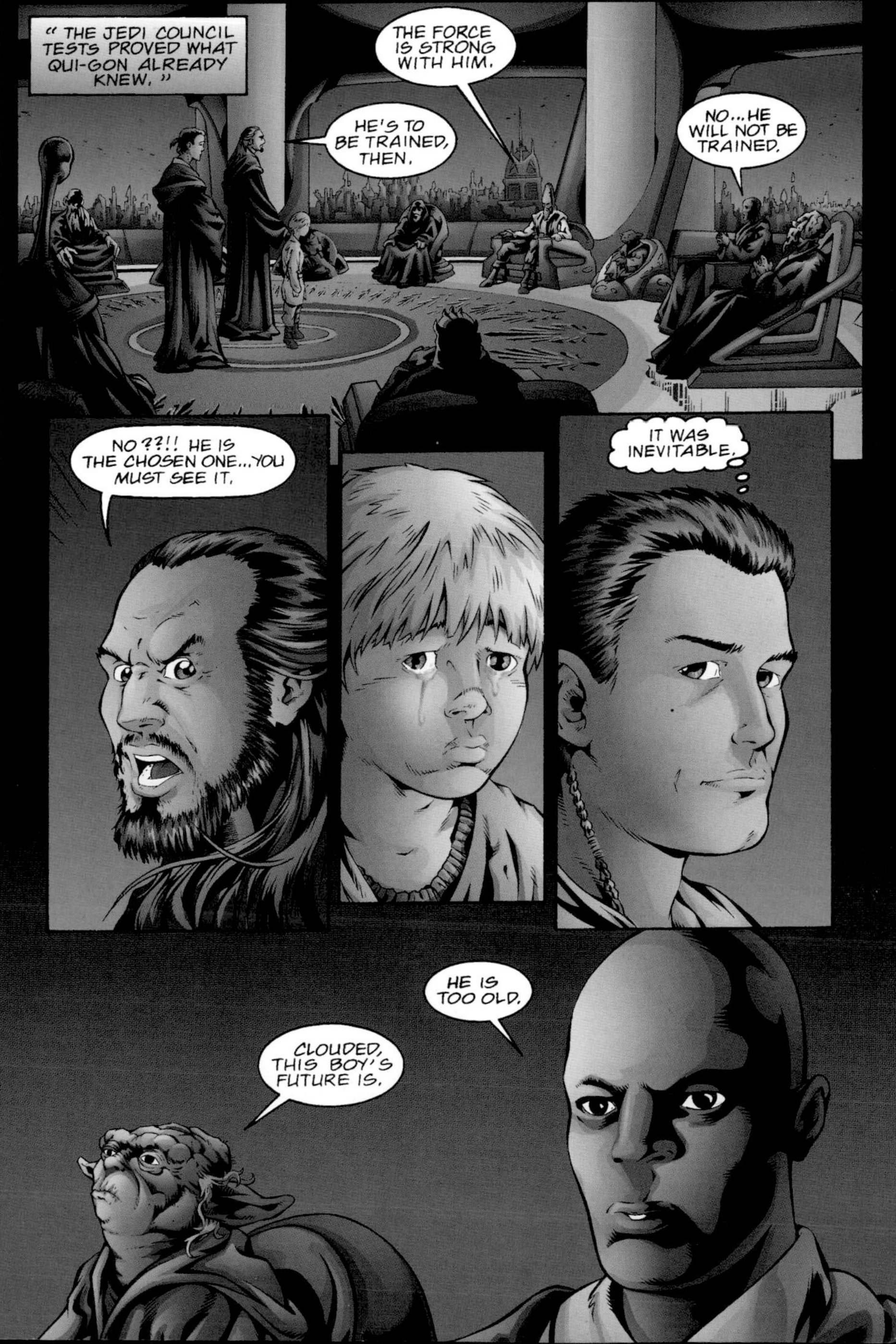
"THE JEDI COUNCIL TESTS PROVED WHAT QUI-GON ALREADY KNEW."
HE'S TO BE TRAINED, THEN.
THE FORCE IS STRONG WITH HIM.
NO...HE WILL NOT BE TRAINED.
NO??!! HE IS THE CHOSEN ONE...YOU MUST SEE IT.
IT WAS INEVITABLE.
HE IS TOO OLD.
CLOUDED, THIS BOY'S FUTURE IS.

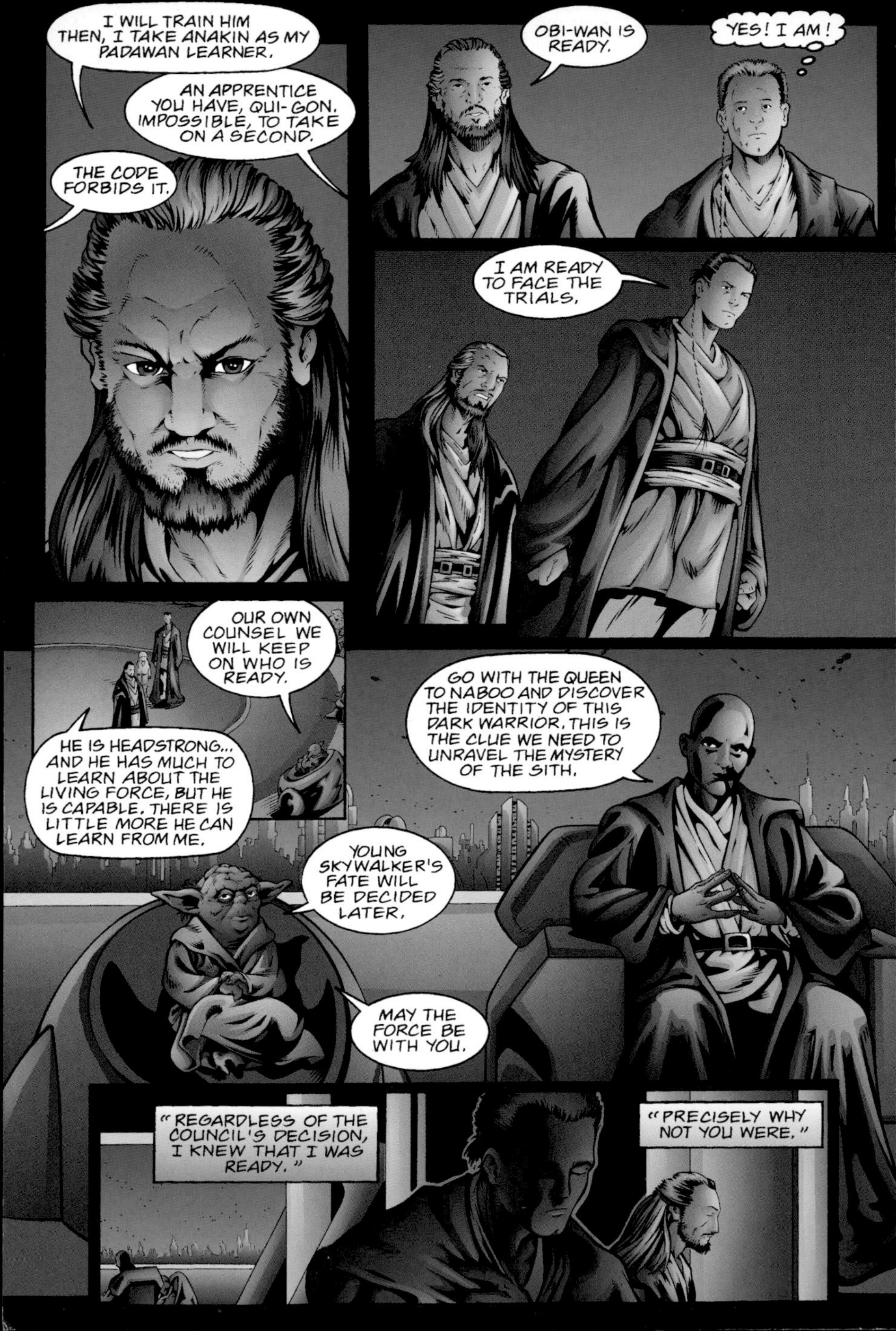
I WILL TRAIN HIM THEN, I TAKE ANAKIN AS MY PADAWAN LEARNER.
AN APPRENTICE YOU HAVE, QUI-GON. IMPOSSIBLE, TO TAKE ON A SECOND.
THE CODE FORBIDS IT.
OBI-WAN IS READY.
YES! I AM!
I AM READY TO FACE THE TRIALS.
OUR OWN COUNSEL WE WILL KEEP ON WHO IS READY.
HE IS HEADSTRONG... AND HE HAS MUCH TO LEARN ABOUT THE LIVING FORCE, BUT HE IS CAPABLE. THERE IS LITTLE MORE HE CAN LEARN FROM ME.
GO WITH THE QUEEN TO NABOO AND DISCOVER THE IDENTITY OF THIS DARK WARRIOR. THIS IS THE CLUE WE NEED TO UNRAVEL THE MYSTERY OF THE SITH.
YOUNG SKYWALKER'S FATE WILL BE DECIDED LATER.
MAY THE FORCE BE WITH YOU.
"REGARDLESS OF THE COUNCIL'S DECISION, I KNEW THAT I WAS READY."
"PRECISELY WHY NOT YOU WERE."

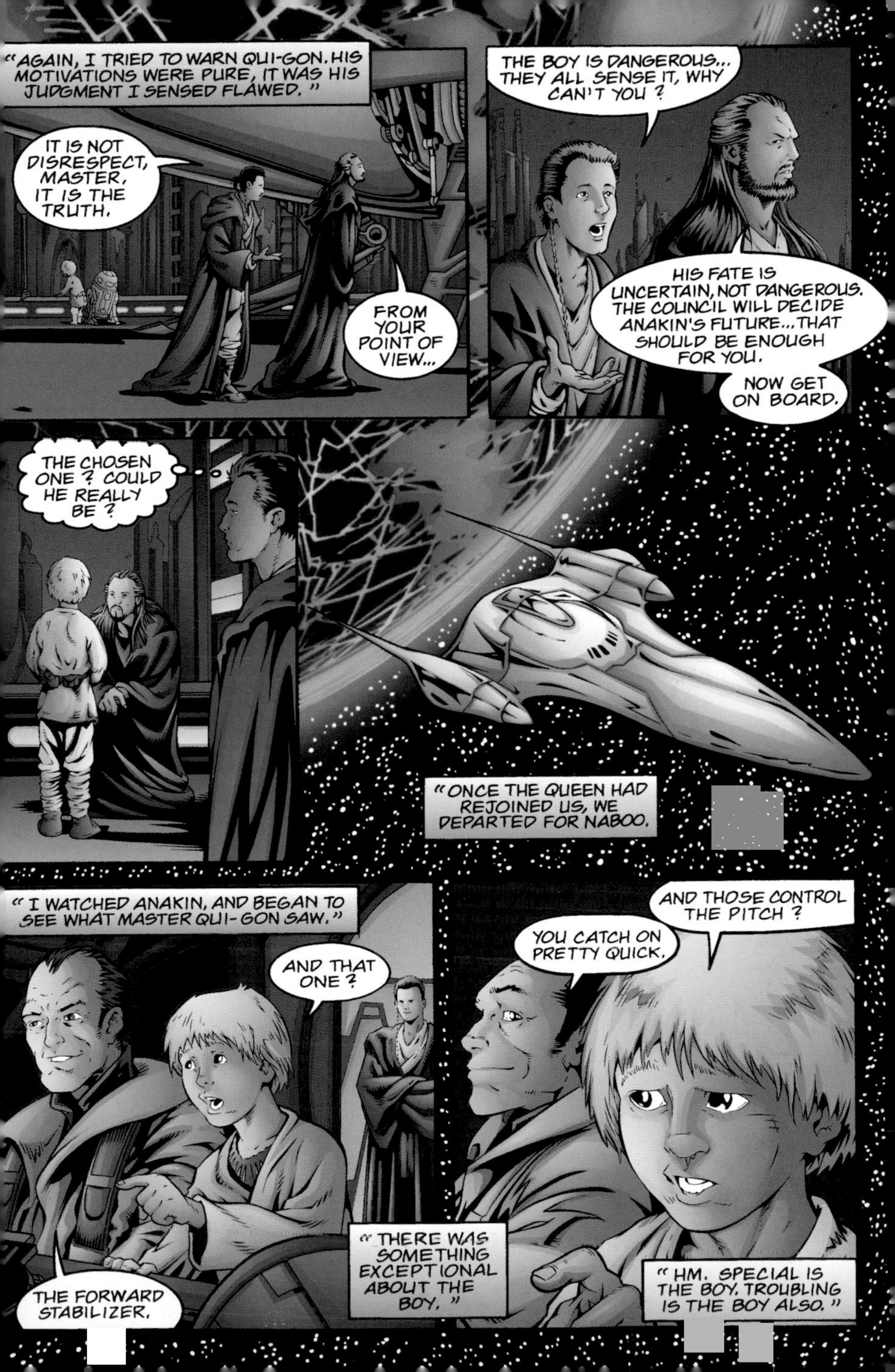
"AGAIN, I TRIED TO WARN QUI-GON. HIS MOTIVATIONS WERE PURE, IT WAS HIS JUDGMENT I SENSED FLAWED."
IT IS NOT DISRESPECT, MASTER, IT IS THE TRUTH.
FROM YOUR POINT OF VIEW...
THE BOY IS DANGEROUS... THEY ALL SENSE IT, WHY CAN'T YOU?
HIS FATE IS UNCERTAIN, NOT DANGEROUS. THE COUNCIL WILL DECIDE ANAKIN'S FUTURE... THAT SHOULD BE ENOUGH FOR YOU.
NOW GET ON BOARD.
THE CHOSEN ONE? COULD HE REALLY BE?
"ONCE THE QUEEN HAD REJOINED US, WE DEPARTED FOR NABOO.
"I WATCHED ANAKIN, AND BEGAN TO SEE WHAT MASTER QUI-GON SAW."
AND THAT ONE?
THE FORWARD STABILIZER.
"THERE WAS SOMETHING EXCEPTIONAL ABOUT THE BOY."
AND THOSE CONTROL THE PITCH?
YOU CATCH ON PRETTY QUICK.
"HM. SPECIAL IS THE BOY. TROUBLING IS THE BOY ALSO."

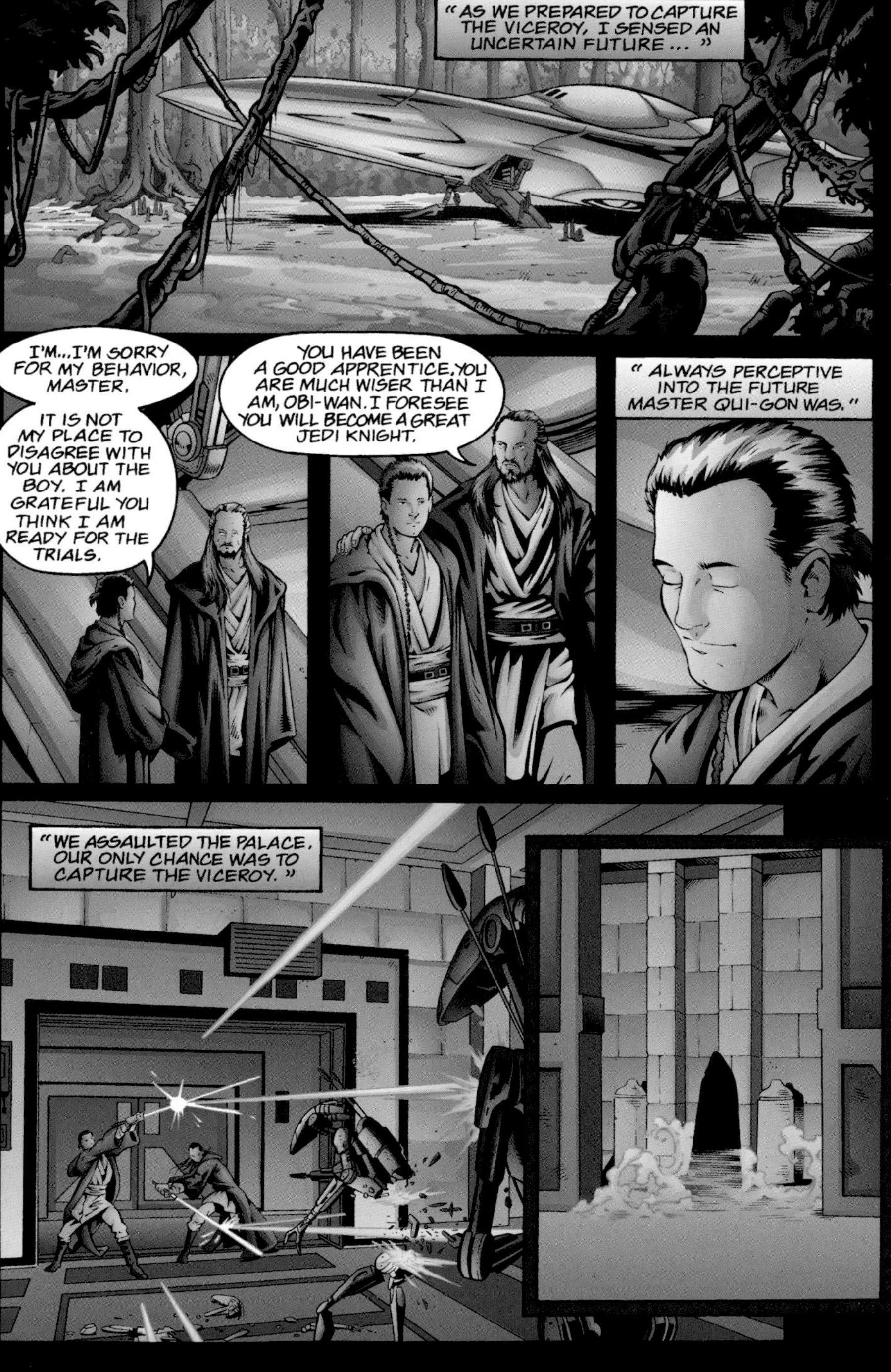
"AS WE PREPARED TO CAPTURE THE VICEROY, I SENSED AN UNCERTAIN FUTURE..."
I'M...I'M SORRY FOR MY BEHAVIOR, MASTER.
IT IS NOT MY PLACE TO DISAGREE WITH YOU ABOUT THE BOY. I AM GRATEFUL YOU THINK I AM READY FOR THE TRIALS.
YOU HAVE BEEN A GOOD APPRENTICE. YOU ARE MUCH WISER THAN I AM, OBI-WAN. I FORESEE YOU WILL BECOME A GREAT JEDI KNIGHT.
"ALWAYS PERCEPTIVE INTO THE FUTURE MASTER QUI-GON WAS."
"WE ASSAULTED THE PALACE. OUR ONLY CHANCE WAS TO CAPTURE THE VICEROY."

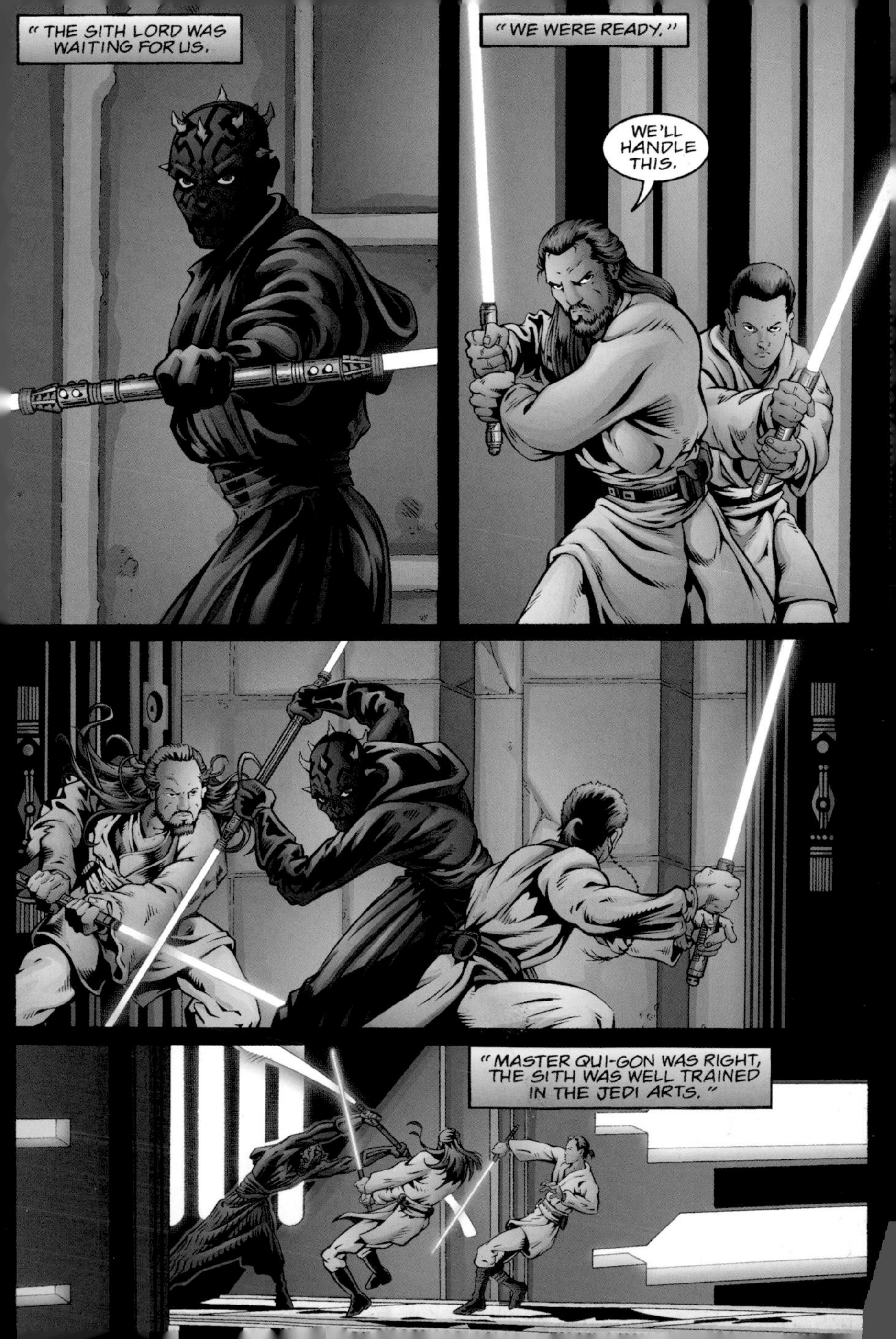
"THE SITH LORD WAS WAITING FOR US.
"WE WERE READY."
WE'LL HANDLE THIS.
"MASTER QUI-GON WAS RIGHT, THE SITH WAS WELL TRAINED IN THE JEDI ARTS."

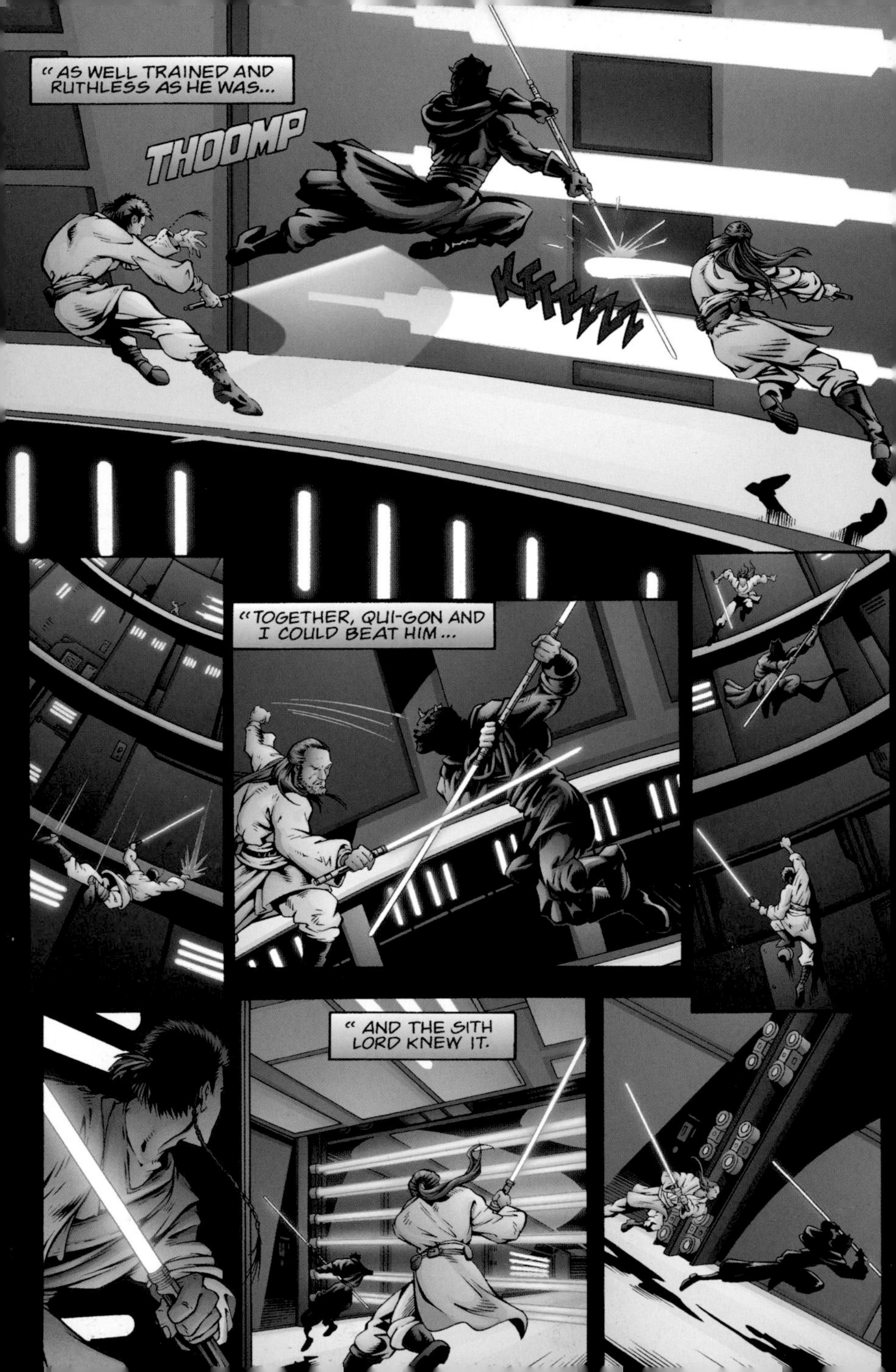
"AS WELL TRAINED AND RUTHLESS AS HE WAS...
THOOMP
"TOGETHER, QUI-GON AND I COULD BEAT HIM...
"AND THE SITH LORD KNEW IT.

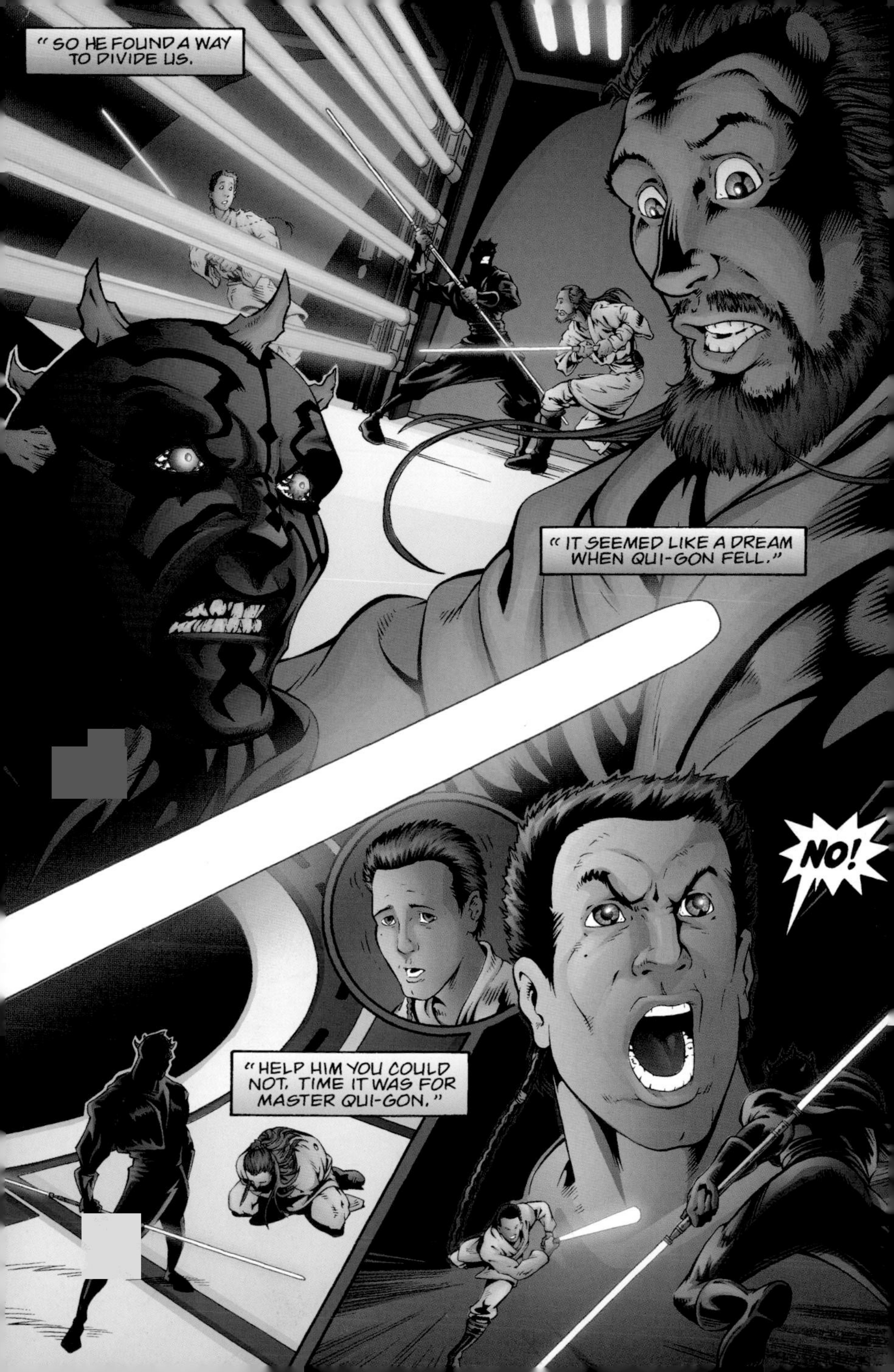
"SO HE FOUND A WAY TO DIVIDE US.
"IT SEEMED LIKE A DREAM WHEN QUI-GON FELL."
NO!
"HELP HIM YOU COULD NOT. TIME IT WAS FOR MASTER QUI-GON."

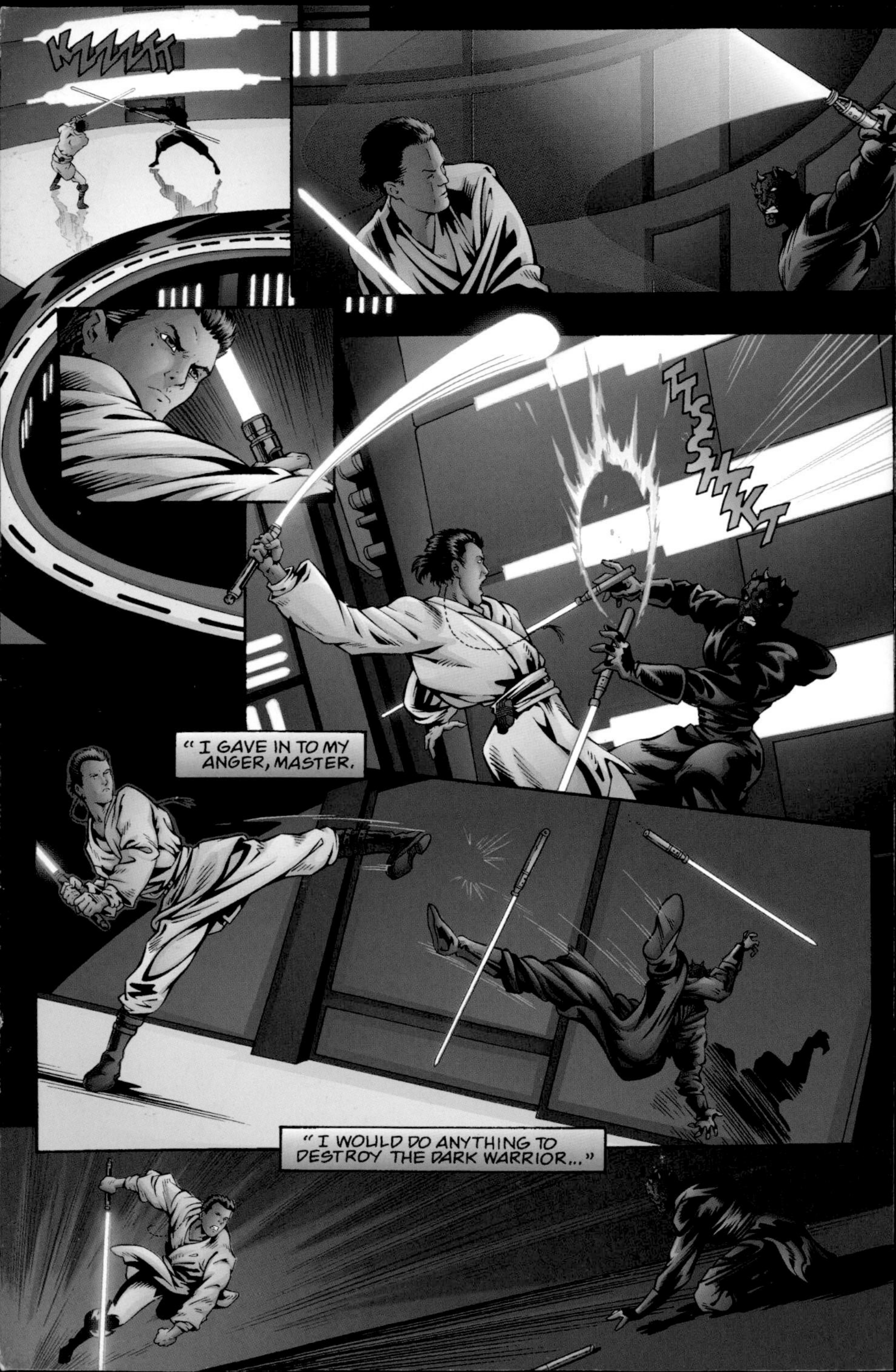
KZZZZKT
TTSSHHKKT
"I GAVE IN TO MY ANGER, MASTER.
"I WOULD DO ANYTHING TO DESTROY THE DARK WARRIOR..."

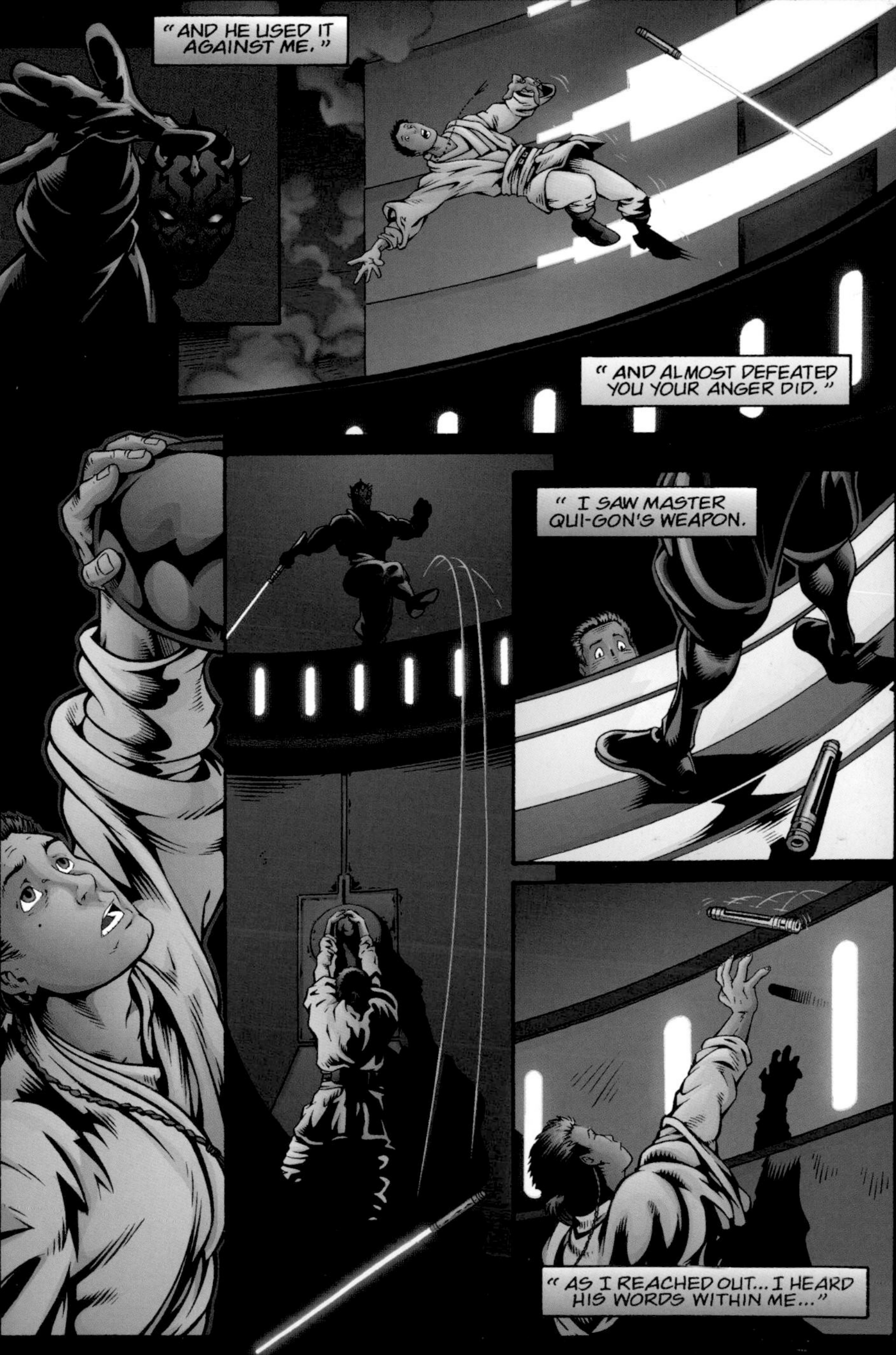
"AND HE USED IT AGAINST ME."
"AND ALMOST DEFEATED YOU YOUR ANGER DID."
" I SAW MASTER QUI-GON'S WEAPON.
"AS I REACHED OUT... I HEARD HIS WORDS WITHIN ME..."

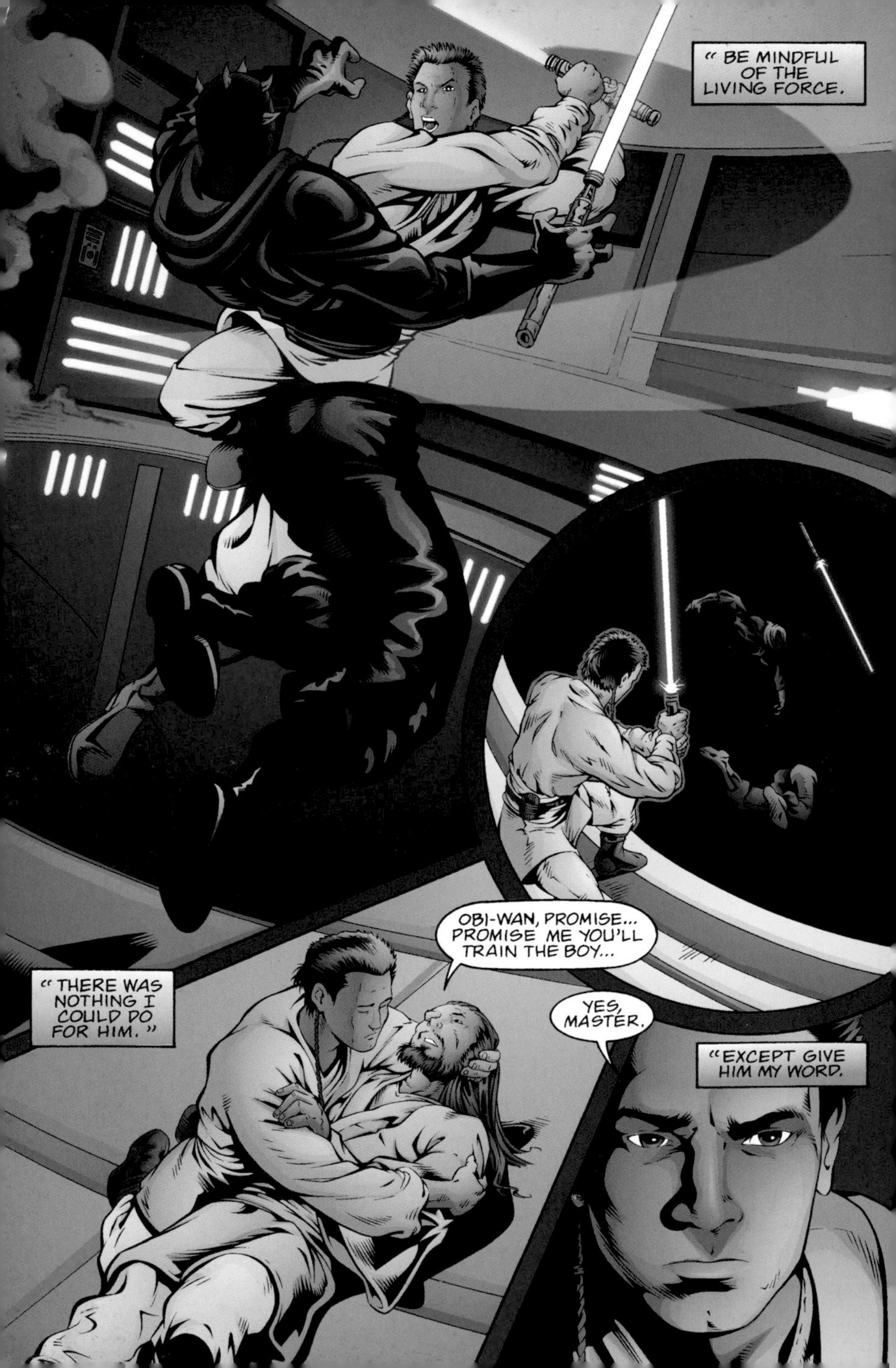
"BE MINDFUL OF THE LIVING FORCE.
OBI-WAN, PROMISE... PROMISE ME YOU'LL TRAIN THE BOY...
"THERE WAS NOTHING I COULD DO FOR HIM."
YES, MASTER.
"EXCEPT GIVE HIM MY WORD.

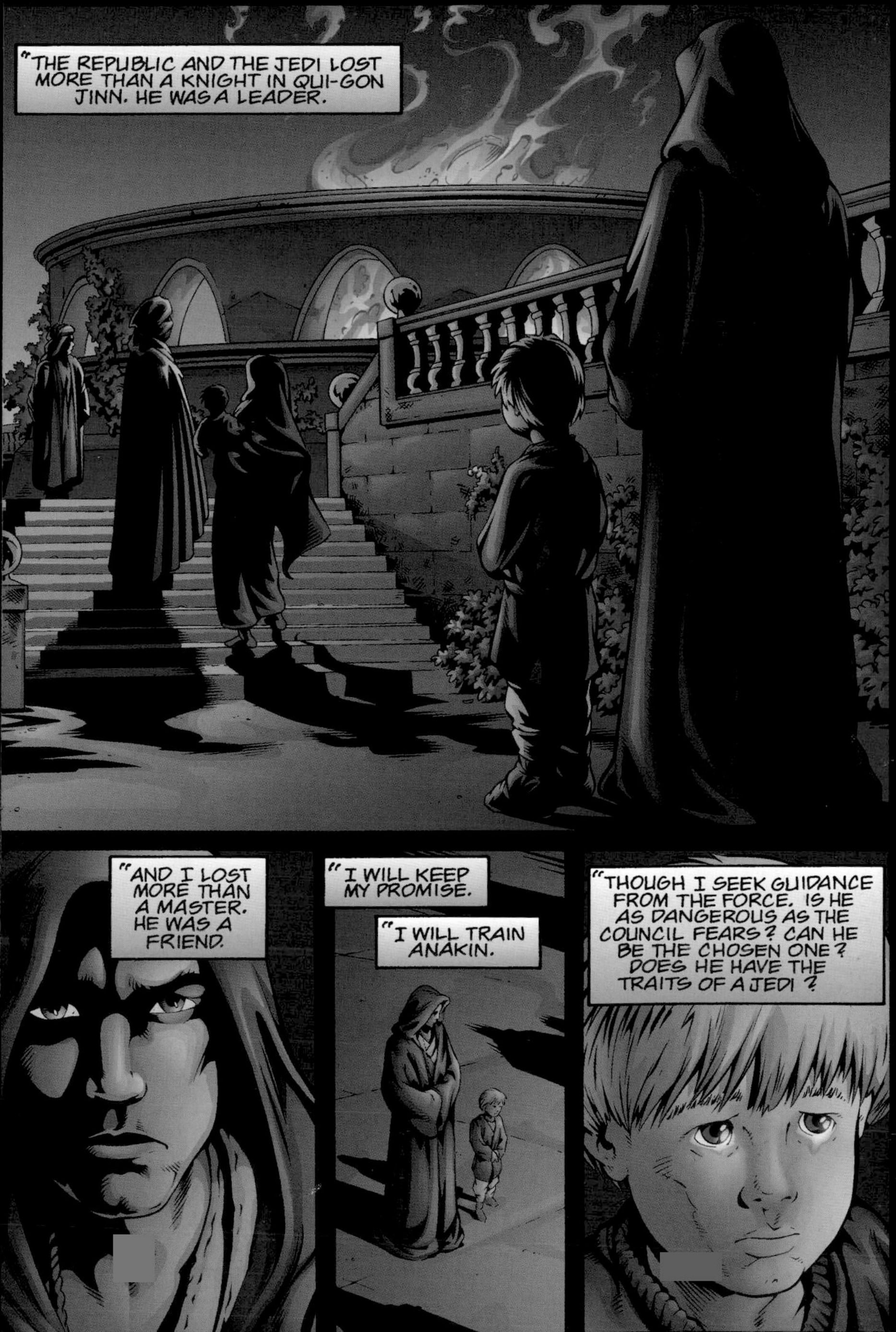
"THE REPUBLIC AND THE JEDI LOST MORE THAN A KNIGHT IN QUI-GON JINN. HE WAS A LEADER.
"AND I LOST MORE THAN A MASTER. HE WAS A FRIEND.
"I WILL KEEP MY PROMISE.
"I WILL TRAIN ANAKIN.
"THOUGH I SEEK GUIDANCE FROM THE FORCE. IS HE AS DANGEROUS AS THE COUNCIL FEARS? CAN HE BE THE CHOSEN ONE? DOES HE HAVE THE TRAITS OF A JEDI?

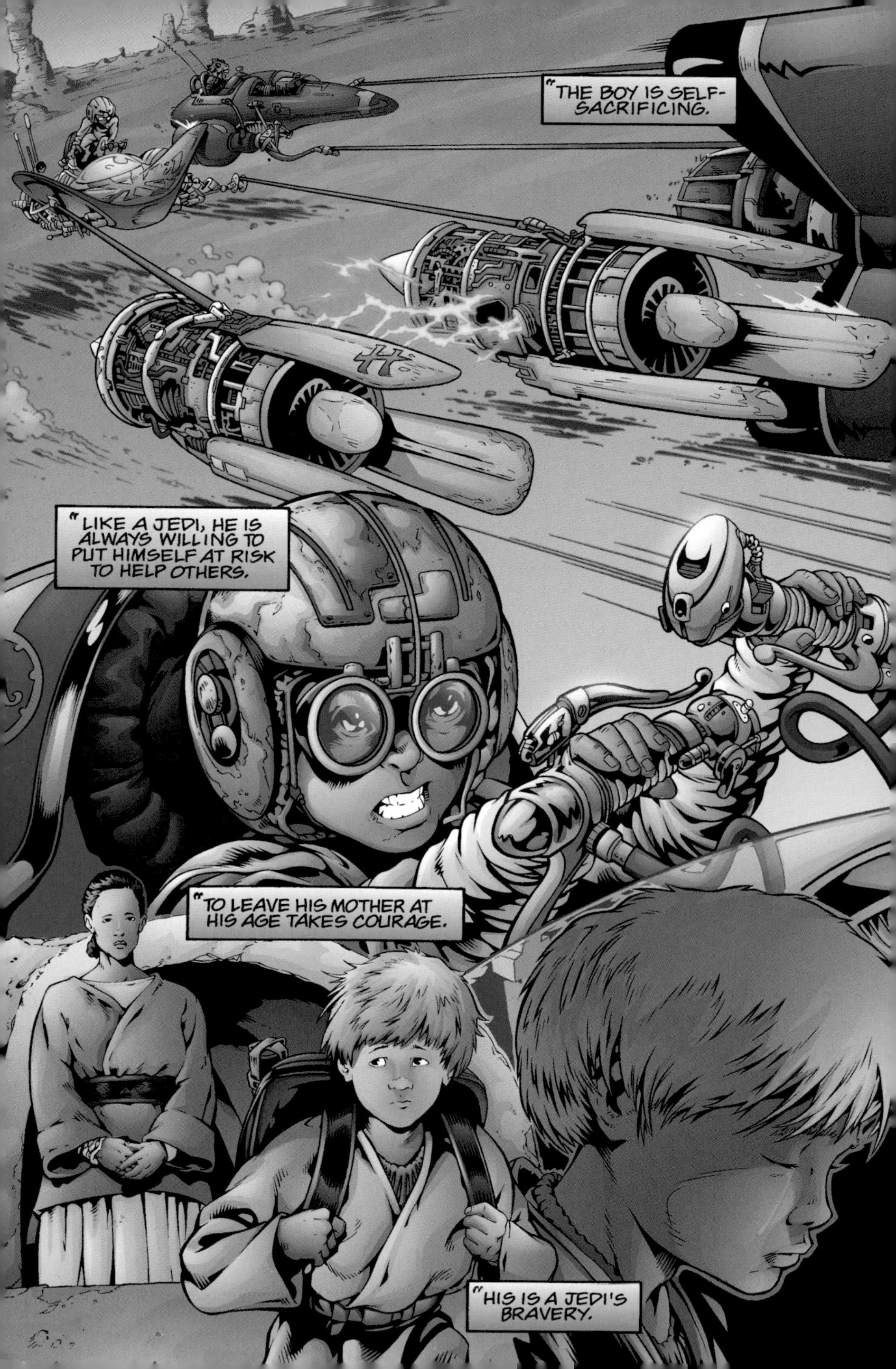

"THE BOY IS SELF-SACRIFICING.
"LIKE A JEDI, HE IS ALWAYS WILLING TO PUT HIMSELF AT RISK TO HELP OTHERS.
"TO LEAVE HIS MOTHER AT HIS AGE TAKES COURAGE.
"HIS IS A JEDI'S BRAVERY.

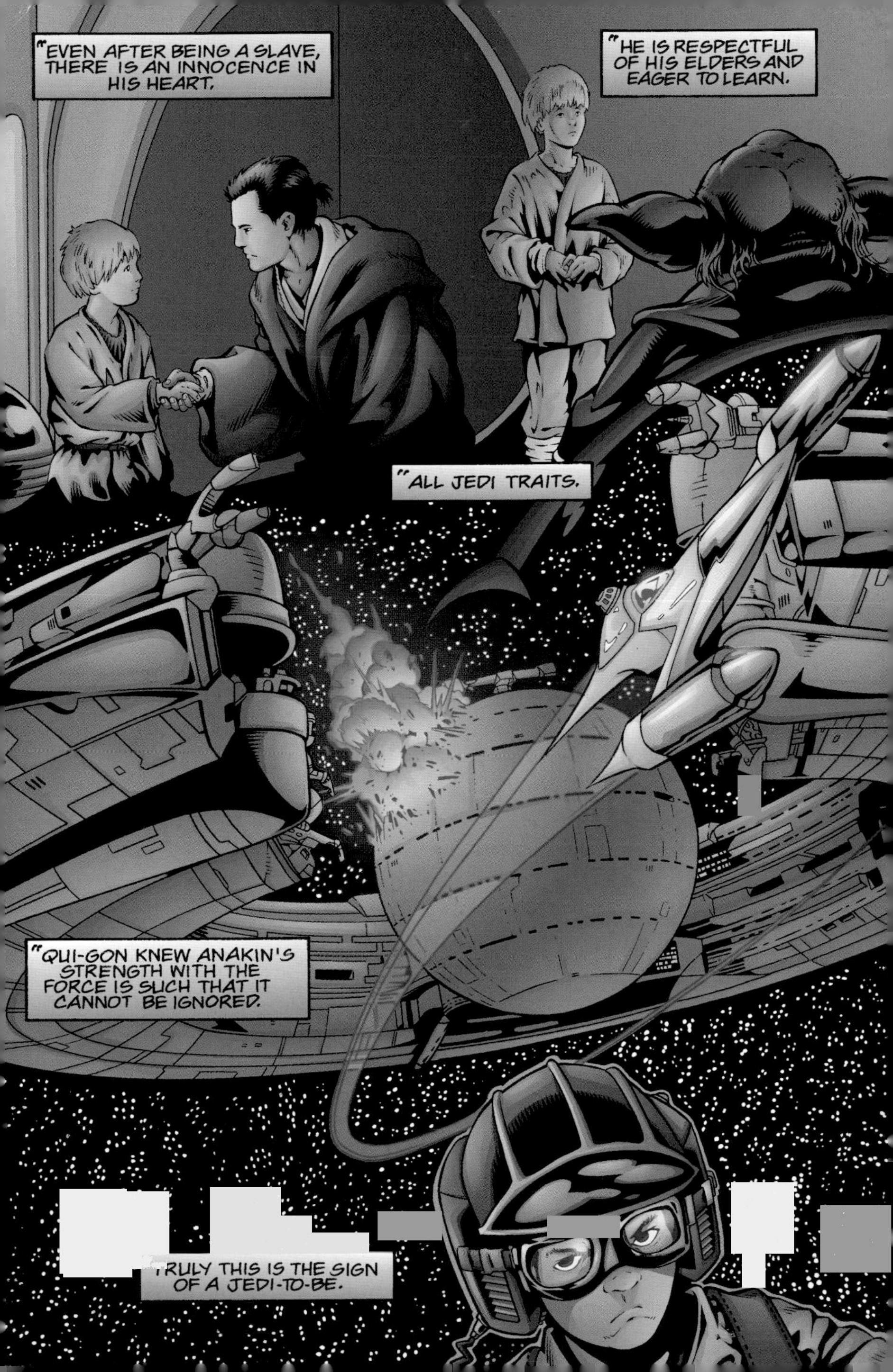
"EVEN AFTER BEING A SLAVE, THERE IS AN INNOCENCE IN HIS HEART.
"HE IS RESPECTFUL OF HIS ELDERS AND EAGER TO LEARN.
"ALL JEDI TRAITS.
"QUI-GON KNEW ANAKIN'S STRENGTH WITH THE FORCE IS SUCH THAT IT CANNOT BE IGNORED.
TRULY THIS IS THE SIGN OF A JEDI-TO-BE.

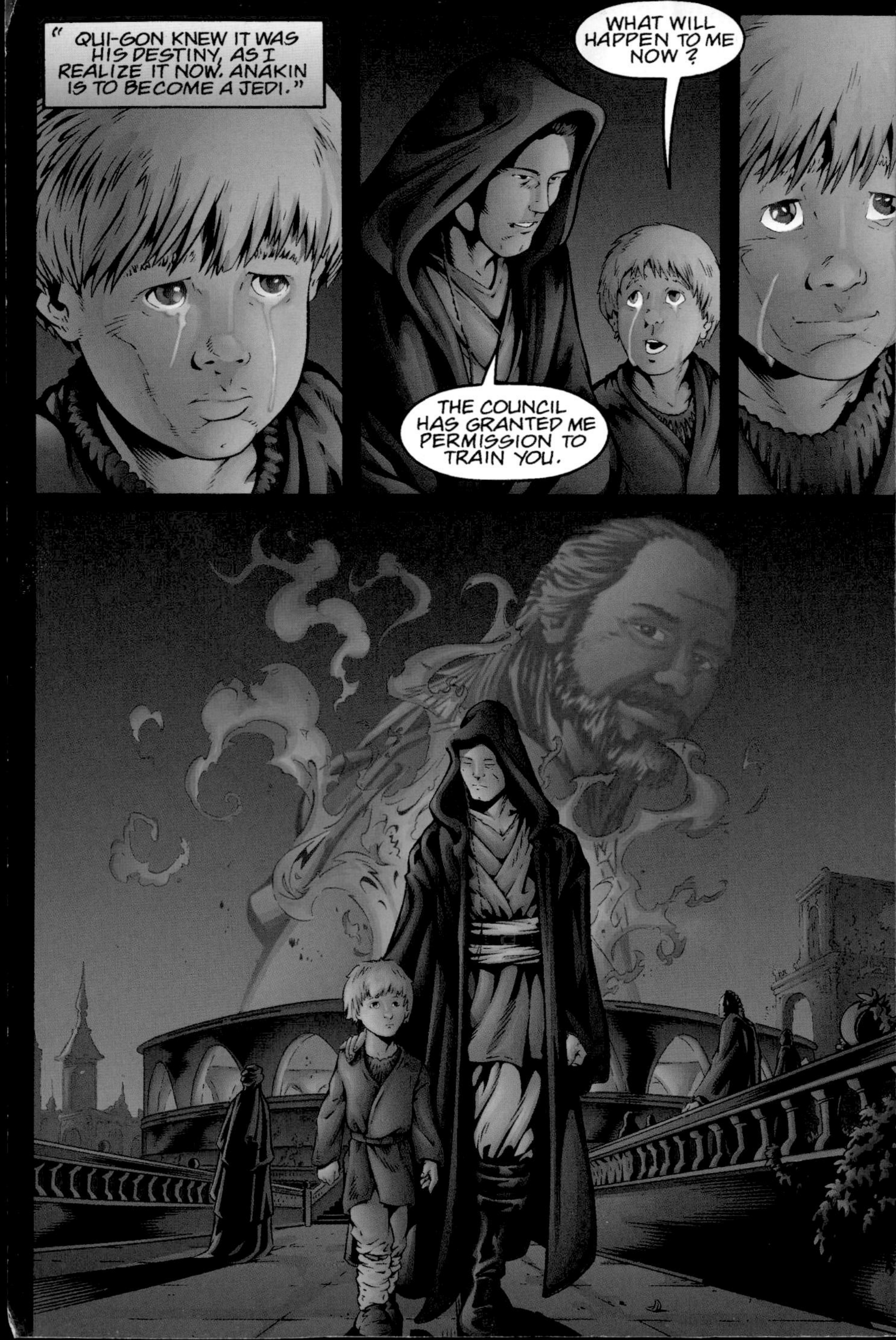
"QUI-GON KNEW IT WAS HIS DESTINY, AS I REALIZE IT NOW. ANAKIN IS TO BECOME A JEDI."
WHAT WILL HAPPEN TO ME NOW?
THE COUNCIL HAS GRANTED ME PERMISSION TO TRAIN YOU.

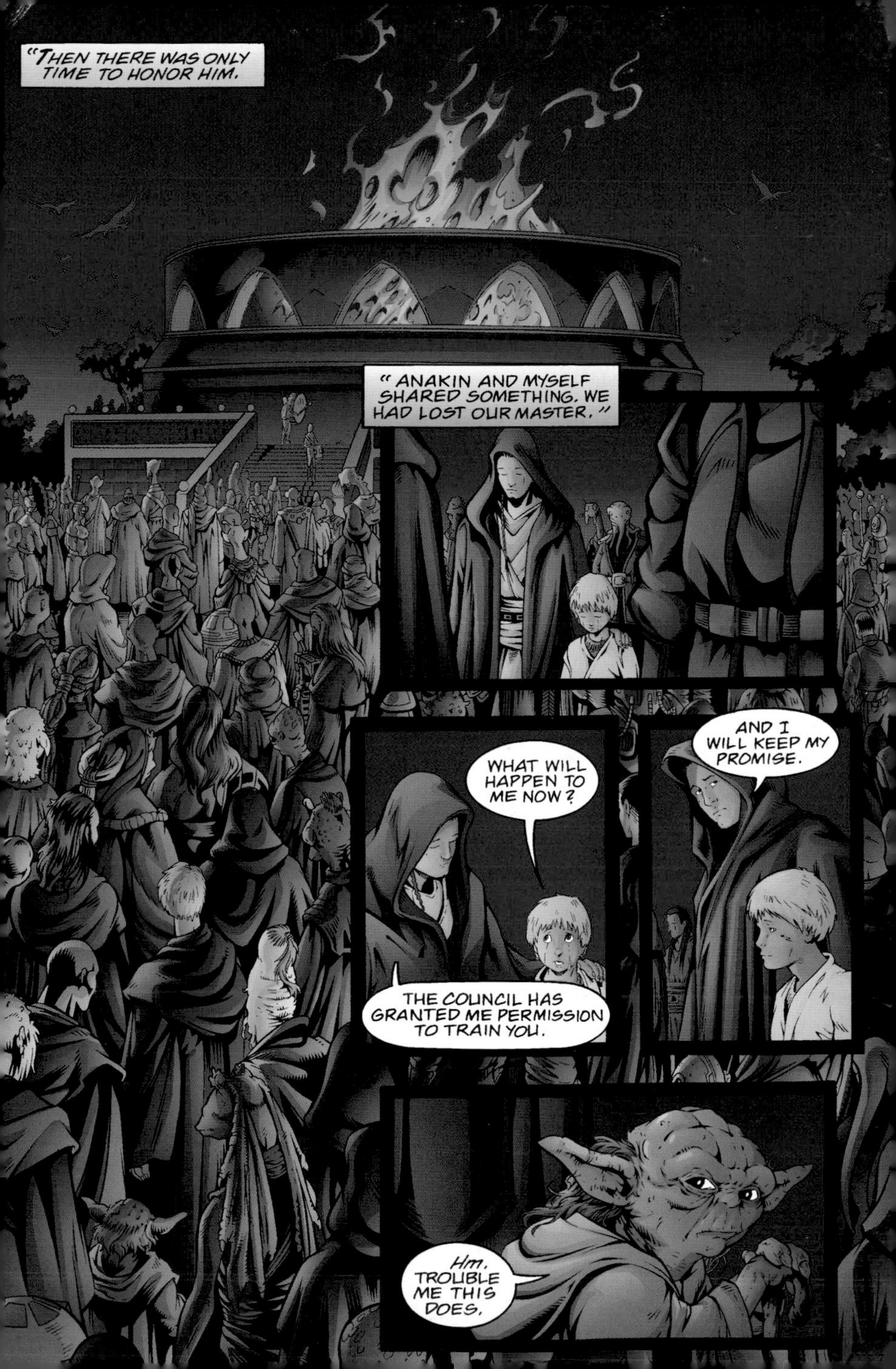
"THEN THERE WAS ONLY TIME TO HONOR HIM.
" ANAKIN AND MYSELF SHARED SOMETHING. WE HAD LOST OUR MASTER."
WHAT WILL HAPPEN TO ME NOW?
THE COUNCIL HAS GRANTED ME PERMISSION TO TRAIN YOU.
AND I WILL KEEP MY PROMISE.
Hm, TROUBLE ME THIS DOES.

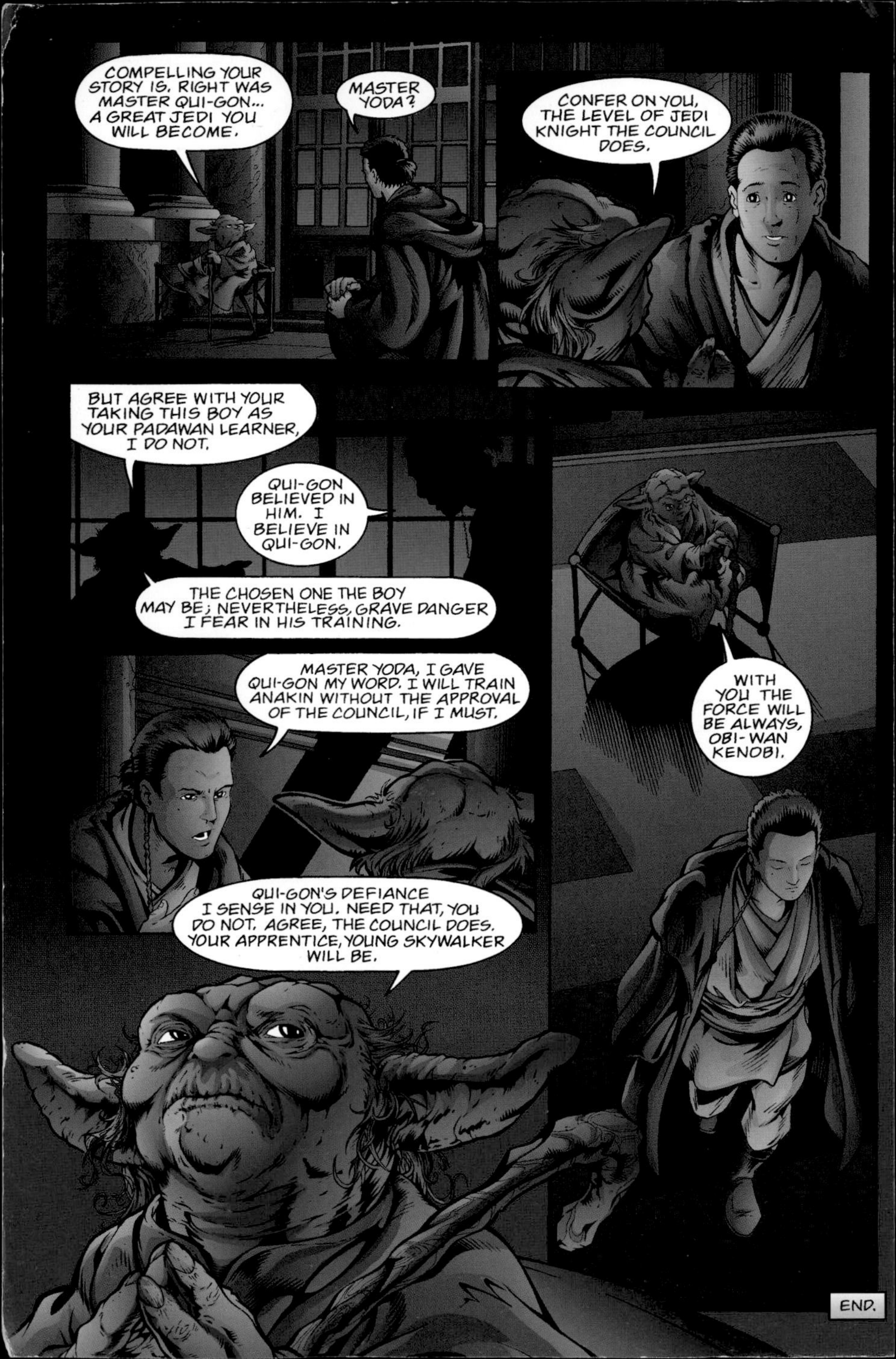
COMPELLING YOUR STORY IS. RIGHT WAS MASTER QUI-GON... A GREAT JEDI YOU WILL BECOME.
MASTER YODA?
CONFER ON YOU, THE LEVEL OF JEDI KNIGHT THE COUNCIL DOES.
BUT AGREE WITH YOUR TAKING THIS BOY AS YOUR PADAWAN LEARNER, I DO NOT.
QUI-GON BELIEVED IN HIM. I BELIEVE IN QUI-GON.
THE CHOSEN ONE THE BOY MAY BE; NEVERTHELESS, GRAVE DANGER I FEAR IN HIS TRAINING.
MASTER YODA, I GAVE QUI-GON MY WORD. I WILL TRAIN ANAKIN WITHOUT THE APPROVAL OF THE COUNCIL, IF I MUST.
QUI-GON'S DEFIANCE I SENSE IN YOU. NEED THAT, YOU DO NOT. AGREE, THE COUNCIL DOES. YOUR APPRENTICE, YOUNG SKYWALKER WILL BE.
WITH YOU THE FORCE WILL BE ALWAYS, OBI-WAN KENOBI.
END.

STAR WARS GRAPHIC NOVEL TIMELINE (IN YEARS)

Omnibus: Tales of the Jedi—5,000–3,986 BSW4
Knights of the Old Republic—3,964–3,963 BSW4
The Old Republic—3653, 3678 BSW4
Knight Errant—1,032 BSW4
Jedi vs. Sith—1,000 BSW4
Omnibus: Rise of the Sith—33 BSW4
Episode I: The Phantom Menace—32 BSW4
Omnibus: Emissaries and Assassins—32 BSW4
Omnibus: Quinlan Vos—Jedi in Darkness—31–30 BSW4
Omnibus: Menace Revealed—31–22 BSW4
Honor and Duty—22 BSW4
Blood Ties—22 BSW4
Episode II: Attack of the Clones—22 BSW4
Clone Wars—22–19 BSW4
Clone Wars Adventures—22–19 BSW4
General Grievous—22–19 BSW4
Episode III: Revenge of the Sith—19 BSW4
Dark Times—19 BSW4
Omnibus: Droids—5.5 BSW4
Omnibus: Boba Fett—3 BSW4–10 ASW4
Underworld—1 BSW4
Episode IV: A New Hope—SW4
Classic Star Wars—0–3 ASW4
Omnibus: A Long Time Ago . . . —0–4 ASW4
Empire—0 ASW4
Rebellion—0 ASW4
Omnibus: Early Victories—0–3 ASW4
Jabba the Hutt: The Art of the Deal—1 ASW4
Episode V: The Empire Strikes Back—3 ASW4
Omnibus: Shadows of the Empire—3.5–4.5 ASW4
Episode VI: Return of the Jedi—4 ASW4
Omnibus: X-Wing Rogue Squadron—4–5 ASW4
Heir to the Empire—9 ASW4
Dark Force Rising—9 ASW4
The Last Command—9 ASW4
Dark Empire—10 ASW4
Crimson Empire—11 ASW4
Jedi Academy: Leviathan—12 ASW4
Union—19 ASW4
Chewbacca—25 ASW4
Invasion—25 ASW4
Legacy—130–137 ASW4

Old Republic Era
25,000 – 1000 years before
Star Wars: A New Hope

Rise of the Empire Era
1000 – 0 years before
Star Wars: A New Hope

Rebellion Era
0 – 5 years after
Star Wars: A New Hope

New Republic Era
5 – 25 years after
Star Wars: A New Hope

New Jedi Order Era
25+ years after
Star Wars: A New Hope

Legacy Era
130+ years after
Star Wars: A New Hope

Vector
Crosses four eras in the timeline

Volume 1 contains:
Knights of the Old Republic Volume 5
Dark Times Volume 3

Volume 2 contains:
Rebellion Volume 4
Legacy Volume 6

W4 = before *Episode IV: A New Hope*. ASW4 = after *Episode IV: A New Hope*.

FOR MORE ADVENTURE IN A GALAXY FAR, FAR, AWAY . . .

**STAR WARS: THE CLONE WARS—
THE WIND RAIDERS OF TALORAAN**
978-1-59582-231-4 | $7.99

**STAR WARS ADVENTURES:
LUKE SKYWALKER AND THE
TREASURE OF THE DRAGONSNAKES**
978-1-59582-347-2 | $7.99

AVAILABLE AT YOUR LOCAL COMICS SHOP OR BOOKSTORE